ALL THE LIGHT INSIDE OF YOU

One woman's quest
**for spiritual understanding
and the gift discovered
for all who choose it.**

A TRUE STORY

KERYL J. OLIVER

 Storia Group, Inc.

[handwritten: Dear Barbara,]

It is a lie—any talk of God

that does not

comfort

you.

Meister Ekhart

[handwritten: Always be a warrior for your inner-light.]

[handwritten signature]

Dedication

For every person who wants to forge a brighter
today in a world of diminishing light.

Contents

PART 3

Heal to Lead, Love, and Forgive

Introduction

Even if you have never opened a Bible, you have probably heard of Adam and Eve, the central characters attributed to mankind's fall from divinity.

Theirs is a story of our birth from the spiritual realm to the world we know today. It shows our intrinsic desire to exert the free will given to us to make moment-by-moment choices, and how we suffer painful consequences from some of the choices we make. It depicts our hunger for knowledge to know all that is good and evil about the world around us, and it reminds us that we are not meant to go through life alone, but rather with a helper.

There are endless debates regarding the *Holy Bible*. Are these stories true? Are they simply allegorical? Are they the words of man, the word of God, or some heavily edited combination of both? No matter what side you find yourself in this debate, according to the Book of Genesis, Adam and Eve are convinced they are separated from their creator, God, and banished from the place where God exists.

That is an extremely compelling thought because, as you might have already discovered in your own life, whatever we believe eventually manifests as reality; profoundly affecting how we live and ultimately who we become. Thus to me, the story symbolizes the unrelenting power of our mind-set.

Only by changing our thoughts can we ever hope to change our lives.

It also delivers the unforgettable message that it's best not to go against the formidable life-force of our universe to appease our own selfish agenda. There is nothing selfish about what swirls in the unseen. It is the purest form of love.

Over the centuries, we have addressed this force of nature using many names: Source, YHWH, Elohim, Jehovah, Divine Energy, Abba, Father, I AM, and of course, God, to name just a few. Although gender-agnostic, we commonly refer to God as He.

God defies the logic of science, turns ordinary into extraordinary, is limited only in the minds of those who don't understand the sheer might of His power, and moves in ways that are impossible to anticipate.

Can a person truly escape the presence of God in their lifetime? It has been my experience that whether one believes in His existence or not, sooner or later in everyone's life, God *will* 'show up.' To state otherwise is merely the effect of ones inability to recognize—or perhaps, acknowledge—the palpable spirit of our Creator.

This divine energy is unpredictable, yet unchanging, has never shown a bias for the vehicle chosen to deliver its endless supply of love and hope, or to demonstrate in an irrefutable manner, that we are never alone. We need only be still and know that He is indeed, God.

He uses a flawed world to teach a flawed world, and quite often, it is in the darkest moments when we are lovingly reminded that He is the Source of all light.

All of these things are what happened to me.

The stories in this book are true accounts of events that took place over the years of my secular life as I found myself striving to understand what I could *sense* since I was a small child, but could not *see*. What *was* this extra something that surrounds us? From where does that inner voice come and why is there such wisdom when it presses on a heart? How and why do some things occur that cannot be explained humanly?

It is segmented into three parts:

Part 1, The Awesome Wonder in What Cannot Be Seen, shares the seasons of my young life when I first became aware there was something more than what I could physically see with my eyes.

Part 3, Heal to Lead, Love, and Forgive, brings readers to where I am today—spiritually wiser, with the understanding that we are intrinsically woven into the massiveness of all that surrounds us, and more aware of the enormous power this gives us in our everyday lives.

Part 2, Where the Mind Goes, is the series of events that brought me to finally identifying the invisible and lifelong companion I had felt since I was a child.

In Part 2, you'll be introduced to a person I brought into my home for 16 months as she battled an insidious and heart-wrenching disease. I take you along on my journey through this challenging season and share with you the many things that occurred to change the lenses from which I normally viewed life, prompting me to see beyond what was obvious. Together we'll travel deep inside my thoughts and the vast array of feelings I experienced during that time.

As you read, you'll come to understand why I deemed it permissible to disclose the medical and personal information shared with me by her doctor, which includes full protocols, personal stories, and more. You'll recognize that no HIPA laws were breached.

Because I want you to feel as though you are with a friend, I wrote this book in a conversational, sit-across-from-me-and-hear-this-story style.

I chose to share my experience for two primary reasons. The first is, without these events it would have taken me a lot longer to identify God as the comforting, invisible companion I had felt since childhood. The second is to show how we can find healing from a negative external condition by maintaining control of our thoughts, staying focused on faith, forgiveness, and love, and basing our every response from these things. You will read about the rage I had to overcome to get to this place and how God, whom until this time had not been identified in my life, made His presence undeniably known to me.

The true name of the cancer patient is not disclosed in this book, nor anywhere else—and I have *greatly* tempered this section to not reveal more than what many already know from the period she was in my home. My intent is not to add to the harm she has already caused. I have come to understand that those who behave in ways we find detestable are suffering enough in their minds and spirit. Our responses should counter that.

I also believe that when our complex brain with its billions of neurons, misfires, it can cause a person to experience life in ways we deem 'not normal.' I ask the question in the book, what defines normal anyway? I am nobody's final judge.

I urge you to read Part 2 with an open mind, filled with curiosity, which I will remind you again in the chapter preceding it. Challenge yourself to find the beauty that lies within these things I experienced.

Throughout the book I share story after story of the many remarkable ways that God was revealed in my life. I weave in the beautiful story of Everett, a then-8 year old boy whose enormous faith will touch your heart and the powerful experience his mother had when she chose to trust what she could not understand.

Without the darkness of the 16 months, I would never have experienced the light of Everett or many other things. By removing the limitation of my thoughts to see beyond what was readily obvious, I was given a gift that will be with me always. One that has created a peace that defies all understanding and supplies me with the resilience to endure challenging situations and interactions. It is what I draw upon to heal physically and emotionally, and to teach the same to those who desire to learn.

I walked through intense fires to achieve this understanding, but the force that walked with me made the heat tolerable. I thought this was worth sharing.

You see, we are in this life together. We are called to support each other with love, and to be a light in this world. Exchanging our stories without fear of vulnerability and judgment is a powerful way to do that. What's more, when you start to compose your story, you shed light on who you are in your truest essence. You connect or reconnect with that wise inner-voice; you become emboldened to face pain from the past or your present, and are guided to the realization that it no longer has power over you *unless you grant it that permission*.

You heal.

Perhaps your story may help someone else to do the same. That is my hope with this book.

Discover your story.

Share your story.

Thank you for reading mine.

PROLOGUE
The Fall (Genesis 3:1-13)

Extracted from *The Holy Bible* (New International Version)

Now the serpent was more crafty than any of the wild animals the Lord God had made. He said to the woman, "Did God really say, 'You must not eat from any tree in the garden'?"

²The woman said to the serpent, "We may eat fruit from the trees in the garden, ³but God did say, 'You must not eat fruit from the tree that is in the middle of the garden, and you must not touch it, or you will die.'"

⁴"You will not certainly die," the serpent said to the woman. ⁵"For God knows that when you eat from it your eyes will be opened, and you will be like God, knowing good and evil."

⁶When the woman saw that the fruit of the tree was good for food and pleasing to the eye, and also desirable for gaining wisdom, she took some and ate it. She also gave some to her husband, who was with her, and he ate it. ⁷Then the eyes of both of them were opened, and they realized they were naked; so they sewed fig leaves together and made coverings for themselves.

⁸Then the man and his wife heard the sound of the Lord God as he was walking in the garden in the cool of the day, and they hid from the Lord God among the trees of the garden. [9]But the Lord God called to the man, "Where are you?"

[10]He answered, "I heard you in the garden, and I was afraid because I was naked; so I hid."

[11]And he said, "Who told you that you were naked? Have you eaten from the tree that I commanded you not to eat from?"

[12]The man said, "The woman you put here with me—she gave me some fruit from the tree, and I ate it."

[13]Then the Lord God said to the woman, "What is this you have done?"

The woman said, "The serpent deceived me, and I ate."

[...]

[21] The Lord God made garments of skin for Adam and his wife and clothed them. [22]And the Lord God said, "The man has now become like one of us, knowing good and evil. He must not be allowed to reach out his hand and take also from the tree of life and eat, and live forever. [23]So the Lord God banished him from the Garden of Eden to work the ground from which he had been taken. [24]After he drove the man out, he placed on the east side of the Garden of Eden a cherubim and a flaming sword flashing back and forth to guard the way to the tree of life.

• • • • • •

The story of Adam and Eve continues in the *Books of the Apocrypha*, which are found in some Bibles between the Old Testament and the New Testament, or as an Appendix to the New Testament, as well as in full volume books of their own. In the following excerpt, the story picks up where the human couple retreat in despair across the stony, sandy, dark, and barren landscape to the Cave of Treasures that was their new home.

[1] But Adam and Eve cried for having come out of the garden, their first home. [2]And indeed, when Adam looked at his flesh that was altered he cried bitterly, he and Eve, over what they had done. And they walked and went gently down into the Cave of Treasures.

[3]And as they came to it, Adam cried over himself and said to Eve, "Look at this cave that is to be our prison in this world, and a place of punishment! [4]What is it compared with the garden? What is its narrowness compared with the space of the other?

[5]What is this rock, by the side of those groves? What is the gloom of this cavern, compared with the light of the garden? [6]What is this overhanging ledge of rock to shelter us, compared with the mercy of the Lord that overshadowed us? [7]What is the soil of this cave compared with the garden land? This earth, strewed with stones; and that, planted with delicious fruit trees?"

[8]And Adam said to Eve, "Look at your eyes, and at mine, which before beheld angels praising in heaven; and they too, without ceasing. [9]But now we do not see as we did; our eyes have become of flesh; they cannot see like they used to see before."
[10]Adam said again to Eve, "What is our body today, compared to what it was in former days, when we lived in the garden?"

[11]After this, Adam did not want to enter the cave, under the overhanging rock; nor would he ever want to enter it. [12]But he bowed to God's orders; and said to himself, "Unless I enter the cave, I shall again be a transgressor."

---

1   *The Lost Books of the Bible: The Rejected Texts, Apocrypha, and Pseudepigrapha* by Dr. Edward Hammond

• • • • • • •

The man and woman ate the forbidden fruit because they were told "Your eyes will be opened." Instead, according to these texts, it appears their vision was greatly diminished. *"...our eyes have become of flesh; they cannot see like they used to see before."*

Which is it? Are our eyes truly open or are they closed? Are we with our Divine Creator or are we separated because of our human mistakes?

It is a matter of perspective and the answer is unique to each person. The choice is yours.

We get to choose how we see the world.

Part 1

The Awesome Wonder
In What Cannot Be Seen

CHAPTER 1

Meeting Everett

Fall of 2016 | Age 49, on the brink of 50

Pushing aside the curtains of my city apartment, I turned to eight-year-old Everett. "Can you see the wind?" I asked him. We both peer outside on this crisp, fall day in 2016—a day of blue skies and bright sunshine. His thickly-lashed eyes were transfixed on a tall, thin tree that separated the brick buildings in the historic garden district of midtown Atlanta. The green leaves were not yet revealing which color they would later become as they rustled with motion from the limbs swaying softly in the breeze. Left and right, back and forth, they danced as though the trees could hear the melody of a song that we could not.

Everett turned away from the window and looked at me, "Yes," he said shyly, moving slightly closer to his mother. I smiled at him "You can? You can see the wind?" He looked to his mother for the answer. Moms know everything when you're eight years old. In a few years she will know very little. That day, she demonstrated her motherly wisdom by remaining silent, leaving Everett on his own to answer this one. He nodded definitively. "Yes, I can see the wind."

I leaned forward and said gently, "Well, I can certainly understand why you would think so. But the truth is you can't really see the wind Everett, because the wind itself is invisible. You can feel the wind and you can see what happens when the wind blows through the trees...how it bends the branches and rustles the leaves." I paused, offering him a reassuring smile "So, the wind is an invisible force of nature, but we can see and feel the effects of the wind, yes?"

Another silent nod.

Such a sweet, shy boy.

He began squirming and it was obvious he was not too happy. He had just come from the doctor's office and was still experiencing pain where his IV had very recently been removed. We put a heating pad on that tender area to soothe and comfort him.

"And what about love, Everett?" I ask. "Can you see your mom's love?"

He stopped fidgeting and gave me a look that said "Now, that's a trick question." He sat there silently, not quite sure how to answer. I decide to approach it a different way. "Can you feel your mom's love?" He smiled and nodded with confidence. I nod back. "Yes you can! And you can see all of the nice, caring things she does for you because she loves you. Right?" His eyes reflect light as he quietly smiles at his mother. "But love itself, the amazing force that causes her to be so caring, is invisible... like the wind." I pause to observe him as he looks at her again. This boy, with his jet-black hair and thick eye lashes, will one day look like a Hollywood star.

"May I ask you one more question, Everett?" He turns back to me as a sign of approval to continue. "Do you believe in God?"

"Yes," he says, still showing shyness but starting to relax, "I prayed before I came here."

My heart squeezes with pleasure at the inherent innocence of a child.

"I believe in God too," I tell him softly. "God is like the wind, isn't He? He is invisible, but you can feel Him around you and you can feel His love." He stares at me with those handsome peepers. "Did you know God's love can also be found inside of you? God's love is inside every single living thing and being on Earth, including you. Like a light that shines on everything."

As he takes in my words, I ask. "Do you want to know how you can actually feel His light?"

"Yes!" He says, no longer looking to his mom for answers.

"Put your hands very close together but don't let them touch," I instruct, demonstrating with my own hands. "Can you feel the heat between them?"

He nods his head.

"You are feeling the energy inside of you glowing like a warm light bulb. Now move your hands apart very slowly.... Good. Very slowly, just a little bit at a time. Can you still feel the heat?"

"Yes," he says softly, studying the space between his hands.

"As long as you concentrate on it, you will be able to feel the light of God's energy with you. It might be invisible, but you know it is there because you can feel it. Just like the wind. Just like love." I watch his face as my words reach him. This is not the time to explain that the energy of love and the energy of God are the same. "Do you want to know something else?" I ask. He nods his head as he continues playing with the sensation between his hands. "It is ALWAYS with you. That is one of God's promises. The love of God is always with us and will never leave us." Reflected on his face is a hint of wonder

3

as he processes this notion that he has a way to physically feel the invisible energy of God. I am well rewarded with another sweet smile, and my own heart smiles. Why must we lose this transparency as we grow older?

"Everett," I say, leaning in toward him. "Now let me tell you the best part. If it's all right with you, I would like to teach you how to use it to help make those pesky migraines of yours go away."

CHAPTER 2

My Constant Companion

So, we fix our eyes not on what is seen, but what is unseen.
For what is seen is temporary, but what is unseen is eternal.

2 Corinthians 4:18

Childhood | Age 6

40 years away from identifying God in my life

The law of relativity tells us that everything in the physical world is made real by its relationship or comparison to something else. We gain our perception of things in this world through the accumulation of our individual experiences over time and how we compare them to those of others. Let's say 500 people register to hear the words of a motivational speaker who typically draws a crowd of 100. To this person, 500 attendees is a large crowd. But when he attends a speech by a speaker who draws thousands, he realizes 500 folks is an intimate gathering.

In other words, it's all relative.

The Biblical figure, Adam, understood this. *"What is the gloom of this cavern, compared with the light of the garden"* he asked.

But seriously, what could possibly compare to the Garden of Eden, to paradise?

To me, there was nothing in the world that compared to the woods across the street from my childhood home in Upstate New York.

I could not wait until I had all my chores finished so I could run across the street and play in them. They were my favorite place to be in all of the world. When mom said it was okay to go, all I had to do was cut across my friends' The Johnston's property, through their backyard, and I was there. Sometimes I could go through the Immerman's yard, but their driveway felt too long. I wanted to get there fast.

The woods were not deep or expansive—they were the perfect size for the young child I was. I loved all of the different sounds I heard coming from the small woodland creatures I could never spot. I would pretend that some of them were magical elves who were not allowed to be seen by humans, but could be heard going about their day, doing the things that magical elves do. I knew for certain that the big mushrooms were where they secretly lived, so I was careful not to step on them and accidentally crush them.

The trees in my woods were so tall that they created a 'roof' above my head. Even when it drizzled, I barely felt it. Only when the breeze would sway their majestic tops to one side would I get a good look at the sky. But the light always managed to find its way in. My woods didn't get dark until the sun went down.

I would play and play and play. I would pretend the rocky cliffs were the different rooms of my outdoor home and the moss was the carpeting.

Any northerner will tell you that there is nothing like Fall in this part of the country. When I stood beneath the gold and

6

orange of the leaves, it reflected on my skin, casting their colors upon me with an illumination that made me look like a glowstick. The crisp air hinted that winter was coming, and would soon lay a glittering, white blanket over everything, turning my special place into a fairyland.

When I first started tromping through my magic forest I was about six years old. It was the early Seventies, a time when parents did not fear for the safety of their children playing outside for hours—even alone—without a cellphone. As children, our greatest perceived danger back then was not making it home in time for dinner or accidentally running into a patch of poison ivy. I got to play in those woods all day long; sometimes with neighborhood friends, but more often alone.

During those times, however, I never felt alone.

It was as though someone caring and safe was standing by my side, watching in joy as I delighted in the beauty and magical feel of nature. Its presence was not intrusive or unnerving, rather, it was comforting and peaceful. I felt it palpably.

I did not have to retreat to the woods to experience this connection, but felt its existence much more deeply in the solitude and tranquility of natural settings. Perhaps this is what our ancient ancestors felt, sheltered by their tents in the desert, communing with nature while receiving divine information from the same presence I was blessed to first experience when I was a child.

My 6 year-old self believed that the winged angels of story books surrounded and protected me; giving me the inherent understanding that, at that moment, everything was okay. I was enveloped in a love so pure it defied the laws of relativity. Nothing was comparable. It's difficult to describe to someone who has never felt it, but it is an awesome thing to be fully aware

7

that we are not alone. We are unconditionally loved by a force greater than ourselves.

Outside of the canopy of nature, it was not really any different, albeit more subtle. I still felt guided by this pressing on my heart. "Do you see that child alone there on the playground? She is lonely and needs a friend," the inner voice would gently urge. "Invite her to join you." My mother still smiles at the memories of those I brought home to offer my friendship.

Somehow I understood that the thoughts that seemed to come out of nowhere, and taking me by surprise, didn't come from my own mind but from somewhere deeper. From where I did not know. However, I listened carefully to this inner-voice then, as I do to this day; and followed its loving commands in a manner that was as natural as breathing. It was the source of my compassion and my understanding that others were not separate from myself—we were all one. I began to see everyone, not so much as individuals, but rather as 'souls on a journey.'

Through my connection to this unseen force, my senses sharpened and I became more aware of the energy of those around me. I was a part of everything, both seen and unseen. Is there a more beautiful way to exist?

As children, we possess an unfiltered spiritual wisdom that I wish we could protect and nurture so that it sustains throughout our lifetime to become the governor of our every response.

Yet, even as a six-year old child, it took no time for me to recognize that not everyone had this sensory. Why can some feel what others cannot? It would be a question I would ask throughout my life.

• • • • • • •

The six-year old me was aware that there was something more than what could be physically seen. I would come to learn, years later, that I was correct. We live in a world of wonders and mysteries that transcend the human eye.

[2]Everything you see around you, from your own body to the planet you're standing on, and the stars in the sky, is made of atoms. These atoms are 99.9999999999999 percent empty space. In fact, [3]if we were to squeeze all the empty space out of all the atoms that come together to create all the people of the world, we would be able to fit the entire human race inside the volume of a sugar cube.

We often hear the phrase, "I have to see it to believe it," or "seeing is believing." Yet, the world in which we live is primarily made of what cannot be seen.

Quantum theory takes modern physics to the tiniest, most minute level of existence, explaining both the nature of energy and matter down to the subatomic level. It is there we would also discover that nothing is solid. Everything in our world is in motion.

Atoms come together to form matter. These atoms consist of electrons, which are subatomic particles attached to the nucleus of an atom, and usually carrying an electrical charge. When you touch a solid object, the electrons that vigorously 'dance around' making up that object do not permit the electrons that vigorously dance around making up your finger to permeate. One pushes back against the other, giving us the perception that both are

---

2 http://www.bbc.com/earth/story/20150824-what-is-the-universe-made-of

3 https://www.scienceabc.com/pure-sciences/can-the-entire-human-race-fit-inside-a-sugar-cube.html

separate solid forms. What is not visible to the naked eye is the displacement of these electrons when such interactions occur. We cannot see the dance. But the fact is, everything in our world is in motion, vibrating at a specific frequency.

The frequency in which solid matter vibrates is lower than that in which energy vibrates. Our minds exist at an even higher frequency than energy. That which we refer to as God vibrates at the highest frequency. God is 'the Most High.'

It's all vibrational energy.

As such, there is much we cannot see with our eyes yet can sense with our bodies. Likewise, there are many messages we cannot hear with our ears but can receive through intuition.

My earliest recollection of this awareness was around the age of six. What was the source of knowing that pressed on my young heart? Do we all start our lives with a connection to this invisible source, but for some it gets lost along the way?

The answers to these and many other questions would come to me as I journeyed through the seasons of my life.

CHAPTER 3

The Light of a Tattered Man's Soul

What fuels your spirit fuels your body.
The power that fuels our bodies, our minds, and our hearts does
not originate in our DNA. Rather, it has roots in Divinity itself.
The truth is as simple and as eternal as that.
Caroline Myss, Ph.D., The Anatomy of the Spirit

1983 |Age 16
30 years away from identifying God in my life

My family moved from my hometown in upstate New York to a small town in Arizona as I was entering my senior year of high school. I traded in the lush green of the Catskill Mountains for the tan and beige of the desert landscape; the constant chill in the air for the dry heat of the unrelenting sun. Instead of deer darting across the road, we slammed on our brakes for giant tumbleweeds. It was as if I were stepping onto a different movie set depicting a vastly different scene. I missed my friends back home terribly, but thankfully I made new ones easily and I was happy to get my first job working at a privately-owned fast food restaurant that was similar to the long-standing KFC.

As I made my way home at the end of each work day, I would drive beneath a particular interstate overpass, and now and then, would see someone sleeping beneath it. Back then, we called them hobos. In old black and white movies, hobos are depicted as jolly, sometimes wearing funny hats, dancing and yucking it up as they drink. In reality, they live a near-joyless, often frightening, and primal existence. There is nothing jolly about homelessness.

Most people have no good idea what to do when they come upon a homeless person. For a moment, they may contemplate giving them money to buy food, but then immediately think, "What if they use it to buy cigarettes or liquor? What if I approach them and they're dangerous?"

There was no room for these concerns as long as my inner voice was guiding me. "He's hungry. He has not eaten in days. Give him something to eat. You are safe," the voice inside would say. By this time in my young life, I had become completely obedient to the voice within.

The restaurant owner was also my boss. I cannot say for certain, but I have a strong hunch that he started the restaurant as a hobby for himself, and to keep high school kids out of trouble after school. He was affluent, very good-hearted, and he put great effort into creating a pleasant working environment for his staff. One of the small perks of working for him was that he permitted his employees to put meals on a tab that would then come out of our paychecks. That was a big deal for a young, poor high school teenager just starting out. Also, it was convenient on the occasion that I would bring a homeless person in to his restaurant for a much-needed hot meal. The overpass was close to work, so it was easy for me to find and transport these men, (they were always men back then), to the restaurant for a heaping plate of chicken and vegetables. I would log the meal so that my boss could deduct it from my paycheck.

My boss was not too happy about any of this. His beautiful heart revealed a fatherly concern that one day I might get hurt—or worse, killed, stopping by the roadside as I so often did, to offer care. And tucked behind the expression of concern, peeking through, was the expression of gratitude for the heart he saw in the young girl standing before him. A gentle warrior who never took one cent of these meals from my paycheck.

This next story was the catalyst for the start of my quest to understand who we are as human beings at our innermost core, what is most special, yet often unacknowledged and never seen — the spirit that sustains us when everything else falls away.

• • • • • •

One evening I brought a homeless man to the restaurant for a meal. He was so withdrawn that I could hardly extract a single word from him. This was unusual, as those before him seemed to crave conversation and company, almost desperate for someone to call them by name. After several futile attempts to draw his attention away from the silent consumption of his meal, I stopped trying. I was very young, and I didn't understand the delicacy of delivering kindness without stripping dignity. What grown man wanted to look at the face of a teenager who had the means to provide him such a basic necessity in life as food, emphasizing that he himself could not? Although he decided to

13

get in my car earlier, once we were at the restaurant, he made it clear that he preferred to be invisible.

Eventually I stopped trying to talk to him and I studied him discreetly from across the table, deploying my teenage mastery of checking someone out without their knowledge.

He looked ancient to my sixteen-year-old eyes. I would guess he was probably early 50s. He was Caucasian with a gray beard and a knit cap. His clothing was tattered, but he didn't smell of street living like many of the others. He wore knit gloves that ended at the knuckles. His fingers were chapped and his fingernails were long, but not dirty. He might have been experiencing homelessness, but there were visible signs reflecting his efforts to keep himself groomed, to perhaps hang on to as much of his dignity as possible.

Throughout the consumption of his meal, thus far, he kept his head bent down, never raising it to look at me.

The other patrons in the restaurant would glance over at us periodically, watching out of curiosity, which was not unusual. Some faces reflected sympathy while others, disapproval. *Too bad, people, this is not your business,* I thought. But their "looks" added to the discomfort I felt from his silence.

I had learned nothing about this person, not even his name, as I sat there as unobtrusively as possible without leaving the table to give him the space he seemingly desired. At that time, it didn't cross my mind that he was probably infinitely more uncomfortable than I was. Hindsight is a teacher that allows you to correct your choices and actions in future scenarios.

All of a sudden, he shifted his focus from his meal. Without even a slight glance in my direction, he reached into his duffel bag on the floor at his feet, and began rummaging through it until he found what he was looking for. He removed a small cloth sack, tied at the top like a bag of coins in a cartoon movie. He put the little bag on the table. I can still to this day see in my mind his partially gloved hands untying and opening it to reveal something wrapped in tissue paper. He carefully unwrapped the tissue paper to reveal even more tissue, unwrapping and unwrapping. *Whatever it is, he has it well protected. Must be important to him.*

When he finally reached the nucleus of this little package, he placed the object on the table, put his semi-gloved finger on top of it and slid it across to me. He slowly pulled his weathered hand away, revealing a small heart-shaped pendant with diamonds and emeralds. It was small, delicate, and well-cared for— a stark contrast from the man sitting across from me.

I glanced at him, making eye contact and asked, "May I?" He nodded and I reached for the small treasure. It was lovely. *Finally! Something to talk about.* However, I could see that his eyes were once again focused on the meal before him.

Undeterred, I put the pendant in the palm of my hand and studied it.

"It's really beautiful. Does it belong to someone special?"
No answer.

I tried again, "Did someone give this to you?"
More silence.

Any remaining hope I had of talking with this man faded. I placed his treasured pendant back on the table and slid it across to him as I thanked him for showing it to me.

Without a single word, he slid the beautiful bejeweled heart back over to me again and the inner guide spoke up. "He wants you to have it."

No! I couldn't! I looked at him in complete disbelief, and with hesitation asked, "Are you giving this to me?" He responded with one silent nod of his head.

"I can't keep this. It's too special. I could never take this from you," I said, tripping over my words.

Again, my inner guide spoke, telling me, "Accept it. He wants you to have it."

He remained silent.

I continued to insist that it was *way* too big a gift in exchange for the food I'd purchased, as my heart felt overwhelmed with a sensation I couldn't identify. He lifted his head to gesture with his facial expression that he wanted me to keep it. I finally stopped protesting and just stared in wonder at the treasure that was now mine. "Thank you. It will be my honor to have this," I told him, feeling awe and completely humbled by his generous gesture of gratitude. He simply lowered his head slowly, returning his focus to his plate. Once again, I stared at the top of his knit cap.

My inner voice pressed on, "You have just witnessed a part of this man's spirit that has not been impacted by the difficult circumstances he finds himself in. Only love could touch this sacred part of his being." I knew with certainty this was a very pivotal moment in my young life and I was moved beyond words.

I could barely hear myself say to the quiet man across the table from me. "I promise you I will keep this for the rest of my life and I will think of you each time I wear it."

He looked up and held my gaze for just a moment, his first real eye contact with me. I felt my eyes fill with tears and experienced a sudden rush of emotions. I somehow knew that I had just connected, in a different way, to the familiar presence of my angels.

Interesting thing is, at this point God was NOT on my radar. All I thought I knew about God back then was that He was great and He was good and we should thank Him for our food.

When I look back on this event now I can't help but think, *if only I had been more aware of God*, I would have known the Source of that which was pressing on my heart and the Source of the powerful, benevolent energy moving through this man that early evening in my youth. I would have had an even deeper understanding of the spark of divinity that lives inside each of us; the light of God we all possess that shone so brightly between this tattered man and my sixteen-year-old self. I did not yet understand that through our interactions, we were heeding the commands of the very same God—the Source of perfect love.

If I had known God back then, I would have known that what I felt that night was God's exquisite, unconditional, constant, and unwavering love as my homeless friend reached across the table to give me what was probably the most valuable of all his remaining worldly possessions. And I would have known that the awesome wave of emotion I experienced, the overwhelming feeling of pure love, is what happens when the Holy Spirit, the action part of the eternal Being of Love, swells inside and overtakes the command center of your body. When this happens, unless you have enormous control, you cannot help it, you will cry.

I did not know any of this yet, but the day would eventually come when I would. If that knowledge was to be delivered to me at then, I missed it. This would prove not to be the first, and certainly not the last, time I would miss a beacon from this Divine Source.

What I did know then was I wanted to discover what exactly it is that can protect someone's spirit so completely that it becomes impervious to the brutal beating life can deliver. What is the source of this inner-warrior that shields? What exactly had I just experienced?

This beautiful man did indeed have a voice, and as I reluctantly returned him to his desolate spot beneath the overpass that night, he used it to say, "Thank you, Miss. God Bless you."

I never learned his name, yet to this day, he is one of the most influential people I have ever met in my life. Because of him I began my quest to understand the source of hope that ultimately resides inside all of us. It would be the start of learning about something so powerful, it would eventually mold me into the person I am today.

It would be the first step on a path that would lead to the understanding that I too possess an inner-warrior for my light.

Telling the story at a speaking engagement. I kept my promise
to honor the gift given to me that early evening so long ago. I
see the gift-giver in my memory each time I wear it.
Photo Credit: Jim Harrison, Atlanta, GA.

18

CHAPTER 4

Disconnected

1988 |Age 22
24 years away from identifying God in my life

The commute was always the worst part of the day, but once I arrived, I loved every minute of my job. I immensely enjoyed the work I was doing and was surrounded by fantastic colleagues. I was in my early 20s when I began to make my way in the world of business, and had started working for a broadcasting corporation with global reach. My days were suddenly filled with all the things that affect our lives when we first become adults—rush hour commutes, grocery lists, conference rooms, work projects, bounced checks, Friday night dates, friends, family, and much more. I was still a stranger to the church and lived my life with a completely secular existence, as far as I knew.

At this point in time I am twenty-eight years away from meeting young Everett for the first time, teaching him about the unseen vibrational energy of love and light that is God, and telling him that if you concentrate on it you will always be able to feel it.

I could have used that lesson on this day in 1988 when the realization came to me out of nowhere, *something's different*. But what? I couldn't immediately put my finger on what had changed, but I knew something was off.

It took me at least half of the day to figure it out. *I cannot feel my unseen companion!*

"When did this start?" I wondered. I had no earthly idea. I hadn't been paying attention to that comforting presence that had been with me throughout my life. My focus had been entirely on the life I was building around me.

How long since I last felt it? Days? Weeks? Think, Keryl. I didn't know.

For as long as I live, I will never forget that day and the new reality that was upon me. To not feel the comfort and love that surrounded me for so many years was extremely hard on me. It left a significant void—like waking up after the loss of a loved one, only to remember seconds later that this person you so loved was gone.

Perhaps like being kicked out of Eden?

What had happened that made the feeling that 'everything was okay' disappear? I didn't know. I had no answers, but I knew I had no choice other than to go about my day. The world didn't stop because I could not feel the angels of my childhood. So, I carried on, and eventually fell asleep with a certainty that the next day would be different.

I was wrong. The next day was just the same. I still could not feel my constant companion, the comforting presence I had grown to love since it made itself known to me all those years prior. What's more, now that I was aware of its absence, I felt it in a profound way.

Having this disconnect altered the lenses through which I viewed everyday life. I could still see the exquisite landscape of a world I loved, but it was changed; somehow it was less vibrant and felt more ordinary. This made *me* feel ordinary. What was this foreign feeling? What had become missing in my life to cause such a feeling of loss? How is something not visible so palpable? Why now? Why did it not impact me when I was not aware of its absence?

So many questions and no answers.

What I did know was that I was now like the countless others who didn't seem to feel what cannot be seen, and I was certain I would never feel that connection again. Ever.

Although I had lived most of my life feeling this exquisite presence, it took only a few short hours for my mind to become convinced it was gone forever. Just like Adam and Eve, who believed they were separated from God.

Where the mind goes, the body follows.

We create what we think and once we decide something doesn't exist, then to us, it simply does not.

We are much more powerful than we know.

●　●　●　●　●　●　●

What makes us so powerful?

If the cosmic energy of our universe is the pitcher, we are the cups. Our bodies are a container of the same life-force energy that swirls in the unseen. We draw from the same energy that fuels the universe and we return energy back into the universe in a perpetual cycle of exchange.

Through the vibration of our brain waves, we transmit broadcast-like signals that are attuned to the emotions of our thoughts. Science tells us that thoughts and atoms are the same. Thus, not only are we created with atoms, but we in turn, create atoms with our thoughts.

When these atoms are observed, they change their pattern of behavior. Scientists have tested this numerously, with the most well-known experiment being the double-slit experiment. This experiment demonstrated that particles of matter behaved differently when they were under observation than they did when they were unobserved. In other words, we alter the patterns and behavior with our observations. As such, it is understood that reality is created by observers.

Pioneering physicist Sir James Jeans wrote: "The stream of knowledge is heading toward a non-mechanical reality; the universe begins to look more like a great thought than like a great machine. Mind no longer appears to be an accidental intruder into the realm of matter, we ought rather to hail it as the creator and governor of the realm of matter. Get over it, and accept the inarguable conclusion. The universe is immaterial-mental and spiritual."

If we believe these scientific findings to be true, then our thoughts and observations make us the co-creators of this enormous universe.

It was American physicist John Archibald Wheeler (1911-2008) who suggested that "no phenomenon is a *real* phenomenon until it is an observed phenomenon." For example, if you don't look at the moon— for you, it does not exist in that moment. It's a hard concept to grasp because one might say "I know the moon exists." Yes, it exists in your brain as knowledge, in your conscious, and in your memory. The moon that you do not see in that moment is merely a thought from your past.

Your reality is what you can observe *right now*.

It's that old conundrum, 'if a tree falls in the forest, with no one to observe it, does it make a sound?' The answer is no. Sound is vibration that is only detected when it passes through the ear canal and into the eardrum. If there is no receiver present, sound cannot exist. If there is no observer present, the occurrence does not exist.

In June 2017, someone very dear to me was the victim of a crime. At one point during the hours that followed with police officers and detectives, I was asked to come in to the interview room to help bring comfort to the raw emotions that poured out from having to relive the ordeal to them. I hugged her closely and gently soothed her. "Quiet your mind and bring it to right here, right now. Right here, right now, you are safe, you are protected, you are no longer in danger." The reality of the danger was in her past and no longer posed a physical threat nor existed anywhere but in her memory. Her reality was right now, surrounded by the safety of those committed to protecting the law, and by my love for her. The challenge she faced now was in over-riding the enormous power of her brain so her emotional body could believe that.

In the same manner that our brain can make something nonexistent, it can also take a memory and make it seem so real, it is as though the event is happening now. This is common with war veterans who battle post-traumatic stress symptoms. The horror of what they witnessed in the past, plays out in their brain as if it were in the present moment.

Thus, healing of a past trauma begins in earnest when we control our thoughts to not reliving it repeatedly in our present—simple words, complex process. Our brains are the most powerful computers in the world.

Not reliving an ordeal does not mean we should stifle or hide any negative emotion. We must address the source of emotional unrest. It means that we feel it, acknowledge it, let it rip through us, and then we remember that at this very moment "I AM whole and strong. I have, within me, the ability to create a different reality, right this moment, by controlling my thoughts, by staying in the now."

Emotions are one of our Creator's many gifts to us in that they help us gauge the disparity between the desires of our innermost self and our current life situation. When we pay attention to our emotions, it allows us to course-correct our thoughts and our lives to consciously create a reality that is in alignment with the deepest part of our souls, where love resides in its purest form.

I think back now and wonder, what event happened in my early twenties that created the feeling I was no longer surrounded by something special? Was it an event at all or did I simply manifest the feeling with my thoughts? My new reality was that I would never feel that comforting presence again.

And that thought created that reality.

In fact, I could not have known it then, but it would be another two decades before I felt my constant companion again. I did not yet understand how to control my thoughts to create the life I desired to live.

We are *that* powerful.

If we focused our thoughts on that which honors our highest-self—positive, affirmative, and steeped in love—we would eventually change our reality for the better.

Now, imagine if everyone alive collectively chose to turn their thoughts to the elimination of a world plague, like hunger, for example. We would impact much more than our immediate reality, we would change the world. We would, without fail, achieve the reality of a world where no child or adult would ever be food deficient again. If the collective conscious of the entire human race determined it was time to eradicate the issue of homelessness, we would create a reality where this travesty did not exist. This can be said for every global situation on Earth.

The greatest way to forging a better life for ourselves and for others is to simply change the way we think and the way we emotionally respond to our circumstances and what shows up in our lives. To act in alignment with our thoughts. It's to bring forth love and stay in the now. We must step fully into this understanding, experience it, and live according to that knowledge on a daily basis. The choice is ours to live consciously.

If in 1988, I had shed the thought "I will never feel my constant companion again," and instead chose to consciously connect to the unseen energy of it, I would have felt it again. A lesson I would come to learn as the years passed.

If there is this much power in our thoughts, there is even more in a thought that is combined with the spoken word. And there is infinite power in a thought, that is spoken aloud, and followed by action. When these three elements are focused on creating a better existence for us and the people around us, the universe conspires to support the effort. Some call this God's will.

In 2016, it would not take long to recognize that deep inside the soulful part of eight-year-old Everett, he somehow already knew all of this.

CHAPTER 5

The Faith of a Child

Fall 2016
Still on the day I met Everett

Everett was not huddling as close to his mother as he had when he first sat down in my city apartment on that fall day in 2016. He had visibly relaxed by the time we wrapped up our introductory meeting. I suggested he should have the evening to think about if he wanted to come back the next day to begin learning how to use his connection to the Divine to alleviate the pain from the migraines that had stripped away so much of his active young life.

To combat theses headaches, Everett had been put on the highest possible dosage of a narcotic strength painkiller that was extremely hard on his small body. Most recently, he underwent a lumbar puncture so the doctors could further examine the cause of his severely debilitating headaches which started six months prior. The doctors were not having much luck with the test results, and his parents were at a loss on what to do next to stop his suffering. They were wearying of the time Everett spent in hospitals, in doctor offices, and away from school. It was then that his mother remembered my strong belief in drawing from the energy of the universe to assist in healing a body. That is how Everett came to be in my apartment, being asked if he wanted to have time to think about coming back the next day.

Everett didn't need time to think. He decided right then that he would like to come back. We set up a time to meet the next day and said our good-byes. I was thrilled he wanted to continue in his healing together.

There is such power in saying yes.

And so much unwavering faith to be found in heart of a child.

● ● ● ● ● ● ●

When Everett left my apartment that afternoon, he turned to his mother and said, "Did you see her candle, mom? I feel like we need one of those candles."

"OK" she says, silently rejoicing that he seemed to be headache-free for the moment. A rare and wonderful occurrence.

"*Now,* mom! Can we go to a store and get one *now*?"

"Now?"

"Yes, now," he insisted.

"OK then...now," she replied, with more than a little curiosity about his insistence.

And so they began their search.

Everett is one special child.

The candle he was referring to in my home has been burning since 2013. It resides in a metal holder with intricate designs that create a beautiful dance of flickering patterns on the walls when I light the white pillar candle inside. Before I burn a new candle, I sit in silent reverence and give thanks for all I am grateful for. I ask God to bless the candle, and I offer prayer for whatever tugs at my heart in that moment.

The candle has been my way of sending positive energy out to the universe for reasons that are as diverse as can be. I have sent prayerful energy for peace in our troubled world, for love and compassion in the hearts of our leaders, for the oppressed, the refugees fleeing their home countries, for those in the path of natural disasters. I have lit the candle to send comfort and strength to the sick, the lonely, elderly, and homeless, as well as our soldiers and peacekeepers, the victims of terrorism, and the children in our world who are orphans. Of course, my candle has burned for family, friends, and loved ones in times of need, and even for myself—for my peace, for the wisdom to hear the quiet whisper of God, and the strength to be true to my highest self.

I set my intention that this candle represents divine light and love, a silent symbol that my home belongs to someone who honors and understands the power that is light. I envision sourcing this light from the vast and endless supply of high vibrational energy that comes from the Most High. I visualize this magnificent force protecting and filling my home with love so that nothing negative or unwanted could ever intrude into my peaceful space. There is no welcome mat in my home for negative energy—with or without the candle—but I light it in honor of my faith and my commitment to conduct my life and my responses in a manner that honors love.

There is nothing about the candle in this holder that would reveal what it represents to me. Unless I chose to share this, you would not know.

Yet somehow, Everett knew.

The time was rapidly coming when I would discover that this young, quiet boy was not only hearing, but was already choosing to heed the wisdom that came from the powerful voice within.

CHAPTER 6
A Monumental Understanding

1996 | Age 30

16 years away from identifying God in my life

I looked at my toddler daughter and once again acknowledged the thought that came to mind each time I did—she owned me. My heart was gone. What beat in my chest for close to 30 years no longer belonged to me, it was now hers—this chubby-cheeked, chortling baby who began infusing rays of sunshine into my soul since her arrival two years prior. I loved being a new mother! My then-husband observed that Madeline brought out a playfulness that must have been lying dormant inside of me, just waiting to be unleashed. I was childlike in my display of love. I kissed her scrumptious little tummy, tossed her in the air, stroked her velvety cheeks, and spent hours just watching her sleep. How can a heart get so big and not explode in its casing? How did mine even still fit in my body? It was a season of love, and a feeling of tranquility dominated my home.

That was, until BAM, out of nowhere—disruption. Like a stone that is thrown into a crystal smooth lake. My father, who had not been a part of my life for most of my adult years, contacted me.

I did not stay in the 'moment of now' when that contact came. My mind automatically hit playback on a movie reel of interaction with my father; one that reminded me with clarity how difficult his harsh manners had made life for the children under his roof. Mom was our glue. She held us together with her gentleness, strength, and easy laughter. She was the opposite of my father, who was quick to show his frustration and slow to show his love.

Now, he wanted to be a part of my tranquil life—the pebble had been tossed into my smooth lake.

"Absolutely not" was the response that surged up from inside of me, immediately spawning an inner conflict. I recognized I was torn. On the one side of the split emotions were manners, the lenses that saw beauty and goodness in all things, believed we could be stronger than what is negative, and quite frankly, my inability to put my own wants in a place of priority over the wants of someone else. On the other side were the memories, the mama bear who didn't want anything negative to penetrate the walls of a wonderfully-balanced home, and who wanted to keep an environment of peace for her little cub. It took less than a minute to know which side would win. No way were we answering this proverbial knock.

Is anything stronger than a mama bear?

Whether that was the right decision at that moment or the wrong one, I cannot say. Nor does it even matter all these years later, it was simply the choice I made. Heartbreakingly, I didn't want the father of my childhood in our lives at that time.

I had not yet learned how to offer love even in the hardest situation, as I do now. A capability each of us possesses but is hard to execute. The experiences that taught me this was forthcoming, but at that point, still a long way into my future.

However, what was upon me at that very moment turned out to be a monumentally important lesson that I would keep for the rest of my life. It was right then I learned that with every situation in life, we could control the manner in which we responded. We could choose what to let in and what to keep out.

I could choose.

When facing a person who was once an authority figure in our lives, we tend to think we must acquiesce to their will and not our own—even as adults. Additionally, we are programmed to do what is habitual, what society deems normal, or what feels polite.

This scenario revealed a new truth, *I was empowered to choose.*

The light bulbs continued to go off in my mind. *I had that same choice with everything.* We may not always have a choice to determine what life hurls at us, but we always have a choice on how we respond and how we let it impact our lives.

I understood with my decision that I could render powerless anything negative that threatened the peace of my surroundings by simply not allowing it in—not just every now and then, but every moment. *I am the chooser.* I have free will—the ability to base a decision on the options available to me. The same free will that had Eve plucking the fruit from the forbidden tree.

We were a mother and father warrior team, who wanted a home that was filled with a positive vibe. We could choose to do whatever we had to do to achieve that.

It's easy to exist in peace during periods of joy and tranquility, like the one we were experiencing as new parents desperately in love with our cheerful toddler. The real challenge is in maintaining that positivity when the peace of your life is greatly disrupted.

How do we stay true to the light of love when injustice is upon us—or tragedy? When someone we love is terminally ill, has been taken from us, or is hurt? When we are wrongly accused, or judged harshly and unfairly? When we are- or a loved one is- the victim of a violent crime that blackens our world, takes from the muscles in our legs the ability to hold our weight for that moment, clutches our heart and squeezes it like a vise that we think will never ever be released? How do we not let ourselves—and consequently, our environment—become poisoned with resentment, hatred, and fear?

The answer is—the very same way. We don't give power to the negative. Words that are easy to write, say and know, but might take years to fully master. Just as we have a choice with our thoughts and our responses, so do we have a choice with what we allow in.

This does not mean that we close the door on all who are not perfectly harmonized, it simply means don't be hesitant to do what you must to not allow negativity to permeate your thoughts, your home, and your life and become a permanent residence.

We have a choice. I had a choice. What a monumental understanding!

I began practicing choosing options that spawned positivity until it became a habit. I began with the most influential part of my life—me. This required learning how to stop the automatic thoughts that raced through my mind like a speeding train. It meant taking a hard look at the habits that were toxic to me and having the fortitude to remove them—not just some of the time, but every time. I had to shine a light on the shadow parts of myself to reveal them. It meant openly examining my responses and my feelings, letting go of things that no longer served me positively—people included—and filling my life with things that progressed and expanded my thinking.

It required that I release painful memories from the past and refrain from fretting about what hadn't happened yet, as well as becoming more intentional in my actions and more impeccable in my words. More than anything, I had to be honest with myself about whether I was letting the fear of my ego govern my actions versus the love in my spirit.

None of these happened overnight. I worked hard to form new habits and shed those that no longer served me. In time, the changes came—slowly but surely. As a result, I was in my early thirties when I discovered mindfulness.

By choosing what was beneficial to me and those around me, by setting my intentions, and looking for the positive in all situations, displaying gratitude for everything, removing my ego where possible, being selective on what I allowed within my boundaries, not letting the words or thoughts of others penetrate me, staying rooted in today, and trusting that I had a connection to the energy around me, my life began to change.

The change was subtle at first. I noticed that life seemed to ebb and flow like somehow it was working alongside me. This put me in tune with myself and my intuition developed, causing my sensory abilities to be sharpened—a mirror of what began for me as a child connected to my constant companion. For example, I had a sense when someone would be calling me. I could more easily detect the vibe of the person next to me, and even across the room. Solutions to challenges at work came to me much faster than ever before which had a positive impact on my career. I became bolder in my intentions as I listened to my inner voice and heard it more clearly. I felt lighter, more rooted in the moment. I even had a better sense when it was safe to be on the streets at night with our city's unsheltered homeless and when I should stay away. I trusted my intuition.

My dreams became more vivid and I became aware that there seemed to be signs everywhere that were in alignment to my thoughts. I paid attention to those signs; and the more I did, the more I noticed them. I took nothing for granted and I stopped believing in coincidences. Life began to display a pattern as though I was living in a reality that was designed just for me.

I started running when I was in my mid-twenties and ran throughout my pregnancy and post-pregnancy. I was already healthy, but I noticed that I was getting sick less frequently. When other mothers of young children succumbed to the germs carried home from day-care, I stayed healthy. Not only that, but should there be an instance where I began to feel sick, I would feel myself becoming bigger than my illness, and soon discovered I could will it away. Mind over matter. Positivity, joy, and gratitude boosted the immune system significantly.

The changes that occurred became less subtle over time— an extra something, an extra sensory ability that deepened. I didn't feel my 'angels' in the way I felt in the past, but I felt a connection to everything that exists in a different way than I had before and became more adept at balancing the energy in my daily life.

I didn't know it yet, but I was well on my way to becoming a true warrior for my light.

At this point in my journey, I still had no idea that the connection I felt was God or Source. But there was no doubt that I felt something tugging at my soul. If that wasn't enough, situations occurred occurred that would show me perpetually how we are never alone, and are watched over by something much bigger than we can fathom.

CHAPTER 7
Vanished into Thin Air

July 2006 | Age 39

Seven years away from identifying God in my life

Bike riding is therapeutic for me, and this day was going to be spent riding with a friend I loved, which made it even better. Sherry and I had looked forward to this day all week. She arrived to my home early on a Sunday morning and was greeted by the gentleman I was dating at the time. He complimented the new bicycle rack that was attached to the hitch on her Acura sedan, and went to work securing my bike to it with ease, using the built-in heavy-duty rubber straps plus a few bungee cords for added security. As an avid mountain biker, he was always hauling his own bike to some new place for an adventure with his group of riding buddies. He would not be accompanying us however, as it was a ladies-only excursion. We were not going to be trail riding anyway; we were taking our road bikes to ride on The Silver Comet, a popular local bike path in Atlanta. Sherry's bike was tied down in the first of the four slots, closest to the back window of the car. Mine was in the second slot, and the two slots farthest from the back-window remained empty.

I loved my bike and enjoyed the Zen of a ride. I had invested in the bike a few years earlier and never had a single regret. I was the mother of a pre-teen daughter and the owner of a thriving business—two things that kept me constantly on the go. The bike was my solace, a way to relax and let it all go for a while. It was silver and blue, designed for the road as well as light off-road use. As I watched it being carefully secured, to Sherry's car, I couldn't help but notice that it still looked brand new. *I really wish I could use it more often,* I thought. I also gave myself a little pat on the back for having taken such impeccable care of it over the years.

Unbeknownst to me, in just a short while, the exact words in this thought would come back to me in the most surprising way.

Early morning will always be my favorite time of day. It marks the beginning of 365 fresh starts and 24 hours of adventure into the unknown, where I could make the new day into whatever I want it to become. This lovely summer morning the air was still cool. We knew the heat was coming, so we decided to get an early start. We drove with the windows down, enjoying the dewy fresh air dancing gently around us; the only real sound we heard as we traveled on the nearly empty interstate. The radio was off, allowing us to speak in normal volume, as we drove on, so looking forward to the day ahead.

The bike path was approximately 25 minutes away down Interstate 285, a major highway that encircles Metro Atlanta.

We opted to start at mile marker zero located behind an elementary school. Sherry pulled into a nearby parking spot, closed the windows and turned off the ignition. She immediately got out of the car as I stashed some things in the bag I was taking, planning to hide the rest in the trunk.

Neither of us were prepared for what came next.

I got out of the car and went around back where I found Sherry staring at her bike rack with honest-to-goodness shock on her face; the kind of shock that hits you when you are faced with something so completely bizarre it takes a moment for your brain to get through the numb zone and begin to process again. "Your bike! Where's your bike?" she exclaimed dumbfounded as she finally found her voice. I stared in total disbelief at her new, state-of-the-art bike rack holding only one bike. Hers.

I was speechless.

She looks at me panicking, "We have to go back! We have to go back! How could this happen? Oh my gosh!"

Still I said nothing. My brain was not yet through the numb zone.

It was at that very moment a vehicle pulled up alongside us. The front passenger window came down revealing a handsome man who spoke to us across the empty passenger seat in an articulate manner, exuding a peaceful confidence that said, "I know who I am." Even in my numbed-out state, I will never forget my immediate impression of him.

"Are you ladies looking for a bike?" he asked.

Sherry whips her head in his direction and exclaims, "Yes!"

He turns his gaze toward me. "Is it blue and silver, looks impeccably cared for?"

I furrow my brow just a little behind my sunglasses. *How uncanny that his words were nearly identical to my earlier thought. And does he know it's my bike and not Sherry's? How could he? There's no way.*

I finally utter my first words since stepping out of the car. "Yes, that sounds like my bike."

Wide eyed, Sherry gasps, "You know where it is? Please tell us where."

"I saw it under the overpass at Roswell Road on 285 Westbound. Looks like someone just lifted it off the rack and laid it there gently."

Sherry and I turn and stare at each other in total disbelief.

He nods politely to both of us and says, "Good luck ladies. Enjoy this day," as we watch him drive off.

Did that really happen or is this a dream?

Interstate 285 at Roswell Road was not exactly just around the corner. The Silver Comet Trail is a trail that spans two states. Who was that man and what are the chances he would pull into the same parking lot and just happen to know we were looking for a bike that he claims to have seen lying neatly on the side of the freeway, beneath an overpass at least ten miles away?

"WE HAVE TO GO!" Sherry exclaimed as she jumped in the car, clearly feeling like it is somehow her fault, because the bike rack belongs to her. I could feel the weight of this falling on her shoulders and could see the distress on her face. As she navigates her car out of the parking spot, the apologies start.

For those of you who have ever secured a bicycle to a hitch-mounted carrier rack, you are likely aware of the force required to pull down the rubber straps that hold the bike in place. Each of the four bike holders on Sherry's carrier had numerous rubber straps. I could see a replay of the straps being checked and double-checked by the avid mountain biker in my life. I could also see the numerous bungee cords that were added as backup, and noticed at that moment, that none of them were dangling empty on the rack that once held my bike.

Yet, that was not even where my mind went first.

"Sherry..." I pause for a minute before continuing. Remarkably, I felt calm. Not in shock, not the numb zone, just simply calm. "We had the windows down and the radio off. The road was quiet, we were speaking in normal tones and could hear each other perfectly well."

"OK...yes?" she said, much more focused on getting us to Roswell Road than to listening to me.

I continue, "If the bike had fallen off the rack, don't you think we would have heard it? I mean, if one of the straps came undone, it and the bike would have started clanging and banging around against your bike and the bike rack, right?" I paused as the image of metal banging against metal crystallized in my mind. "But let's say all the straps somehow, unexplainably snapped away at the exact same time, including the extra bungee cords. Even then, the bike would have had to have been lifted off the padded rack, fallen between the bars, then under the rack, and then somehow be swept off of the road to beneath the underpass." I pause again. "Are you following what I am saying, Sherry?"

But I might as well have been talking to the empty space between us as we sped down the divided interstate heading East on I-285. She was too focused on getting to our exit to even hear a word I was saying.

"Oh! Here's Roswell Road! This is where he said it would be, right? Let me go past it and come back down the other way. Do you see it, Keryl?" she asks as she slows down and gets off at the next exit. She turns left, then left again, and we are back on I-285 going West just as we were less than an hour before, when we were excitedly anticipating the Zen of our day with two bikes on a rack. No more than a minute had passed since I had spoken, but my mind was churning rapidly.

"We would have heard it, Sherry. We would have heard my bike fall off the rack. We had the windows down, the radio off, we weren't talking loudly. We definitely would have heard my bike

40

make a racket as it came loose, got tangled under the rack, and kicked out onto the interstate."

I heard the mystery man's words again, "It's like someone lifted it off the bike rack and laid it there gently."

At that very moment, I knew I would not see my bike under the Roswell Road overpass. Although I could almost see it in my mind, laying there, carefully placed, I just knew I would never see it again. Sherry was utterly distressed, and laser focused on finding it. She still had not acknowledged one word I'd said. She circled the area twice, as if it was there and we were somehow missing it.

What was my inner voice saying to me? *This had to happen.*

Okay, but why? *Why* did this have to happen? Why was my bike not on the bike rack when we arrived? Why did we not hear it come untethered from its double grip and slip away from us? Who was that man and what was it about his energy that felt so different? So peaceful.

My beautiful friend, Sherry, did not want to accept the inevitable, that my well-kept investment of a bike secured to her new bike rack less than an hour ago was somehow gone. I could see, however, that it was starting to sink in. She looked at me with great sadness.

"Sherry it's okay." I said, still calm, despite my loss. "Someone obviously needed my bike more than I did." This was the only thing I could come up with at that moment. I thought maybe there was a father out there who lost his job and desperately needed a way to get to work. Or maybe a family needed the money it would bring them if they sold it. I didn't know. All I knew was that this would not have happened without a purpose. The only thing that made sense to me was that someone must have needed my bike more than I did and it was no longer mine.

I looked at my friend. "Really, Sherry, I'm okay. And this is not your fault." She reached for my hand and squeezed it, grateful for my understanding. We drove back down the interstate exactly as we had the opposite direction less than an hour before, windows down, radio off. It was the same cool air gently touching our faces, the same serene atmosphere and very light traffic. The only difference was this time we didn't say a word, and Sherry's new rack carried only one bike.

We got to my place where she dropped me off, and we said goodbye.

It was strange not to see my bicycle hanging on its hook in the garage for the next two days.

I told the story to my office staff and they were just as perplexed as I was. They too offered, "Things happen for a reason."

The next evening, I had the television on in the background, tuned in to the local news. With the reporter's next words, I swear I felt the ground shake beneath my feet.

"Missing woman on Silver Comet Trail."

Oh my God.

A mother of three was reported missing by her husband when she didn't return home the previous night. She was on the Silver Comet Trail, where she rode a regular 50-mile out and back route; the very same bike path we were thwarted from riding just two days prior.

I had to sit down.

The reporter continued, "Her family began to worry when she didn't return by 8 p.m...."

Again, I replayed the seemingly significant words I heard in the parking lot. "It looks like someone lifted it off the bike rack and laid it there gently," the mysterious stranger had said

The next day they found her body. She had been brutally murdered in the woods along the route Sherry and I had planned to be on that early morning, had we had two bikes upon arrival and not just one.

"We would have heard it," I recalled telling Sherry that fateful day. "We would have heard the bike falling off."

My heart was crushed for the family who had lost their loved one. Turns out the victim of this violent crime fought off her offender so bravely, he was arrested because of the visible defensive wounds she inflicted upon him. A neighbor of his became suspicious after hearing of the missing woman and then noticing his significant injuries. She unfortunately lost her life, but there is no doubt she saved the lives of many other potential victims, perhaps two women setting out for a ride on a quiet Sunday morning.

Brave soul.

My heart continued to hurt for days.

For as long as I can remember, I have listened to and heeded my inner voice, but I did not hear it that morning we left for the bike ride. Did it try to stop me from going, but I wasn't listening? Did this amazing woman who lost her life that day, also have an inner voice, and if so, was there something that afternoon that told her not to go on her regular ride? We can't know, but I wonder, how many of us receive intuitive messages we automatically dismiss? How many times have we heard that inner voice urging us not to do something we have done routinely so many times before and for some reason we listen? For example, we follow the gut instinct to take a different route home, and we later learn there was a terrible accident on our normal route. How many times do we dismiss it?

Through our connection to the Divine Energy of this universe, we receive messages constantly. God speaks to all of us in so many ways. Are we listening? Sadly, not all of us can avoid disaster. As

I think about this woman, I realize that the courageous spirit of a beautiful woman who went to her eternal home far too soon for those who loved her, lives eternally now where only love exists. I am a stranger to her and yet I have never forgotten her.

I keep a photo of my lost bike on the refrigerator to remind me to stay open to mysteries and miracles when they occur. And I am certain that somewhere someone's prayers were answered when they found my impeccably-kept bike lying on the Atlanta interstate like someone had just placed it there for them to find. Like a gift from God. Again, I am certain it was delivered to that faithful person who needed my bike more than I did.

I will not begin to identify God in my life for another seven years. When I do finally come to know God's perfect love, this will be one of the many things I look back upon in utter awe.

This photo of me with my blue and silver bike is kept on my refrigerator to remind me of the power and mystery of God.

CHAPTER 8

Hard-Wired for Connection

²And indeed, when Adam looked at his flesh, that was altered, he cried bitterly, he and Eve, over what they had done. "What is our body today, compared to what it was in former days, when we lived in the garden?"[...] ⁸And Adam said to Eve, "Look at your eyes, and at mine, which before beheld angels praising in heaven; and they too, without ceasing. ⁹But now we do not see as we did; our eyes have become of flesh; they cannot see like they used to see before."

Adam and Eve were no longer able to see themselves beyond their human skin—their flesh and bones—as they had before. They were unable to experience what is later described in the book as their 'bright nature.'

Dr. Jill Bolte-Taylor is a brain scientist who delivered one of the most riveting TED Talks, titled "My Stroke of Insight." In it, she describes what she experienced when a blood vessel exploded in her brain, temporarily shutting down the left hemisphere and leaving only the functionality of the right. The right hemisphere of our brain, she explains, responds to the kinesthetic nature of our world—the moment of NOW.

"It is the right here, right now, what this moment smells like, feels like, tastes like, and sounds like, part of our world."

She goes on to say, "I am an energy being, connected to the energy all around me through the consciousness of my right hemisphere. We are energy beings connected to one another through the consciousness of our right hemispheres, as one human family.

"And right here, right now, we are brothers and sisters on this planet, here to make this world a better place. And in this moment, we are perfect, we are whole, and we are beautiful."

Without function in her left brain, Dr. Bolte Taylor was no longer able to discern where she, as a human being, ended and the universe began. It was as though she was no longer a solid, individual form but rather she was one with everything around her.

Quantum Physics tells us that when two atoms are created together, a link is forged. If you move them away from each other, even at a great distance, they remain connected through what is known as a quantum wormhole; a bridge between the two separated objects. Because science has determined that all the matter in the universe was created at the same time—a theory commonly known as the big bang—this would mean that every atom in your body is connected to every atom that exists in the universe. This is known as the Theory of Entanglement.

We are all entangled. One. Fueled by the same universal energy.

Try, if you can, to imagine a world where we could physically see our oneness with each other and with all that exists. Think of how we might conduct our lives if we carried that visual with us; if we were able to perceive each other as extensions of ourselves, each of us drawing from the same breath of life, our unique forms morphing into one another while remaining wholly unique and sovereign. Would it matter what color skin we have or that the shapes of our eyes are different if, when we were standing next to someone, we couldn't fully distinguish where one person ended and the other began? "Love your neighbors as yourselves" (Mark 12:31, The Holy Bible), would certainly have deeper meaning if we could actually see that our neighbors are, in reality, a part of ourselves.

Despite the unimaginable suffering Dr. Jill Bolte Taylor endured from her stroke, she received the gift of seeing what most cannot—and she found exquisite beauty in this.

While Dr. Bolte-Taylor's condition was temporary, there are many who go through their entire lifetime in such a state. Our brains are like complex machinery. We should not immediately judge people who claim they can see or experience certain phenomena others cannot—like auras and visions, undetectable sounds, or the appearance of certain 'paranormal' beings or energies. I find it troublesome that our society is so quick to place labels such as 'mentally ill' on those individuals who experience life on a different frequency. I find it even more troubling at how quickly modern medicine and psychiatry suggest the use of mind-altering pharmaceuticals to try and make them 'normal.'

What is 'normal' anyway? Who defines that?

As it turns out, we are hard-wired for connection to the unseen. One does not need to suffer a stroke to connect to the divine.

Located in the middle of your brain, just above eye level is the pineal gland, which is about the size of a pea. Despite its very small size, it is an extremely important gland, and given its name because it is shaped like a pine cone. The pineal gland is often referred to as the third eye.

In the 17th Century, Rene Descartest referred to the pineal gland as "The Seat of the Human Soul." It has also been called

47

the God organ. In the Bible, when Jacob claimed to see the face of God and lived, he named the place where this occurred Peniel.

Pineal, Peniel. Sounds pretty similar. You do the math.

This powerful little gland is responsible for producing serotonin and melatonin, and acts also as a transducer, which is defined as to convert from one energy to another.

A windmill takes wind and converts it into electricity, which gives us power.

A battery takes chemicals and creates an electric charge, giving us power.

And a water wheel is turned by powerful water currents that produce electricity, generating power.

These are all transducers.

It is understood that our pineal gland actually intakes information from the universal energy around us, translates it into an understandable thought, and moves it to the frontal lobe which holds it as an idea. Do you know those palm-to-forehead moments when a flash of brilliance manifests in the form of an idea? Trust me when I tell you there is a lot happening to create that moment. Your brain has taken a message from the spiritual realm and transduced it into a thought.

Dr. Bolte Taylor explains that the endless chatter in our minds comes from the left hemisphere. Maybe you've heard the saying, *quiet the mind and the soul will speak—a quiet mind is able to hear intuition over fear.*

Quiet mindfulness brings our subconscious and conscious thoughts together in one space, allowing us to connect to the divine energy of the universe, to infuse our mind with its infinite wisdom, and to palpably feel at one with all there is.

What's more, this practice is beneficial to our emotional and physical wellness. Findings after findings have shown this.

Dr. Bolte Taylor, a studied scientist experienced it firsthand, in a manner that was incredibly profound. I encourage you to watch her TED Talk video.

She ends her powerful testimony with an observation born of her enviable experience, "So who are we?" she asks. "*We* are the life-force power of the universe—with manual dexterity and two cognitive minds. And we have the power to choose moment by moment, who and *how* we want to be in the world.

"Right here, right now, I can step into the consciousness of my right hemisphere, where we are—I AM—the life force power of the universe. I am the life force power! The 50 trillion molecular geniuses that make up my form; at one with all that is.

"Or I can choose to step into the consciousness of my left hemisphere where I become a single individual, a solid—separate from you, separate from the flow. I *am* Dr. Jill Bolte Taylor, intellectual, neuroanatomist. These are the 'we' inside of me.

"Which would you choose? Which do you choose? And when?

"I believe that the more time we spend choosing to step into the circuitry of our right hemispheres, the more peace, we will project into the world and the more peaceful our planet would be."

Every person should watch this TED Talk.

CHAPTER 9

The Boundaries of Faith

2011 | Age 45

One year away from identifying God in my life

2011. I was no longer married. That season of my life ended years earlier with a mutual agreement between my former husband and I that our relationship was more suited to a platonic friendship. The bond we both had with our 17 year-old daughter was not impacted. It was a strong one.

I was still running the business I had launched in January 2000 and had been fortunate to have had successfully nurtured it into one that generated multi-million-dollar revenues.

Even though I still could not feel the presence of my unseen companion in the manner in which I did as a child, I felt an integrated flow with life, and I could still hear the wise inner voice that pressed on my heart.

Something was shifting inside of me and I felt it strongly. I could feel a pull to transition to a different phase in my career. I craved one that focused on a more purposeful service. This pull began in 2010, but at first, I largely ignored it.

I recognized this pull. I had heard its whisper years earlier in the final days of 1999, when I made the decision to leave my corporate job to launch my company.

It had been much easier to listen to the call of a major transition when the impact of the decision was primarily on me. Now the situation was different. I had a company with employees who had families, children, and mortgages. There were standing legal contracts to consider, as well as multiple clients who were depending on us. It would be a complicated process to disentangle from all of this.

Not to mention the fact that I was single, which meant I was solely responsible for my mortgage, bills, and overhead. Most importantly, I was responsible for being a present mother and role model to my teen-aged daughter.

I did my best to ignore what was pressing from within.

Big mistake. There is nothing more powerful and relentless than a beckon from the Divine. Thus, two years after the first whisper in 2010, I finally found myself making the arrangements necessary to wind down my company. I understood it would take years, but I was finally ready for whatever would come next.

Unbeknownst to me, I was about to stand in the doorway of what would become a season of enormous challenge; of faith discovered and tested, and of endless situations that pushed the boundaries of my mind.

Looking back now, it was as if God was the sword maker and I was the unshaped metal.

I was put into a scorching fire to strip away the non-pliable rigidity of what I was, and held there until I could no longer bear the heat. I'd be pulled out—but only so the sword maker could fold the metal over to mold and shape me. Before I could even fully cool off, I would be thrust back into the next fire to be made pliable again. Each process burned away what was not needed. Each subsequent fold strengthened me. Each pounding shaped me into a new version of me, until what was meticulously, lovingly, and boldly crafted had the strength to withstand any fire that life brought.

Yes, that was the season I was about to enter.

This period would also reveal to me—a secular woman in her mid-forties—the infinite, mysterious, unending power that exists in the life-force that is God, and how the inability to grasp the boundlessness of God is a common human affliction.

Rather than expanding our thinking, we tend to shrink God down to the confines of whatever we can realistically believe in our quite limited minds. Intellectually we might understand that this Source is omnipresent, unwavering, and mighty, but the moment something happens that is even slightly outside the boundaries of what we can logically grasp, we don the lens of skepticism.

We shout the glory of this power in our hearts, and we mute it in our actions. When push comes to shove, we choose doubt. If we witness an act transcending our limited boundary of faith, we condemn it, dismiss it, and crucify it.

In the Christian faith, it is believed that Jesus of Nazareth, empowered by his oneness with God, was able to perform many miracles. Many Christians also believe that the *Holy Bible* is the true word of God. But if you ask almost any Christian of today if they believe that they themselves can perform the miracles Jesus did, they will most likely tell you no.

Yet, in the book of John, chapter 14, verse 12, Jesus says: "Truly, truly, I say to you, he who believes in me, the works that I do, he will do also; and greater works than these he will do..."

Greater works. It sounds to me like we are meant to exceed the boundaries set by Jesus.

Peter, I would soon learn, was a dedicated and devoted student of the teachings of Christ. He was also a man with the gumption to try to accomplish something that defied the perceived confines of being human.

(Matthew 14:28-31) *28Peter said to him, "Lord, if it is you, command me to come to you on the water." 29And he said, "Come!" And Peter got out of the boat, and walked on the water and came toward Jesus. 30But seeing the wind, he became frightened, and beginning to sink, he cried out, "Lord, save me!"31Immediately Jesus stretched out his hand and took hold of him, and said to him, "You of little faith, why did you doubt?"*

I have not spent any time trying to walk on water, but I lived my life attempting to believe in that which is beyond my finite understanding.

Perhaps this is why I experienced what was coming next; because I had a lifetime of listening to the voice within and not the voices around me.

Quite frankly, I have speculated the many 'whys' for this season I was about to face. Was something greater than me trying to show me in a grand scale just how powerful we are or that we, as Jesus stated, can become much more than what we limit ourselves to be? Was I learning the truth in what is said—God does not call the prepared, He prepares those who respond to His call?

Perhaps it was me who sent out the beacon that said "I'm ready to be shown more. Bigger please. I can handle Your boldness."

Was that it?

Maybe I just needed to be woken up and this was the hard shake that did it.

Whichever it was, I was about to enter a wickedly challenging boot camp.

In the midst of it, I would discover that no matter how insidious something may seem, there is still beauty and light to be found if one chooses to seek it. When they are revealed, there is nothing more powerful. Darkness has nothing on the light of love.

In the next part of my book, I am going to share with you a series of events centered around an individual whose path converged with mine.

During this period, I archived a large amount of communication that took place via digital formats—e-mail, instant messenger, cellphone voice recordings, and more. 'Something' pressed on my heart to archive these communications in numerous mediums and keep them safe. As I always do, I heeded this voice.

From the archives, I carefully selected only the parts I believed were relevant to my story of discovery.

Let this part of my story wrap you in curiosity—perpetually wondering, just as I did, what was the *why* behind it. Think not from your brain but from your spirit. Read it with a detached and open mind, understanding that God has no bias in whom or what event He chooses to use to teach His creation, and guide us to Him. Without these events, it might have taken me much longer to identify God in my life.

Perhaps you can relate.

Part 2

Where the Mind Goes

CHAPTER 10

The Cancer Patient

2012

In a swimming pool in the Southeastern part of the United States, a woman in her late thirties, named Allison, was swimming routine laps. As she moved through the water, she noticed something wasn't right and soon discovered a strange lump on her left knee.

Its presence troubled her.

At the time, she was engaged to her fiancée, Eric, an affluent man with a heritage rooted deeply in the South. Eric urged her to make an appointment with a doctor as soon as possible to have this strange lump examined. She chose a local doctor who immediately ran a battery of tests. When the results came back, the news was not good. She was diagnosed with bone cancer. The physician she chose wanted to remove a good portion of the bone in her left knee to ensure it did not spread. Because she wanted to be able to continue her active lifestyle, she decided against this particular treatment and hunted for another doctor.

She finally found a doctor who would take her case, promising her there would be no invasive removal of bone. This doctor, who I will refer to as Dr. M., was a pediatric oncologist. Why a pediatric specialist? Because something very odd was discovered about the type of cancer from which she suffered. It was a cancer that is usually only found in children.

At first, Allison shared this information with select individuals in her social circle. I was not a part of this small, particular group of friends, and had never even heard mention of her name. Turns out however, she and I had a mutual friend who encouraged her to disclose her diagnosis to me. He believed me to be a good friend to others, as well as a source of comfort, and she really seemed to need both.

She reached out to me at a sporting event where I was a participant and she was a volunteer; and after talking for a while she decided to tell me about her diagnosis. She shared that it was almost an exact mirror of round one, which thankfully, was defeated several years earlier.

Allison's appearance was extremely robust and healthy, not what one might expect from someone battling cancer. My immediate thought upon hearing her story was "How scary that this can happen to anyone." Her vibe was one of understandable uncertainty and insecurity, but she was friendly and eager to connect.

She explained how her family was not available to assist her in battling her illness. They loved her, but her mother had to care full-time for her ailing father, and her only brother lived in another state.

I listened in stunned disbelief to all of it—the diagnosis, the rare form, and especially the absent family. As a mother, it was difficult for me to understand why mountains were not being moved to be by her side.

"What happened to your fiancé?" I asked her with genuine concern.

"He could not handle it, he left," she responded, forlornly.

How terrible. I could not imagine how devastating and hurtful that must have been for her.

Allison informed me that she had a friend who was driving her to her early morning radiation appointments. She said that other than these two friends, and now me, she wasn't really telling anyone. She was determined to face her illness alone.

No way.

My compassion for someone so in need had been activated. I extended an offer to help and opened my home to her as a place she could rest immediately after her treatments—a temporary place to regain strength for the next treatment.

Admittedly, I am quick to open my heart, but not normally quick to open my doors. This was a first. However, I felt the pressing on my heart from my inner voice, and as I had for all of the previous years of my life, I heeded the voice, even if the instructions didn't make sense to me. I knew it was never wrong.

While she was a complete stranger to me, I was under the impression she was an integral part of a running group where we shared mutual friends. For that reason, I did not see any possible risk in opening my home to her as a place to recover after certain medical treatments.

It would be much later that I would learn she was only on the periphery of this group. In fact, I would learn a great deal in the months that were ahead of me.

My online search of Allison's Dr. M. revealed a man with impressive credentials. Almost as soon as I offered her my help, she informed me she was granting me the rights to access her medical information so that I could act as her health care proxy.

She presented documents bearing her signature that named me as such.

Once those papers were sent to the doctor, I heard from him immediately. He informed me that he would be using e-mail and instant messenger to communicate protocol and other treatment-related information. I should expect to receive messages preparing me for the symptoms she would be experiencing, and I was asked to please report back on how his patient was handling the treatment. This method of communication would permit him to have an archived log for his medical records. Subsequently, I would also have an identical log on my end. Given the importance of this study, I immediately set up an archive system so nothing in our exchange would be lost.

I would not have known then that I would find myself referring back to my archives countless times beginning in December 2015 as I sought to gain understanding of the events that transpired with this cancer patient.

At first, I was largely unaware of how special Allison was to Dr. M. My first inkling was when I was informed that he ran a background check to be certain there was not something in my past that would show up unexpectedly and disrupt his work.

I had to be who I said I was.

"Is that normal procedure?" I had asked.

It was for him. She was instrumental to a research study he was leading, and he would not take any chances on who he entrusted to be a caregiver for this patient.

Secret research, background checks, cancer fighting. I felt a little bit like a character in a fictional novel.

Allison presented me with a letter written on the official letterhead of the hospital and bearing the signature of the president of the medical institution. The letter confirmed her participation in a proprietary research study, as seen by the small excerpt included here, which reads: *"This letter is to inform you that you have enrolled in the Stem-5 Intonalviral Research Protocol as of this 1 day of February, 2012. Continuation in this program is subject to the biological response of all submitted biology and physiology. _____, MD is the physician in charge of the research protocol and all resulting treatments for your case."*

This letter is to inform you that you have enrolled in the Stem-5 Intonalviral Research Protocol as of this 1 day of February, 2012. Continuation in this program is subject to the biological response of all submitted biology and physiology. ▆▆▆▆, MD is the physician in charge of the research protocol and all resulting treatments for your case.

She had been chosen for this research because of the way her body responded to traditional treatment during her first round of cancer. For some reason, she did not lose her hair or show any of the visible signs of treatment commonly seen on a cancer patient. Because of her extremely rare physiological makeup, we were told she would not really look sick.

Furthermore, she whispered to us that the hospital was using her blood and tissue to formulate a new cancer treatment for children, and that it was already showing great promise. It was also explained that very few from the medical institution would even be aware of this research. *So, mum's the word.*

No wonder he ran a background check.

It was amazing. We felt so honored to be part of something new that was healing children. 'We,' now included friends in my circle who also jumped in to help her.

From my perspective, Allison loved the attention she received from these folks. They seemed to lift her deflated spirits and help take her mind off the disease that had invaded her body.

While they- and many others- saw firsthand what was unfolding in my home, it was one person from my running group who really stepped up to help throughout this challenging period. Gary would be the one to offer nearly non-stop support. He would, as a result, become the primary witness for many of the unbelievable things to come; eventually becoming one of my closest friends to this very day.

From the start, her doctor behaved quite differently than what one expects in that he lacked what I would consider to be a typical clinical bedside manner. "Cancer," he wrote in his communication tool of choice—email, "is three pronged. It's the disease, the medical, and the emotional. She will live the third prong with you. I will put her through incredible pain in her treatment and then turn her over to you to deal with that pain and the emotion of it; a hard task for any doctor and a humbling one to say the least."

This third prong was indeed turbulent. The news that arrived via e-mail or messaging was never good. It seemed that cancer had unfortunately found a body it felt comfortable calling home. Ironically, it seemed our cancer patient felt perfectly comfortable calling my house home as well.

On the days it was imperative that I go into my office, Gary would drive over from his house, foregoing his office, to work from my home so she was not alone. Gary also took over the task initially handled by her other friend who drove her to radiation treatment. He drove Allison to her medical appointments at local hospitals chosen by Dr. M. While she was inside with the doctors, Gary would sit in the lobby with his laptop and work.

The radiation treatment was done out of sight, but we would both see by the marks on her leg, where the isotopes had been inserted. They greatly resembled the marks one would experience if they were accidentally burned by the cigarette lighter contained in an automobile. Each mark would have a circle drawn around it with a Sharpie Marker so the technician knew where the tumors were that were attached to the bone.

While it was terribly uncomfortable for her, radiation didn't appear to cause illness in the patient. That was good.

After some weeks, we settled into a fairly normal routine, if there was anything normal about fighting cancer. Updates from the doctor would pour constantly into my inbox while I was at work and Allison was at my home full time now versus only after treatment as originally discussed.

It was dawning on me that an initial offer to help through treatment was growing exponentially into something much bigger.

The compassionate part of me made it difficult to tell a cancer patient who had no supportive friends or family that they had overstayed their welcome. When does one send someone 'packing' who is so in need of support? Thus, days turned into weeks and weeks turned into months.

We witnessed spiked fevers, nose bleeds, neuropathy, and more. We never questioned the boxes of syringes that mysteriously appeared at the doorstep of my home because of the secrecy of the research that was taking place. The medical protocol that arrived via e-mail said they were filled with Naproxen and Ativan to help ease the pain of her treatment and decrease her anxiety.

While she slept a good portion of each day and showed erratic emotional behavior, she never looked sick. In fact, friends began to comment that with the fatigue that was beginning to show constantly on my face, I was the one who looked like I was battling cancer.

Outside of my home, the world went on as usual. Inside lived a woman whom I thought was in a battle for her life. Allison behaved as someone who believed she was deteriorating—and she plummeted into emotional despair.

What had I gotten myself into?

• • • • • • •

Many years prior, I came across a book called *Anatomy of the Spirit,* by Caroline Myss, Ph.D. Her book discusses how many of the diseases that invade the body begin with an emotional component. She writes, "Moreover, certain emotional and spiritual crises correspond quite specifically to problems in specific parts of the body. For instance, people who come to me with heart disease have had life experiences that lead them to block out intimacy or love from their lives. People with low back pain have had persistent financial worries; people with cancer often have unresolved connections with the past, unfinished business and emotional issues; people with blood disorders often have deep-seated conflicts with their family of origin." She continues, "The more I studied the human energy system, the more I realized that very little is created 'randomly' in our bodies or, for that matter, in our lives. The links between our emotional stresses and illnesses are best understood in the context of the anatomy of the human energy system—the anatomy of our own spirits...."

When I read this years ago, it aligned well with what I practiced in balancing energy in my own life—and my belief that where the mind goes, the body follows. There is no separating the emotional and physical bodies. Thus, it is imperative to select which energies you give power to, and which you don't. I recalled how my health increased when I stayed in a state of positivity and conscious of the emotions that I permitted to course through me. Thinking about this, it occurred to me I should ask Allison if she had any unresolved emotional issues that needed healing.

To say that her list was long is a major understatement. She told stories of unimaginable horrors that mortified both Gary and I. It seemed her life was one long series of nightmarish events. *No wonder her physical body wasn't able to fight back.*

"We are so much bigger than any of this." I said to her one night, "You must begin to use your mind to combat what isn't working inside your body. The importance of the mind-body connection cannot be stressed enough. You must pull strength from the loving, healing energy around you. Whenever we utilize combined mind, body, and spirit approaches to bolster our intent to get well, we stand a better chance of fighting back for our health."

I stood like a warrior before her, *willing* her to become bigger than her body. Rallying with her to remind her that everything she needs to overcome anything was *already* inside of her. She just had to visualize pulling from that Source and removing anything unwanted within her.

I didn't know it then, but these comments would become the catalyst for a large part of what was to come.

CHAPTER 11

Chemo Day

March 2012

Meds. Check. Food. Check. Fluids. Check. Syringes. Check. Alarms programmed into phone. Update reminder for Allison's mother. Check, check. Back-up helper for the end of the day. Major important check. I was grateful that I was able to cross off that last one. Sometimes I had to go it alone.

Everything was in order. The next 13 hours were mapped out, the calendar was devoid of any social engagements, and soon I would begin. I looked at the watch on my wrist. 7:00 a.m.

Perfect. On time.

So far, so good.

It was chemo day. A day meticulously planned with a routine that became refined with each subsequent occurrence of this day, which happened three out of four weekends each month. Ironic that the effort needed to save Allison's life, meant destroying my social life. But it was worth it. This was important.

Chemo day was not really a day, but rather a weekend because—for both the patient and the caregiver—the next day was spent recovering from the effort. The 13 hours it took to get through chemo day was physically and mentally exhausting.

The pre-planning stage was all me. Through past experience, I had learned that she would get distressed before we even began if she was part of the planning. She had only two tasks on her own checklist prior to the start. The first one was critical to her physical well-being. Rest. She needed to be well-rested.

The second task was puzzling to me but appeared to be critical to her emotional well-being. Before the first dosage, she would take the silver ring off her ring-finger and place it on my middle finger. A silent ritual she performed.

No explanation was offered and none was asked.

The poison that was cleverly disguised as pills had arrived the day before, the protocol came via the standard e-mail from the doctor's account.

They were detailed and filled with information on the medicine, when to administer it, and what to watch out for, as seen by the one included below. (Only the names have been changed.)

—— Original message ——
Subject: Chemo protocol
From: _____
To: keryl____@____.com
CC:

Early morning now K-- Hoping the party at your house went well tonight. Let's see if I can do a better job with the following protocol:

Today is chemo day. This is a big chemo treatment for Allison and for all of us. The first of two that will tell us whether or not both of you will need to come to [city] in a week for an extended period of time.

Here we go - -

What meds need to be administered tomorrow?

Oral chemo (7 pills - Daunorubicin, Adriamycin/Cistplatin, Cytoxan, low estrogen and Phenergen) 3X - 4 hrs apart. 'Super' chemo - very, very strong. She will be ill for 30 min to an hour after ingestion and she will experience high pain in her pelvic region and upper left femur early on. Important - once again, she must not vomit up the oral chemo pills in the first 15 min after she takes them. Cytoxan and the new drug Daunorubicin take longer to digest and they are both harsh chemo drugs. Daunorubicin has the potential to make her more anxious and it will give her CNS (central nervous system) and larger awareness of the pain she is going to experience today. She might be more emotional. This would be a good thing for [Allison]. She would release emotion/ pain more than holding them both in. It is going to be harder for her to stay calm and not vomit up the drugs in the first 15 min. Allison has been stellar about holding out in past chemos but you both need to be more vigilant about making sure she holds to the 15 min time limit.

Atarax (hydroxyzine) - 100 mg = 100 units. Injections. Atarax is a powerful drug for anxiety and will drop her into a deep sleep fast. A normal injection given pre and post anesthesia/high anxiety is 50 mg. Use less if you like once you get a feel for it. Make sure when you give it to her head is propped up on pillows higher than her chest. This is to prevent choking if she falls ill after you have administered it. These injections hurt so the faster you can get them in her the better. She will need Atarax all three rounds and maybe once in the middle of the night post chemo but I think you had better luck switching to the Ativan post third

67

round. *As you noticed last week she will most likely experience post nausea/vomiting from 1.5 - 2.5 hrs after administration of Atarax. IMPORTANT: You can choose Atarax or Ativan today. If you choose to give her Atarax instead of Ativan you can only give Atarax to her once every 4 hours and it cannot be overlapped with Ativan. Multiple doses of Ativan can be administered after the 4 hour Atarax time limit or completely in place of Atarax altogether. Overlapping Ativan and Atarax will cause vomiting.*

Percocet (hydrocodone): 1000 mg every 4hrs (this is a very high dosage)- Once with the administration of Atarax (or Ativan in place of Atarax) post each round of chemo. This will help with the expected severe pelvis/femur pain. Pain will be high today.

Fentanyl: 100 mcg in a soluble water solution - this is a last resort pain drug K! Do not start with this drug in round 1. If by round two/three she is in debilitating pain and Percocet did not work as well in round 1 then go ahead and give her Fentanyl. You should have five of these injections K - use only two today and leave the other three for this coming week if she needs them at night.

50 mg Ativan - Note: 1 injection of 30/50Ativan needs to be administered 20 min before the first dose of chemo. This will calm her and allow her to fight the urge to vomit the first dose of chemo. Post rounds 1-3 - as much as you think needs to administered throughout the day (if you are using Atarax remember to use Ativan accordingly) roughly 15 min post the last bout of vomiting. Sleep is not an option today. It needs to forced even if she does not want to sleep. She won't be able to fight it. It might be the only way she can deal with the vomiting and the pelvic/femur pain.

Naproxen - 500/1000 mg as needed for pain before or during vomiting. You did a superb job observing that she needed to have some pain meds when the pelvic pain started last week during vomiting. Ativan and naproxen will not hurt her and she cannot overdose on them on a chemo day. She can still take as much Naproxen as needed with Atarax BUT once you give her Percocet or Fentanyl stop Naproxen until the beginning of the next round. She has a larger mixture of drugs in her body this week.

What are signs of abnormalities and possible emergencies? Bloating in the stomach, swollen face, hands or feet, fevers of 105 or higher - be watchful for these especially with the high fatigue levels, Flash fevers might also occur today - short, high fevers that cause a large amount of perspiring. Flash fevers are ok. Vomiting more than 1.5 hours violently post chemo administration each time, dry, hot skin on the face or neck - sign of dehydration, coughing up blood more than 2TBSP to 1/4 cup of blood if applicable, pelvic bleeding that is a constant flow, large amount of blood in the urine and blue or purple lips. These are extreme and she has not presented with any of them except for high fevers. You will need to take her to [local hospital] if any of these things occur. Ask the ER Doc to notify me, Dr. Y[...] or Dr. E[...].

You have post round eating and hydration down. She is going be in more pain today from round 1 on. The above meds sounds like today will be horrible. Today will be manageable with meds only. It will be hard to watch. Check your resolve and get her through it. Put her out as soon as you can. Make sure you prop her up on the pillows just in case illness post administration occurs.

So to recap:

Ativan 20 min before round 1

take chemo drugs

15 min of calm before nausea

Vomiting and stomach distress - pain in pelvis/femur begin - administer naproxen

15 min after last bout of vomiting - administer Atarax

Repeat for rounds 2 and 3 (except for Ativan 20 min before chemo drugs)

You can do this K. I will be with you. [Local hospital] will be on the ready if you need to take her but she will be ok. Pain will be high today. Remember to release with her if you need to. The two of you are stronger together than apart, especially on chemo day. Today will pass and tomorrow she will be stronger. I hate this for her and for you. Time for these tumors to disappear! We have real work to do today. Good luck and god speed to you both!

Dr. M.

PS - I talked to Allison before she headed to bed at 10:30 PM. She was in good spirits but very nervous about the chemo but not about doing it with you. Her mom was giving her a hard time but she weathered that storm. She is in a good place for today.

To someone seeing this for the first time, it might look like a lot to absorb, but I had become adept at the process and it was timed down to the minute.

The first injection preceded the first dosage, which would be taken at 8:00 a.m., and we could expect it to begin its attack on Allison's internal system by 8:30. Of the three rounds that were administered, dosage one had the lowest level of impact on her, with the shortest period of gripping stomach pain and nausea. It usually subsided by 8:45 a.m., including the dry heaves in the bathroom. We had to ensure that she didn't vomit for the first 15 minutes, and then after another 15 minutes passed where she wasn't sick, she was cleared for an injection of Naproxen which would help her rest. With these factors, the injection was usually an hour or so after the ingestion of the pills—9:00 a.m., or shortly thereafter.

Allison then slept for three hours. I had been reminded to be sure there was food in between. Something mild like fruit or yogurt, nothing that would be too hard on her stomach. There is little difference between these pills and traditional chemotherapy. I was told that I should expect Allison to have the same reaction as what would traditionally be administered in the hospital.

Given her priority status as an important research patient, Allison was given the luxury of chemo at home. On standby in a local hospital was a doctor or nurse, whose names only Allison knew. Dr. M. would provide Allison with a direct phone number to these medical personnel, but for some reason, she never shared those numbers with me.

Her own name was given to them as an alias. This research was so secret, that affiliated personnel could not know the identity of the patient.

"What name should I give?" she would ask, fingers hovering over her phone's keypad as she typed the chosen name directly to the doctor.

Dr. M. conceived this special setup after several attempts to administer chemotherapy in the traditional hospital setting proved to be disastrous for his coveted patient. Her emotional state continually caused quite a few dramatic scenes in the room where she had sat, receiving a drip with the other cancer patients battling this invasive disease. It would take two people to hold her in the chair when the drug reached her blood stream. Even so, she would always overtake them and tear away the IV as it dripped the liquid fire into her veins.

To avoid this level of stress on Allison, and even those around her in the treatment room, it was determined she should receive her treatment in an environment that would provide comfort. The doctor's team of researchers developed the pills in a laboratory located many floors below his office at the medical facility where he was based. He informed me that she was the first patient in the United States to be given chemotherapy at the house.

When I heard these words, an odd feeling came over me. I could swear that I had heard of oral chemo being shipped to homes before. Was I mistaken? I did a little research and learned I was not. Others have had oral chemo administered at home, typically after they had already undergone traditional chemotherapy. I think he must have meant this particular chemotherapy for this particular research study. I wasn't about to question him on this. He was the expert and I was just a newbie caregiver. Weeks old.

The scene he described with Allison getting hysterical was easy for me to see in my mind. Her emotions were like a roller coaster with steep dips and twisted turns. They ran extremely high in the safety of the haven that was my home. From fear, to anger, to showing nothing at all, it was impossible to know what would show up on any given day. The only thing that made this manageable for me was the deference she showed to me. It was easy to have her swayed to my perspective on the things that distressed her, which often calmed her down. Nevertheless, roller coasters were never my thing and this emotional one exhausted me.

In the end, I would remind myself continually to be patient. How could I ever know what it feels like to have a disease that was rapidly multiplying inside my body and not be able to stop its invasion inside of me? Overall, I thought she showed great strength and courage. At times, she made it look so easy, it was hard to believe she had cancer at all.

I'll deal with the emotions as they come. This disease may win a few battles here and there, but it will not win this war. Not on my watch.

The pills arrived in an unlabeled foil padded package inside a white Styrofoam cooler. The total contents of the cooler was like a chemo kit. Inside were the different pills plus the pre-filled syringes marked for each dosage.

At 11:45 a.m., one and a half hours after Allison closed her eyes, I would wake her. She would consume the simple meal of fruit and other non-invasive nutrients, including an abundance of liquids to ensure she did not become dehydrated from the vomiting, and we would repeat the sequence of dosage one.

I used to marvel at two things. One, she never lost her appetite. She was always able to eat every bit of what was put before her. Two, the incredible mental strength it must have taken to swallow those pills, knowing what they would do to her body, and the pain that was just a few minutes away.

Sheer determination to live. That will go a long way in fighting this disease.

At 12:15 p.m., dosage two pills would be taken. The gripping pain would start at 12:30; more intense and more frequent that its predecessor. They would last a lot longer too, and the countdown would ensue for the period of 15 minutes with no symptoms, when the injection could be administered, providing the relief she desperately needed.

There was little I could do except encourage her and tell her she could do this, as I watched the intense pain of the recently ingested pills. She would flail on her bed, grip her stomach with a face contorted in pain, and cry out. Many time she pounded her fist on the bed, venting the deep frustration and impatience she was feeling with this invader inside of her. It was hard to watch.

Eventually she would end up in the bathroom, vomiting the healthy nutrients she had consumed upon wake-up at 11:45.

Allison was a pre-med student before she changed her major to early childhood development. She seemed to know as much as her doctor about the composition of the pills he was prescribing. She seemed to know as much about the side effects and a host of other things medically-related to cancer and the treatment. The doctor and the patient were completely in sync with treatment and operated like gears on a machine, each one helping to turn the other.

I could not help but notice how they would sometimes phrase things identically in two different e-mail mediums. I aksed, "Are you receiving the doctor's protocols before I receive them? You and Dr. M. are using so much of the same language."

The answer was always no, explaining that she had asked him to communicate directly with me. One of her degrees was in speech pathology, she explained, and it was common to begin to mimic speech and language patterns of the doctor given the connection she had as a patient who was completely reliant on this scientist to cure her.

Okay, then.

She had received seven degrees over the course of her many years of study; jokingly calling this remarkable achievement, 'accidental,' with one degree accidentally leading her to the path of another and so on.

Pretty impressive, I thought. And I was not alone in my sentiments. I began to notice from correspondence I received from her doctor, that he appeared to be somewhat in awe of his cancer patient. His e-mails perpetually built her up.

Through him I learned about her extensive education, the numerous languages she spoke, her elite Olympic-level skill in swimming, her strategic mind, compassionate spirit, and even her angelic-like singing voice. These things and much more poured from this man whom I was now convinced was unlike any doctor I had ever come across in my life. The two, I could see, were intrinsically woven with a bond that I could only guess had formed from their joint effort to remove from her a disease that was ravaging her body.

"Did she tell you about the chess match in Italy? That's an incredible story, ask her to tell you," he once wrote.

In another message he said, "I heard this angel voice coming from the other side of the room, and I looked over to where Allison was in bed. She was singing to get through the pain. Jenna [the doctor's wife] and I were transfixed. We have never heard a more beautiful singing voice. See if you can get her to sing for you."

It wasn't just her spirit that captivated the doctor. "The bone density that is measured in Allison is double that of another human being. If her bone density was that of a regular person, this cancer would have taken her leg. Her father has the same trait."

Allison explained to me that her father did not speak to her for one year after she dropped out of her pre-med studies. I tried to see that side in the gentle man I had met only once at that time. He was indeed battling his failing health, had a difficult time doing anything that required mobility, and an even harder time with language. But there was something special about him. Of the members of her family I had met thus far, his energy struck me as the most authentic.

Maybe there was more to the year of not speaking than I was being told. It was not my business. I knew nothing about Allison's family other than what she told me—how they could not be there for her, just as they were not there for her in the past.

Because of the collective dosage of chemotherapy medicine in Allison's body, it would take her longer to recover from the side effects of dosage two. I was dreading dosage three and I was not even the cancer patient.

By 2:00 in the afternoon, we were all-clear for the second injection that would put her to sleep for the next three hours. She would be asleep by 2:30 and I would set the timer to wake her up at 5:15 p.m.

The less than three hours I had in between each dosage were not enough time to do what I needed to do for me, as a single working mother running a business, a house, and full-time caregiving. Weekends usually included laundry, grocery shopping, and yard work. Plus, I too needed to have a bite to eat to keep my energy up. I also used this time to prepare the wake-up meal, and sometimes accomplish a few minutes of work-related tasks. In addition to all this, I tried to immediately answer the check-ins from well-intentioned friends (everyone knew about chemo days).

The time went by in what felt like mere seconds.

Sometimes the friends who were in the area, or wanted to show me support, would drop by to visit. Depending on how Allison was faring, and if she was awake, some would peek their heads in to say hello and offer her encouragement. On other days, a good friend from the running group would come and take care of my inground swimming pool, which was becoming sorely neglected. Sometimes he would do things around my yard and one time even planted flowers in my window boxes.

I was grateful for him and for my other friends, but it was Gary who was the primary supporter. He would stay in the background around the house, doing things out of the way but nearby in case I needed anything. He frequently brought dinner in a crock-pot which was extremely helpful because that was one less meal for me to make. I thought chemo days needed to be private, and tried hard to protect that, but I also needed all the help I could get. Since her family was not around, this left my friends.

I would smell the dinner simmering in Gary's crock pot and wonder again how she never lost her appetite. It was beyond me.

With all these things that had to happen in between dosages, time was a commodity I didn't always have. As such, on one particular chemo day, I had failed to deliver an update to Allison's worried mother.

On this day, my phone rang and I glanced at the name on the screen. "Hello there," I spoke into it.

"I haven't heard from you, I was expecting to hear from you," came the curt greeting.

"I'm sorry, I haven't had the time to—"

"I'm here and I am worried. I need to know how my daughter is," she interrupted.

I know where Allison gets THAT personality trait, a little thought nicks my brain. That was a huge problem. Allison was always interrupting a person or a conversation to talk about herself. I had to remind her one day, "There are three people who live in this home. Two of whom don't have cancer. This house will not be a house of illness, but a house of healing. We will share our stories equal time."

She usually apologized after her interruption, explaining that it was one of the effects of chemo. "Chemo brain," was a term she flung around like a frisbee.

"She's sleeping right now," I responded to her mother on the phone, shrugging off the irritation that blanketed me from her tone. Irritation I was sure was caused by my fatigue and the indignation that such rudeness would be directed at the one person investing so much in caring for her daughter. *Does she have any idea the amount of effort I am putting forth here? Where is she in all of this? How dare this woman! Where was she during this time?*

My irritation was not shrugging off.

"What is the doctor saying? I hear nothing from the doctor. I am completely in the dark here. I don't know what's going on. How is my daughter?" Her voice was becoming familiarly hysterical, yet another similarity to the emotional outbursts I endured frequently with Allison.

"Listen, I know you're upset, but there is so much that goes into these days. Today I have not had the time to update you, but I assure you—"

I am interrupted again. This time by her screaming into my ear "IF MY DAUGHTER DIES, IT'S YOUR FAULT!"

That did it. I had had enough. I pulled the phone away from my ear and carried it like a poisonous snake into the bedroom where Allison lay in her drug-induced sleep. When I tossed it on the bed, it landed next to her and woke her up. "Control your mother," I said with full-blown irritation.

Patience gone, I turned and walked out of the room.

I would not have know then that I would repeat those exact words to her in December 2015.

As I left, I heard Allison speaking into the phone with a tone that was inquisitive and soothing, as she was forced to borrow from the energy of rest and healing to calm her hysterical mother.

What on Earth am I doing? I asked myself for the hundredth, if not thousandth time.

I went to the other side of the house where it was sunny, peaceful, and devoid of the drama that swirled in the chaos that seemed to be attached to Allison.

One more dose. One more dose. One more dose. I buoyed myself to shake off the fatigue AND the memory of the screaming voice in my ear.

The message I received from the doctor shortly after that scene, insinuated that he knew this behavior well and had put strict boundaries on the interaction that occurred between Allison's mother and his office. He informed me I was the only person authorized to receive information, and reminded me that Allison is protected by HIPA laws and doctor-patient confidentiality. I should not be giving *any* information to her mother. If she continued to harass me or anyone in his office, he would not hesitate to put a restraining order on her.

He was sorry for what I had to endure on such a taxing day and ensured me it was almost over. He urged me to find peace and to please update him after the final dosage, adding that he'd call her in the morning.

Oh! I almost forgot. Update the doctor. Check.

Our bodies are not meant to be poisoned. There has to be a better solution than this. By the time the sequence in dosage three was complete, it was evening. 13 hours after it started, chemo day was finished.

Depending on whether there was a back-up supporter present or not, I would visit for a short while, and then crawl exhaustively into my bed.

Hopefully the pills developed by the dedicated staff who worked for Dr. M. achieved what they were designed to and the cancer that existed under the roof of my home would be gone.

Onward.

CHAPTER 12
The Cancer Fighter

March 2012

From: Dr. M<___@.com>
Date: March 13, 2012 11:23:49 PM EDT
To: Keryl
Subject: Update on [Allison]

Keryl - [Allison] did beautifully today. I demanded a lot out of her and I got a winning attitude and a great fighter. It was a difficult day and she approached it one more time with grace. We battled cancer on the front lines and had a few victories today.

The morning procedures: I started the biopsies and the implant procedure this morning only to find through a small camera that I inserted into the biopsy needle that there were smaller tumors growing around/under the larger tumor near the head of the tumor. I stopped the procedure on the femur and examined the two tumors in the area of the pelvis called the ischial tuberosity (lower pelvic region). They were not surrounded by other tumors and were close together - a centimeter apart. A small victory. I biopsied them and performed the same procedure that

Dr. McG[...] performed last Tuesday at [Atlanta Hospital]. It was a success. It is only a matter of time before these tumors disappear.

I decided to not perform the same procedure on the tumor in the hip. Instead I made a hard call and after some consultation I decided to perform arthroscopic surgery and totally remove the tumors on the femur. Arthroscopic was less invasive than opening the hip and she will heal faster, especially while she is taking chemotherapy. My surgical team and I found that the larger tumor and the smaller tumors lifted completely and cleanly away from the bone. The bone had not been penetrated by the any of the tumors. A GREAT sign. This means that the strontium 104 and the chemo is doing its job. It also gives me a better understanding of why these tumors might be duplicating so quickly. This was a big discovery of a big piece of the puzzle in fighting [Allison]'s bone cancer. I will have more information to give you once I complete more tests and research over the next few days.

Current Status: She is at my home now sleeping and resting well. I have made her comfortable and she is not in any conscious pain. When I left the house earlier after stopping by for a few minutes she was out cold. Jenna is tending to her most of the night tonight while I work at the hospital on [Allison]'s and another patient's case. Tomorrow will be a rough pain day as I slowly bring her off the high dose of today's pain meds so that she can take intravenous chemo on Thursday AM. Tomorrow morning at 10:30 I will be implanting the rest of a large series of new strontium 104 implants - 22 to be exact. They will once again go up and down her legs and in and around the pelvis. She also has acupuncture in the early afternoon to help with the pain management. I am trusting that her 'sports psychology head' will help me to help her fight pain tomorrow and Thursday. The rest of the day tomorrow will be devoted to rest at our home and recovery. Jenna will try to get some food in her and lighten up the day while our boys are in and out from school. It is all I can do to keep them out of her room.

This is a lot for anyone to handle Keryl. [Allison] is strong still and she will recover just fine over the next few days. I did not have to cut much muscle this morning and that will help her heal quickly. By Friday she should be moving around with a cane just fine. Don't be surprised if her texts, emails or phone calls tomorrow or Thursday reflect some of the pain she is experiencing. [Allison] reminded me that you had shoulder surgery at Christmas so you know what some of this pain feels like.

I will update you again tomorrow and let you know what the schedule for Thursday will be. I loved seeing her walk down the hall this morning. What a trooper. I know she has a love/hate relationship with [Cancer Center], but we love her here. She has great rapport with my medical team.

Back to work. Know that our girl is just fine and is doing well. She is on track to beat this cancer out of the ballpark.

Dr. M.

The doctor Allison chose was unique indeed. Night and day, he devoted his life to fighting pediatric cancer. I would come to learn that his passion came from the devastating loss of his own son to the disease—a precious young boy with an insatiable love for fire trucks who would never make it past single digits in years. The total heartbreak that this family suffered spawned the unstoppable quest to stem the tide of this disease in children. And with each child who went into remission because of Dr. M.'s militant care and strategy, he thought of his son. He was a fierce warrior.

Maybe all doctors are this devoted. I would not have known. For most of my life, I had been able to thwart illness. A rare flu was as big as it got for me.

I had hoped there were many more like Dr. M.

His devotion showed in every message, every late night he worked on his tireless research, every extraordinary thing he did for Allison. I mean, really, how many doctors took their research home with them in the most literal sense? He knew that by opening his home to Allison so she was not alone in the hospital, it would ease her distress; and he saw it as a small gesture for her generosity in giving blood and tissue samples for research.

Besides that, his wife Jenna, and two sons, Steven and Thomas flanked Allison when she was there and loved her being in their home. She confirmed the same when she spoke with me.

Yes, he was definitely unlike any doctor I had ever come across; and I would find myself thinking repeatedly how lucky she was to have become so intrinsically woven into the fabric of this good man's being.

CHAPTER 13

Teresa

March 2012

6 months away from identifying God in my life

I could hear the sirens in the distance that warned nearby residents of the severe weather that was approaching. It was evening and their plaintive wails added an eeriness to an already somber evening. I wasn't yet worried about retreating to basement level. In fact, I wasn't planning on moving from the large screened porch that overlooked the pool in my backyard.

I responded to text messages from concerned friends with levity. "When I see a woman flying in the sky on a bicycle, I will go inside," I joked, referring to the famous scene from the Wizard of Oz.

The sign on one of the walls read "What's said on the porch, stays on the porch." Very appropriate for this comfortable spot in my home that was a favorite gathering area for deep or causal conversations with loved ones and friends.

"We were childhood friends. I was 6 and Teresa was 4 when we met...."

Allison was telling me a story.

Moments earlier she had taken the phone call from Dr. M. He told her that the last treatment wasn't working. None of the tumors had shrunk and more were growing. They were still relegated to one leg but starting to travel toward the pelvic area. He was frustrated and Allison was devastated.

I couldn't imagine.

"I can't do this," she said as I listened compassionately. I'm certain she was tiring of the defeats and I knew she must be getting to a place where the battle was getting harder for her to wage.

My assumption with her words was that she couldn't continue to go through chemo days, nor receive the heartbreaking news that seemed to come after each MRI scan the doctor ordered. I could see she was heading toward one of her emotional outbursts.

Understandably.

"I can't do this. I won't do this. I won't have you go through what I went through with Teresa. I won't do it. I can't bear it."

The change in the direction of her message took me completely by surprise.

"I'm not sure what you mean," I said, confusion splattered all over my response.

Out came yet another story of tragedy.

Once she finished, I was certain this would be the one that puts her emotional body on the path toward recovery. I'm thinking specifically of Caroline Myss' wisdom in the book *Anatomy of the Spirit*.

Teresa was a childhood friend. The girls grew up playing for hours at each other's homes, holding hands and running, skipping, and jumping like little girls do. Teresa was an only child, unlike Allison who had one younger brother. Her father was a professor who made the girls sit at the table and write paragraphs each time they were together in his presence.

The girls were inseparable—sisters of the soul. As close as real siblings and with a bond that could not be broken.

They looked nothing alike, according to Allison. Where Allison was large-boned and broad shouldered, Teresa was a petite blond with a small frame.

When it came time for college, Allison chose a university in the southern part of the United States. Teresa would follow one year later, versus the two years it should have been had she not advanced a grade. Teresa was brilliant.

They remained as close as ever during their first year together in the same school and joined a Christian-based women's study group.

Allison didn't speak much about her religious beliefs. I had not witnessed regular church activity in her life, but I recalled the story of the church members she had referred to as 'care Nazis' so I knew it was at least a part of her past.

Also, the ring she put on my finger each chemo day was silver with a small cross on it. Allison appeared to carry her faith in her heart, privately and silently, like many do.

The girls were not fond of the lessons taught in this study group; both feeling that the views were too conservative, maybe even judgmental. But they stayed with it. They took from it what resonated with them and filtered out what did not.

As she told her story, I listened attentively. The wind howled around us and the night sky got darker. I could see her face illuminated by the lights on the porch. It looked like she was watching a movie that was playing in her mind. A reel from a lifetime ago.

It was at a retreat with this group that Allison and Teresa came upon two identical rings: silver with a small cross on the top. In lieu of class rings, they chose to purchase them.

In the middle of the freshman year, Teresa began to feel poorly. Thinking at first she was experiencing a virus or flu, there was little to no concern.

However, the symptoms persisted and worsened. She began having sharp pains in her abdominal area and eventually went to see a medical professional to find out what was happening.

Teresa was diagnosed with cancer.

The girls were devastated and the families even more so. The Wildes had only one child and she was their world. They vowed that she would get the best treatment they could find.

But the cancer was venomous and within a few short months the best they could do was keep Teresa comfortable.

The pain of this memory was etched across Allison's face as she spoke. Or perhaps it was because the memory hit so close to what she was facing that day. I couldn't tell.

I sat still, unaware now if the storm was still raging around us. There was a bigger storm, it seemed, in the heart of the storyteller in front of me.

Allison developed a new routine during those final weeks of Teresa's life. On Friday night, she would leave campus and drive to Teresa's family home. There she would relieve Lily and Robert Wilde of their duties and would take over the care of Teresa so they could refuel for the week ahead of them when Allison had returned to school. Plus, it gave the girls time to be together.

Allison would sleep on the sofa in Teresa's room or sometimes even in the bed beside her. She made a promise to be there until the end.

On the days or moments when it became especially hard, and whenever they needed to rally, the girls developed a ritual. They would exchange rings. Teresa would put hers on Allison's finger, and Allison would put hers on Teresa's. Given the size disparity, the rings went on different fingers, but that didn't matter to either girl. What was important was the symbolism of love, strength, and support behind the simple ritual. What was important was that both girls could feel the energy of the other in the simple silver rings they exchanged. It was the talisman each wore in a pact to never give up—to fight, fight, fight. Together they were stronger than separate.

"Capture the sun for me, Allison," the soft gentle voice came one day from the bed where Teresa lay. "Capture the sun and bring it to me so I could have it with me."

Teresa died before she reached her sophomore year. To Allison, it felt as though Teresa took the sunlight with her. Her world became darker with the loss of her soul sister and lifelong best friend.

I sat with my eyes on Allison, but I wasn't really seeing her. Instead, I was seeing my own movie reel. It was the gesture that occurred each chemo day when Allison silently took her ring off and placed it on my finger. There was no exchange, because I didn't own a matching version of the ring. I wasn't Teresa. But I was touched beyond measure at the gesture that I had never questioned. It was her rally cry. Her symbolism of strength and support.

"I begged Mr. and Mrs. Wilde for her ring after she died. It was the only thing I wanted. But they never responded. In the aftermath of losing their only daughter, it became so chaotic. And then time passed..." She sat silently for a moment, "I never saw the ring again."

ALL THE LIGHT INSIDE OF YOU

There is no pause before she returns to the present moment and immediately says, "I don't want you experiencing the pain I experienced when cancer claimed Teresa's life."

I ignore her statement and instead I ask "Are you in touch with them now? Are they still living in the same place?"

"Lily died five years ago. For the first few years after she died, I stayed in touch with Robert, but I have not heard from him for more than two years. He has not responded to any of my messages."

This woman.

So much heartache in her life.

CHAPTER 14

Robert

March 2012
The next day

Mitchell and I walked along one of my favorite places in Atlanta—Inman Park. We had been dating since February 2010 and normally had an easy relationship. However, lately our time together was greatly impacted by the arrival of Allison into my life. On this day, we were enjoying a rare few hours away from my home.

The weather was mild, which is usually the case in Atlanta; and there weren't any signs of the storm that had ripped through just the evening before. It was only a few hours ago that I was listening to Allison's heartbreaking story, but when I left the house I tried to leave everything behind me, so it felt like days ago.

One of the many things I learned in my earlier years of becoming mindful was how to exist in the present moment—'in the now.' This practice removed a lot of the self-placed anxiety we tend to create when we worry too much about the things that have already happened and are gone or what was yet to come.

In that moment, all that made up my life was Mitchell and our relaxing walk in and out of the shops and stores of Inman Park.

It was a Saturday afternoon and we were thrilled to have this time together. Allison had woken up feeling much better that day. Perhaps it was the cathartic effect of a long-held pain being placed out in the open, where there was much more space than confined in our bodies. Or maybe it was simply a good health day, but she seemed to have rallied and I felt comfortable leaving her at the house to add some fuel to my own well.

We chose a little pizza dive spot and gave our order to the waiter. As the waiter left our table, my phone lit up. I looked at the screen. A message from the doctor.

Oh no.

Reading the message, I was surprised it had nothing to do with Allison. He wanted to share something and asked me to please forgive him for this moment, but as someone who is entrenched in fighting cancer, he knew I would be empathetic. As I continued to read, I could feel my heart begin to break at the words on my screen.

Putting my hand over my mouth in shock and then moving it to my heart to somehow stop the pain, I looked at Mitchell. There we were, two people, both healthy, both able to walk away from the battle and put it behind us, while others like Dr. M. could not.

The message informed me that he had lost a patient that morning. A young boy. The doctor was beside himself. No matter how many years he invested in this field, losing a child was hard on him.

I felt devastated for this good, compassionate man.

Mitchell furrowed his brows. His patience had begun to be stretched by the constancy of interaction that seemed to come from either the doctor or from Allison. "And this is appropriate to share with you?" he asked.

"Absolutely! He's not divulging anything proprietary. There's no medical information in this message."

I could hear the defensiveness in my tone.

Mitchell looked skeptical. His facial expression was asking the question, why is this doctor sending me so many messages? And while he held his tongue, I could feel his annoyance.

But now I felt terrible about the food we were about to indulge in when this precious child a few states away would never taste food again. I felt terrible about wanting to get away from the house when doctors everywhere were still fighting to eradicate this wretched disease.

The day lost its brightness and my heart felt heavy.

Lately I had begun to wonder if maybe, by the time this was all over, I would need a heart transplant. It seemed to be the only muscle getting a workout these days. What an incredibly tough thing this organ is. The endurance it has is comparable to that of an elite athlete.

I glanced at Mitchell and at his dear face. When I put myself in his shoes, I couldn't say I blamed him for feeling annoyed. The arrival of Allison had greatly impacted our relationship, and while he was still committed to me and to Madeline, it had become much harder with this person in my home who required attention night and day.

I thought of Dr. M., and I thought of that boy's family. I thought of my own child who had already lived three times longer than he had, and I knew I would continue to offer my home as a haven for this cancer patient.

By now for me, it was much more than not being able to send her packing—with no support network of her own that I could see. Rather, I was determined that the illness would not defeat her. *Not on my watch.*

It had become personal to me.

And although it was as hard as it could be at times, I could not forget that my inner-voice had prompted me to invite her in. I still knew and believed one thing about that voice, and that is, even though I might not understand its guidance, I had witnessed repeatedly that it was never wrong.

Allison had not yet begun to show the signs of illness at all. Her face was unchanged, as was her weight. If anything, she was putting weight on living under my roof. We were told she would not look sick, which was why they were using her blood tissue and cells in their research for a pediatric cure. They were right. She stayed in her room sometimes for days from the fatigue of this disease, and we continued to witness nose bleeds, fevers, neuropathy, and other symptoms that her body was under attack. Other than these, the biggest sign of cancer on her was in the ups and downs of her emotions.

I wonder if Dr. M. is going to tell Allison that he lost his patient. Can she withstand so much heartbreak?

These thoughts raced through my mind in less than a minute as I sat with Mitchell, waiting for our pizza. Mentally I knew that I needed to put a cap on how much longer Allison could stay with me. I knew I should implement a plan to have this burden be shared across others who would help, besides Gary and I, and let the cancer headquarters be her own home, which was not far from where we were sitting that day.

My mind went to her home. There was something about her home that always made me shudder. I never understood why I had this response to it, but it was intense. I would walk in and immediately feel the need to protect my energy. I would grab my upper arms as though I was walking through a cold wind-storm and trying to stay warm.. I never wanted to stay longer than necessary and knew that the environment that existed there would not perpetuate healing.

I had vocalized my feelings to her about her home numerous times. If they hurt her or startled her, she was gracious enough not to show it. Still, I wondered many times why I felt that way, and the only thing I could rationalize was that the energy of the despair from learning she had cancer still lingered in her home, reluctant to leave.

Well, that PLUS the countless stories of heartbreak she shared with Gary and me.

The pizza arrived.

And with the pizza came another message. This time, from Allison. "Keryl, you must come back. I have something I want to show you. Hold your heart, you are going to need it. Please hurry I won't open it without you."

And so it was that I permitted any reprieve we might have had that day, any chance to fill our depleted spirits to be thwarted, as the entire meal became filled with messages that were coming from both the doctor AND from Allison.

How easy it would have been to turn off my phone and be in the moment. But I did not. I chose to let the intruders invade my meal, my afternoon, my energy, my life.

• • • • • • •

6 p.m.

94

I am sitting at the end of Allison's bed in my pretty guest bedroom. She is opposite from me, using the headboard to prop herself up and wearing her usual outfit, gym shorts and a baggy T-shirt. In front of her, in between us, is her laptop. The screen was facing her. My view was silver and with a white apple that had a bite taken out of it.

"Shortly after you left this morning I received a phone call." Pregnant pause. "Keryl," she says in a lower more dramatic tone, "It was from Robert Wilde, Teresa's father."

I am stunned. Literally, completely stunned into silence.

She is pleased by my reaction and I'm sure, by the look on her face, that she must have had a deeper version of the same when that call came in. I mean, it was *just last night on the porch*, that she told me it had been two years since she had heard from him.

Laws of attraction, I immediately think. In our metaphysical world, if you think it, so will you attract it to you. We are all connected. We are all one. Maybe I am not so stunned, after all.

But I am *thrilled* to experience this moment of oneness manifested. Wow!

I told her not to keep me hanging, I *had* to know what he said. I could barely contain my curiosity. I love this. What an incredible world we live in.

"Keryl," she said and goes silent as though she is formulating her thoughts.

Once she had her thoughts gathered, she went on to tell me that Robert Wilde had woken up early that morning with a feeling of urgency to call her. He had something for her. Something that was left by his Teresa. He had spent most of the hours in the morning looking for it, so sure was he that it was supposed to be received by her today.

It was a letter—a *handwritten* one. *Oh to be able to see Teresa's handwriting again.* She was extremely emotional, but they appeared to be the good kind of emotions.

Another pause.

Robert Wilde typed out the letter from the daughter he and Allison both loved who died 23 years ago. It was in her inbox, and she wanted me there before she opened it.

She explained what she had learned on her emotional phone call with Robert.

Teresa had made her parents promise that they would hold this letter and only send it to Allison if one of two things happened. One, they both died, in which case, it would be left in their will. Or two, they learned that Allison was in a place in her life that this letter was needed to deliver strength and support.

I could not believe what I was hearing. Amazing.

She hadn't read it yet and had wanted to read it with me. She was saying that it was as much mine as it was hers.

"No. No. No. You can't read it aloud for the first time. There might be something private. Read it first and if you want to share it, then you may do so." I was shaking my head vigorously as though that alone would stop her from reading.

She looked at me for a moment, then turned her eyes to the screen. Her face reflected every emotion she was feeling, and I can see her eyes become watery.

She reiterated that this letter was indeed as much for me as it was for her. She choked up. "I am forwarding it to you. It is yours."

She clicked a few keys on her keyboard and although my own computer was stored away in another room on that Saturday evening, I knew something very special was making its way to my inbox. It had now been gifted to me. A moment of pure selflessness and giving. I am in awe of the strength of the woman in front of me and the love that is in her heart.

How could I ever have exercised thoughts of sending her away?

Looking at the computer screen she had turned to face toward me, I read the words sent by Robert Wilde; and for the second time that day, I put my hand over my mouth in surprise. When I move the hand to my heart, this time, it is to hold in the beauty, and not keep out the pain.

I will need a heart transplant, no doubt—the thought is almost constant these days.

Names have been changed, noted by [brackets], private information removed [noted by ellipses in brackets], and any misspellings unchanged.

*"From: Robert Wilde <rwilde***@_____.com>*
Date: Sat, Mar 3, 2012 at 5:51 PM
Subject: from Robert Wilde

[Allison]:
Please let me know if there is anything else I can do for you. It has been years but I would love to see you. I will be in Atlanta in May. Can I visit or can we get together for dinner?
I am saddened to hear about your struggle with cancer. I was hoping you would never have to battle the monster that took our beloved Teresa away. What I do know is that you are much stronger than Teresa and I know you can win this battle and any to come.

I think to Black Mountain and remember how frustrated you would get with Teresa's progressive cancer. You used to leave the house and head out into the woods and tell Teresa that you were off to gather the sun to bring back inside. You always said you would only be a few minutes and sometimes you were gone an hour. The sun you gathered and brought in would last her through the night. It was always in the strength of your smile. Let me gather some sun and send it to you. Think of me and Lily and Teresa. Never forget what she told you about finding joy in her life. She found joy in you always.

Text of Teresa's letter is below. I have been holding onto the letter for years hoping that I would never have to part with it. I am sorry that Lily and I opened it a long time ago not realizing what it was. Our hearts melt when we read her words to you and for a second her spirit and electric personality are alive again amidst us. I finally had to tuck the letter away. Lily would read it and miss both of her girls so much she started not eating. Upon her death I read it one last time at her request along with a stack of other letters and papers from Teresa. I hope you will understand why I kept it all these years. I know that reading the text will not be the same as reading her handwriting and feeling the paper, but I hope it will give you comfort and hope going into the next week. I will send you the letter Monday via Fed Ex.

All my love to my second daughter,
Robbie"

I looked at Allison before continuing.

I was about to read a letter from a childhood friend who died 23 years earlier. My look asked the same question I asked a lifetime ago as a teenager, when my homeless friend pushed his great treasure across the table to share it with me. "May I?" She understood the look and nodded.

I braced myself and read on.

"My sister, my soul, my laughter through the ages and my lasting memory,

Serious huh? Darn right but I mean every word of it. If you are reading this it is because you are at a place in your life younger or older where you need me to bring you some joy in the darkest of your hours. Joy, joy, Joy! I had mom and dad hold onto the letter until you needed it or until they passed away. I hope if you have opened it now it is only because you needed to.

I always told mommy and daddy that I worried you would get sick someday and not be able to pull yourself back out of the darkness again. Mom always told me I worried too much, but I think she knew I was right. You feel so passionately. I was afraid that if you got ill your passion would dwindle to much to help bring you back. I am writing this letter as a request from you to me. Read and it and do what you need to do. Protect yourself and LIVE your life once and for all. Don't look back and rekindle your passion for life.

I am always with you and never really left. I know you carry a piece of my soul inside of you. I also know that you are being as stubborn as a jackass mule when it comes to relinquishing your feelings and letting go. I am right aren't I? Uh, huh! Think of the joy in my life that I found because you allowed me the space to find it and find your release there if you need to. I have enough for both of us to last forever.

I know that I only have a few weeks left and I am at peace. I see the strain in your face every time you come back from school. You are worried and I know the road will be hard when I leave. You have done as I requested and never left my side. The bond we share will never be diminished but will be carried through death, rebirth and life again. My heart is as big as the world and it cries for the tears you will shed soon for me. I will them to be tears of joy every day.

I think often of what you will look like in your later years or who you will be happily married to or who your children will be and what kind of career you will chasing. I only hope for the best of life of for you always.

I don't know what you are fighting. It could be cancer, or depression or a another loss of a loved one. I want to let you know that you are the strongest of both of us. I knew from my first diagnosis that I would never beat cancer. I could never tell you. I fought as hard as you fought for me but my body did not have the strength you had every day for it. Lord there were days when I willed it to take the strength you were so willing to give it.

Your time is not now. Your time is the life of now. Fight whatever it is you are fighting and come back to your life. Share our story with only those you trust and love and heal yourself completely. Come out of the darkness and back into the light. You are a survivor first and foremost.

[...]

Remember this, "Jump, jump back, never look back." We used to sing it on the playground [...]. Remember? We would stay outside for hours playing and singing. It was as if we willed ourselves to live. Will yourself to live now and jump, jump back, never look back. Quit looking back once and for all and look forward to what the rest of your world holds for you.

See me and go one last time. Smile for me and then move on and heal yourself. We had the gift and blessing of God on our side. You have it always.

Keep me alive always in joy, joy, joy and know that I am always with you. You never have to look for me or look back to the darkness anymore.

My sister and my soul - I love you always deeply, fully and completely. I will miss you every day until I see you again.

Heal and be healed,
Teresa"

I stared at her computer screen for a moment after I finished. This was so big. How does anyone get their arms around just how big this was? This was universal connection, quantum sciences, one-ness, love, and life all at once.

I was without words.

Just yesterday she had spoken of this family in her life, and the pain of their absence. Today, the last living member finds her, because 'something told him' he needed to. That same something had pressed on my heart since childhood, showing its wisdom in great ways and small.

I brought my mind to responding. I didn't think Allison was expecting a critique of the letter. What does one say to something like this?

"And the letter is coming to you?" I asked.

"Yes."

"OK, Allison," I say with a pregnant pause of my own as I begin to process an idea that comes to my mind. "I'm going to propose something to you. I am sure you are desperate to see Teresa's handwriting again after all of these years. Is that correct?" It is correct, she affirmed softly.

"Then, when that FedEx package arrives to you. I am going to challenge you NOT to open it until you are completely cancer-free. Make it your reward. A reason to will yourself to fight alongside me, alongside Dr. M."

With surprise on her face, she agreed. She likes the idea.

Deal.

Done.

Good.

"As for me, I will not open this e-mail again until that day comes. Thank you for the gift of this. I will use it as a reminder that we are never alone."

I looked at the message on her computer, with the little banner noting that it has been forwarded. I thought to myself "I have this man's e-mail address now. I wonder how much she told him about how sick she was."

• • • • • • •

Cancun was a special place for my daughter and I. Years earlier, I found myself with a great desire to get out of town. It was February and cold, and I had been in the midst of a long spell of all work and no play. I wanted to go somewhere.

It was a Thursday when this thought that I desperately needed to get away crossed my mind. Once the seed is planted, it was next to impossible to remove. I looked at my work calendar. *Maybe I can take tomorrow off and enjoy a long weekend.*

I have had many moments like this, when an urge would come over me to get away. I didn't respond to all of them, but I knew I was going to be responding to this one. Sometimes when they hit, I would ask Madeline one question that always excited her, "Do you want to go on an adventure?"

What young teenager is going to say no to that?

Where was she this evening, I wondered. *With her dad? With friends?* The schools were closed on Monday and Tuesday because of teacher work days. Maybe we could find a place to drive to for the weekend. Madeline always had plans but perhaps I could entice her to cancel them to be with her mom.

Not likely. But worth a shot

In the midst of this pondering, I fielded a phone call from my friend Greg. "Hi there. Did I catch you in the middle of something?"

"Yes, actually. I was planning a weekend escape."

"Do tell. Where to?"

"I hadn't gotten that far. What do you think? Any suggestions?"

"Go to Mexico," came the response. With a hint of humor, he added, "Bet the airfare is dirt cheap these days."

Mexico had been in the news a lot lately. There were drug-related crimes happening more frequently and the media was reporting that Americans were beginning to become a little wary of traveling to the country.

"That's not a bad idea at all," I respond. I had always felt a sense of when I should do something or not, and my inner-voice was not cautioning me to consider an alternate destination.

Three hours later I had two seats on a flight and a hotel booked. We were leaving the very next day. Madeline did indeed have plans but it was easy to pull her away from them for a tropical, spontaneous adventure. Her father dropped her off, so she could pack.

That was years ago and Cancun had become my place of peace and relaxation.

On this day, March 30, 2012, Mitchell, Madeline, and I were on a bus bumping along the back roads of Mexico, on our way to a day of adventure that included zip lining, cave kayaking, rock climbing, and exploring Mayan ruins. We were sitting near the back of the small bus filled with eager tourists like us.

The trip was long, and we passed the time easily, teasing each other and especially Madeline about the perils of zip-lining in the back woods of Mexico. The feeling between us was light and fun.

I don't think I looked at my phone one time.

Hours later, we were making our way back from our day of adventure; tired in an exhilarated way, and more mellow, we settled into our own thoughts.

I pulled out my phone.

I promised that I would not read that note again and I intended to keep my promise. I did, however, want to see the unopened e-mail so I can look at the address. I navigated to the message but all I could see in the unopened e-mail was Allison's e-mail address since it came from her. *Open the e-mail, get the address, close the e-mail.* Clearly the temptation was there to open it otherwise I would not have to say these things to myself. A promise is a promise and I did not plan to break this one.

I opened the e-mail and looked only at the address.

Once I had Robert Wilde's e-mail address memorized, I opened a new e-mail and from the back of the bus in another country, I composed my note:

"From: Keryl Oliver <___@___.com>
Date: March 30, 2012 4:50:21 PM CST

Subject: A friend of [Allison's]

Dearest Mr. Wilde

I hope with all of my heart that the decision I've made to write you does not cause offense.

You and I share in our love for a very dear woman – To you, a second daughter ... to me a sister of the soul. I guess you could say, that in some ways, this makes us family of the heart. I've learned in my 45 years of life that these family members are just as special as those whom are blood.

I know you and [Allison] spoke not long ago and during this time she told you of her latest battle with cancer. I have been caring for her in my home for the past three months and we have become partners standing on the front lines in a battle for life.

There are two reasons for this note. I'll start with the first. [Allison] had reached Advanced Stage IV with a ruthlessly aggressive bone cancer. I'm certain she down played it when she spoke with you because that is her way. To [Allison]– It's less important that you know of her battle and more important that she never be a cause of worry for you. Yesterday (Thu) I drove her to the airport to board a plane to [City Name]. She had surgery today to remove the 20+ tumors that had grown inside her pelvic area and throughout her femur. I want you to know the doctor and his family love her dearly and are determined to eradicate this cancer from [Allison] once and for all. He was very aggressive and he successfully removed all of the tumors.

At the end of this note I will insert the text from the email sent to me by the doctor. Blessfully I was kept updated throughout the surgery today, which lasted close to 4 hours.

While I pray – as do many – that this ugly disease does not come back into [Allison's] life, I know that in the end, her fate lies not in the hands of her friends, her family, or even this amazing medical team – but rather in the hands of God. I have never prayed so much in my life. Breathe pray breathe.

You are undoubtedly aware that the battle with cancer is also in finding the emotional strength to keep fighting. That brings me to the second reason for this note – Your beautiful daughter Teresa. I wish she knew the strength her letter has injected into [Allison]. I can try to convey this to you but I'm sure I'll do the magnitude of this a disservice.. [Allison] has the words from her letter memorized — and to me, Teresa materialized by my side on the front lines. It is empowering to have a warrior with her insight and wisdom by my side. I thank you for delivering her at the exact moment she was needed.

Mr Wilde, I'm the mother of a 17 yr old – She is my only child. I hurt for your loss and have cried so many tears for [Allison] and Teresa – long before the letter arrived.

I have always believed that the souls that are most evolved and have learned all they could learn in a lifetime are the ones that depart before we are ready to say goodbye. Please know that your daughter lives – in our home – through the memories and the stories and the never-ending love of a childhood friend who carries a piece of her soul with her wherever she goes.

My home is open to you for your visit in May. And if you don't accept – I hope I have the opportunity to meet you. Thank you for "gathering the sun" and for delivering the strength just when it was needed. A stranger in Atlanta is eternally grateful.

Best to you
Keryl

PS. An excerpt from Dr notes follow:

Out of surgery and in recovery. She is in great shape! I removed all the tumors in the left pelvis, left upper femur and left mid femur. I removed some bone in the left mid femur and put in two small plates that the bone will grow over in the next few months. Her range of motion and the structure of her femur is fully preserved. She is a very lucky girl! I cleaned bone and tissue with wide margins to insure that there is no more tumor growth based on the past existing tumors. I also irridiated the left leg and pelvis with a special chemical and electrodes to kill any remaining cancerous cells.

A completely successful surgery! She will recover well over the next few hours. She is a trooper! I will have my nurse update you more as the day progresses.

Sent from my iPhone"

Later that day, from the hospital in a city 1,390 miles from Cancun, Allison sends me a message. "Your compassion knows no bounds, Keryl. Robert called to ask me about you. He will write to you in a few days."

"From: Robert Wilde <rwilde***@____.com>
Date: April 1, 2012 3:36:53 PM CDT
To: keryl___@___.com
Subject: Re: A friend of [Allison's]

Dear Keryl,

How do I respond to your letter of a few days ago? I have nothing to lose now. I have become an old man in the years since my wife died. It has been ages since a stranger has shown

107

me the consideration and compassion that you reached out and blanketed me with. I almost don't know how to respond. I have nothing to lose in my life now at 70 years old with no living family (but [Allison]). I took a chance and reached out to her yesterday morning in response to your letter and asked about you. I choose now to respond in full to your correspondence because I heard Teresa in her voice when she described you. I have not felt my child in so long and I have felt her again more this past month than I have since my wife was alive. The darkest corners of my soul cry for that connection. If I write nothing else know that the gift of having [Allison] back in my life and your recent letter brought her back to me. I need a whiskey...

The greatest gifts God bestowed in my life are my wife and my children - Teresa and [Allison]. My wife and I felt always like [Allison] was ours. Jokingly, I used to jibe her father and tell him that if he needed more time with his son he could relinquish his daughter fully. Imagine the response I incurred time after time. Someone looking in from outside would ask what more could a man ask for? The ethereal and physical absence of these women from my life and my daily musings has left me with a vacuous heart.

I have suffered from depression for years since my wife's death and for the last 9-12 months I have turned the world away from my doorstep. My wife was my rock after Teresa passed. She gave all her strength to me and in the end of her life left none for herself. Two years ago I started sending [Allison]'s letters back to her unopened. The pain I experienced while reading about her daily life was too much for me to endure without my child and now my wife. I was reminded of my losses. I focused only on my own pain. The self pity crushed me. Selfish bastard as I was I tried to break the bond that [Allison] and I shared. She never relented and never gave in to my ridiculous behavior. I kept my distance until my phone call to her in March. To this day I still receive cards from her for all the major holidays with short notes about her life. I just received an Easter card from her a week ago.

I am a retired college and English and History professor. I taught at Georgia Tech, UAB, Georgia State and Emory during my 41 years of teaching. I remember sitting Teresa and [Allison] down at the kitchen table and teaching them to write their first paragraphs. They hated it. Big wheels and bikes always called louder. Now at 70 I don't care about my scholarly ego. In the grand scheme of life I care about the people not in my life for the first time in a long time.

I can't pinpoint what made me reach out to [Allison] a month ago. I woke up that day with her heavy on my heart and went rummaging through Teresa's papers for the letter she wrote to [Allison]. Hours went by before i dug it out of my wife's keepsake box. I read it for the 100th time and knew I had to call her. Thank god her number was the same. The overbearing sense that I was harboring something that did not belong to me hung heavy in the air. It was a half a day and several whiskeys later before I summoned the nerve to call her. The self pity in me told me that she would not pick up. I was so wrong ...

I did not deliver that letter to [Allison]. That was my Teresa. In my heart I know this. My eyesight has been very bad and that day when I realized I needed to send it to her via email (which I check every couple of days) I had an hour of clearer vision than I had experienced in months. It was as if another hand and heart guided me that night.

Your soul sister and my child is all I have left in this world. I have been in turmoil since I spoke with her on the phone. She spoke of cancer and my heart and mind went into panic stricken overdrive. Correct you are. I did not know it was so advanced and aggressive. [Allison] was always concerned about hurting or imposing on others even at a very young age. Thank you for letting me know. Countless nights of no sleep followed that phone call. How right Teresa was. She knew [Allison] to the depths of her soul. She predicted that she would be ill later in life. Several times I came close to boarding a plane to Atlanta to see her. Several times I picked up the phone to call her parents. We have been estranged for years. I plan on contacting them in my own time over the coming weeks. Please let me do this.

Relief! For the first time in a month when I read your email the other night relief washed over me. I know my child is with both of you step by step. I will go out on a limb for the first time in 20 years and say that if you know of [Allison] and Teresa then you must know of their guarded history. Knowing this gives you an added understanding of why they are soul mates for eternity. Love is stronger than any bond we can form from one lifetime to the next. Teresa must know she is with you healing and if so then I hope it brings rest to my child. The unspoken hurt she had when she realized she had to leave [Allison] to live out her life without her to break the spell of their childhood fears ate at her spirit. Her letter to [Allison] was partly born of this.

You said "A stranger in Atlanta..." Family of the heart is of strong warrant in our correspondence. You took the time to pull me out of despair that you had no idea I was wading in. I went out of the house for the first time in a long time and called upon old area friends who were more than happy to have me to dinner. I have sent [Allison] emails and old pictures and poems this week. I have tried to be there for her. God has provided a miraculous person in you just as he provided [Allison] twice over for my child.

Wherever you are, whatever you are doing, whatever you believe in know that God guided us together. What God guides and creates he does not put asunder. Please continue to take vigilant care of my child and grow and love in life with her. She is one of a kind. God is grand!

I am coming to Atlanta in May and would love to see you and [Allison]. The ramblings of an old man. You read them all. Please don't share this letter with [Allison]. Inform her only that I replied to your email in full. I don't want to upset her more than she already is or could be. She needs to channel all her strength to healing.

Contact me any time and please, I beg you, keep me posted on how [Allison] is healing. Her doctor in [City Name] sounds like he has her cradled well in hand.

Profusely and humbly thankful,
Robert Wilde"

That would be the last message written by Robert Wilde. He died that day, but Allison would not know this for another week. By then we had both returned from our respective trips back to Atlanta.

We met in the kitchen one morning in front of the coffee maker. "I haven't heard anything more from your friend Mr. Wilde," I told her. "Have you?"

She hadn't either she said, adding how it was funny I should mention it because before she came in, she had called the authorities in Florida where he lived, and was waiting to hear back.

"Something's not right," I told her.

She agreed.

* * * * * * *

The phone call came later that day. She was crying and besides herself with distress. She learned that he had suffered a massive heart attack and had died with no one to claim his body. He had been cremated, with no fanfare, and his ashes, along with a box of letters would be shipped to her home.

Will these heartbreaks ever stop coming?

The executor of his Last Will and Testament contacted her. Robert Wilde left everything to Allison. His home, his car, his personal belongings—everything was left to the second daughter with whom he had just reconnected. I would never be given the opportunity to see him. He no longer needed that heart doctor appointment in May.

Maybe I should take it in his place. God knew my heart was still getting a workout.

She would end up remotely closing that chapter of her life long-distance from Atlanta, as she concurrently battled a disease she could not shake.

Incredible strength.

I felt the sadness in my heart. Even more so, weeks later, when I saw his ashes that had arrived to Allison's home.

Yet, I could not help but think, *He performed his last earthly duty when he sent her that letter. Of course, he should now be with his wife, and the daughter he lost too soon.* It gave me peace to know they were all together. Three warrior angels now, looking out for Allison.

I would not have known it at that time, but that thought was much more accurate than I could have imagined when it crossed my mind.

April 1, 2012 would also not be the last time either of us heard from a member of the Wilde family. This God that they spoke of so easily had other plans.

CHAPTER 15
An Extra Something

*For He will command His angels concerning you to guard
you in all your ways; they will lift you up in their hands so
that you will not strike your foot against a stone.*

Psalm 91: 11-12

April 2012

Something was happening in my home. I felt it distinctly,
and the more I became aware of it, the more I felt it. It began
with a subtlety, but it wasn't long before it was blatant.

It was the feeling that someone was in the room with me
all of the time. Even if I was completely alone, I felt not alone.

I would look over my shoulder, or turn around, fully
expecting either Allison or Madeline to have come into the
room, but no one would be there.

It didn't scare me, it didn't unnerve me, it just simply *was*.

What's more, my house seemed to be making an unusual
amount of noise during those days. They were the popping
and cracking kinds that are heard when a house was settling.
It seemed to be doing that louder and more frequently than I
had ever heard it before. Sometimes it sounded like a crack of
electricity.

Ever the homeowner, I just hoped the foundation wasn't about to create a fissure that would end up becoming a costly repair.

I asked Allison if she had noticed the same, and she exuberantly answered, "Yes! I thought it was just me. I wanted to say something but didn't know how to."

What was this extra something? What was I feeling? Why did my house feel different?

●　●　●　●　●　●　●

I had known my friend Kara since my very early days at the corporation in which I had worked from the late 80s to the end of 1999.

She had lost her mother to cancer not too many years prior to this period in 2012 and I attended the funeral to honor her memory and support my friend.

I walked out of the church that day, making a mental note to tell Kara that when my time came, I wanted it to be her who planned my funeral. The celebration of life and the joy of the ceremony was what I believed all memorial services should be. Light, love, joy, laughter, fun stories, and the peace of knowing that whatever pain her mother had suffered in the latter part of her life, including the cancer that eventually consumed the body, was now gone. There was only love where her soul existed now.

I didn't know God, but I knew somewhere in that part of me where divine wisdom is the sole inhabitant, that when we die only love remains.

Remembering something Kara said to me during that period, I reached out to her via telephone. "What was your house like when your mother was nearing the end of life? Did you feel anything different?"

"In fact, I did. And I even made mention of it to the hospice nurse. She told me that people tell her this all of the time. She believes that God sends His angels to escort a soul home when someone is near the end of life. She has witnessed unexplainable things many times and with many patients. For us, we began to see things out of the corner of our eyes and felt like we were not alone. We just accepted it and started to talk to these unseen beings like they could hear us."

Her words clung to me like a second skin had been put on me.

Once again I thought, *No. As beautiful as that is, that is not going to happen. Not on my watch. No soul was being escorted anywhere by whatever it was I felt in my home.*

After that call, I started a little ritual at the end of each night. Shortly after Allison received her injection of medicine to rest, I would close the door to the hallway leading to the part of the house that hosted the bedrooms.

I would then step into the great room just outside the hallway, look around at the invisible air and say "You are in the wrong house. Go back to from wherever it is you have come. You are not welcome here. Not on my watch."

Nightly. This was the adamant thought I sent out to the universe—to God's angels. *Go back, you are not needed here.*

I never questioned the words of my friend.

I too believed they were angels. There was something about them that was familiar to me.

I also never questioned any other reason for the feeling that somehow my house was surrounded and protected by these beings. I didn't have to know God to know that there was more to our world than what we can visibly see.

That was simply the way of world in which we lived.

It just *was*.

CHAPTER 16
Hands of Light

July 2012

6 months after Allison arrived to my home

By the time July 2012 rolled around, I had been dating Mitchell for two years and five months. He continued to show great patience during this particular period that turned upside down the time we were able to spend together.

Although Mitchell's professional life was corporate in nature, he had spent years studying martial arts, which taught students how to make a choice about the best action to take with day-to-day situations that brought them face-to-face with negative energy. It taught students how to become conscious of energy and how to become masters of their own energy flow. They referred to this energy as chi.

Over the years Mitchell not only learned how to connect to chi energy, but also had achieved the ability to pull this energy into his hands to generate a healing heat, and then pass this energy on to others to stimulate healing and bring comfort to specific parts of the body.

A modern-day laying on of hands.

He had performed this technique numerous times on a shoulder I had injured years earlier in a serious bike accident. What came from his hands calmed the pain whenever it became uncomfortable for me. There was a tingling. A heat. A balm. Something wonderful.

I loved it.

Allison's cancer was not responding to treatment, according to the reports from Dr. M.

So, one day when she complained about being in high pain, I had the thought that we might be able to use Mitchell's technique to help her find relief. She claimed to be experiencing a headache so severe, it was causing nausea like a migraine. We could hear her retching in the bathroom where she was kneeling in front of the commode. She was desperate for relief.

On this terribly painful July day, we had her lie down on her back and close her eyes. The sun was just beginning to set and we further darkened the room by closing the curtains and dimming the lights, creating a relaxing atmosphere that felt much like a room at a Day Spa.

I didn't know exactly what Mitchell was going to do, but I realized I should probably inform the doctor.

Sitting next to him on a bench in the darkened room, near to where she lay on the bed with her eyes closed, I silently tried to reach the doctor using my phone's messaging app. Minutes passed with no response. I waited a bit longer and made a second attempt, and then waited some more. Still, no response. *A constant barrage of messages from you and now that I need you, I get nothing but silence. This is not the time to disappear,* I thought to myself, willing a message to pop up on my screen.

Mitchell began his process anyway. He pulled the energy from within, drew its heat to his hands, then held them close to

119

her head, sending peace and calm to the area where her headache was most severe.

Five to ten minutes later my phone lit up.

The message said "Energy work is fine, K. Just do not put any pressure on the left frontal lobe. Find me again when you are finished and give me a report."

Oh good. We're safe.

I touched Mitchell's shoulder and motioned that we had been cleared to continue. The very moment my hand made contact with his shoulder, Allison's body jolted on the bed. Wow. *That was a strange coincidence,* I thought, *near perfect timing.*

I settled back to watch with my mind more at ease, knowing it was okay to continue. The room darkened slowly, allowing my eyes to adjust in synchronization with the changing light.

All of a sudden, I noticed a subtle movement directly above where Allison lay. *What was that?* I took a closer look and tried to focus my gaze. *There it was again. What was that?*

Hovering just above her body, was a very light gray mist. It was wavy and fast and looked like dancing vapor. It looked like what you see when the heat rises off a pavement and distorts what's in the background, except that it had a white tint. *What am I seeing?* I looked to the left of Allison where I had tossed the throw pillows on the bed to see if the mist was visible above the pillows, but the answer was an obvious "no." Whatever I saw, it was not dancing above the pillows, so it was not my eyes playing tricks on me. I looked at Mitchell's hands which he held just above Allison and saw that the mist was not there either. But when I looked back at her outline in the darkened room, sure enough there it was.

My eyes traveled up to her head where the headache was supposed to be, and the mist was even darker—like a deep charcoal gray. I was completely riveted. *What in the world am I seeing?* As I watched this darker mist, it dawned on me that there was intent in its movement. It appeared as though it was trying to enter her head! As it bumped against her head she would moan in pain. I continued watching in fascination. I glanced over at Mitchell who was solely focused on sending her healing energy. *Does he see what I see?* It happened again. The dark shadow bumped up against the side of her head and she moaned in pain.

Wait a minute! Am I seeing pain?

I closed my eyes and opened them again like I was rebooting a computer, but it was still there. Light colored mist hovered over her entire body except near her head where it was a darker mist.

Repeatedly, each time it banged up against her head she would moan. I'm either seeing the energy of pain or the energy of something very dark. It appeared to be that the barrier of light Mitchell created around her blocked it from gaining entry.

I was filled with immense curiosity and complete fascination.

In that moment, there was a familiar pressing on my heart. I knew intuitively that whatever path I had taken to get to this very moment had been the right one. This was supposed to happen. I just didn't know *why* this was supposed to happen.

● ● ● ● ● ● ●

6A FEW MEDICAL FACTS

- There are 50 trillion cells in our bodies.

- Neuroscientists believe that some—***not all***—diseases that manifest in the body are a direct result of the mismanagement of our thinking.

6 Project 101010 Pill or Perception - Documentary

- It is a known medical fact that 1/3 of all healing is a result of the placebo effect.

- The placebo effect works only when the patient believes they are getting an active ingredient. Our minds are that powerful.

A FEW FACTS ABOUT ENERGY HEALING

There are many kinds of energy healing being used today. Some are centuries old, like Polarity Therapy, which combines Eastern and Western techniques to unblock energy in a body. There is Qi Kong, which is used in China by physicians as well as healers. Of course, a commonly known modality is Reiki, which focuses flowing healthy life-force energy on the chakras, meridians, and nadis. Massage is the most common form of energy healing, which by hands-on touch, moves a person's energy through the body and removes both physical and non-physical blocks.

The type of energy healing that best describes Mitchell's technique is called Therapeutic Touch (TT). However, there was no physical touch involved.

[7] *Therapeutic Touch was created by Dolores Krieger, PhD, RN, formerly a professor at New York University, and Dora Van Gelder Kunz, a natural healer, on the premise that the human body, mind, emotions, and intuition form a complex, dynamic energy field. Practitioners believe that in a healthy person, the energy field is governed by pattern and order—and that disease occurs when the energy is characterized by imbalance and disorder. Today, TT is accepted in a growing number of hospitals and universities throughout the United States, Canada and*

7 Prevention.com: Mind-body, Natural remedies. How energy healing works

around the world, and has a number of clinical studies attesting to its usefulness.

When you visit a TT practitioner, she will begin your session by getting a sense of the imbalances in your energy field. Holding her hands two to six inches above you, she begins at your head and works down toward your feet. Some practitioners say that a balanced energy field feels like a barely perceptible but steady breeze; others sense it differently. Imbalances, they say, may feel tingly or slightly cooler than other areas, and areas with deficient energy may feel empty or congested. A practitioner "balances" the energy field with her hands, using various techniques.

The kind done by Mitchell looks like this: The person requesting the healing session lies down and is guided through visualization techniques that bring them to a state of total relaxation. In this relaxed state, they are able to disconnect from their physical self enough to get out of their own way, if you will, so that they don't block the healing, and gains a stronger connection to their spiritual body. The energy healer uses their hands to help create a current of energy flow through the body—like a gentle magnet capturing and directing the flow. The hands do not have to touch the recipient.

Because of the power of our thoughts to alter reality, it is imperative that the energy session be performed with benevolent intention. The recipient must believe with complete faith in the results.

In the *Bible* Jesus repeatedly states, "Because of your faith, you are healed." In the *Bible,* the placebo effect is revered. We call it God's miracle.

For all the years I had been successful in keeping the energy balanced both within myself and my home, helping someone else with their energy was not anything I had participated in before. Being a witness in this session with Mitchell was really the first.

Also, this dancing mist was something I definitely had never seen before, the darker mist near the head and the lighter mist over the body was a brand-new experience. There was a lot going on that I could have closed my mind to, could have made excuses about, and ultimately could have outright dismissed. I chose not to do any of those things. Somewhere in the deepest part of me, this learning experience felt right. This feeling increased as I re-centered myself and felt the familiar pressing on my heart as the message was delivered and received, "I am here."

My curiosity of the mist I could see was now being replaced with complete relaxation as I sank deeper into the moment.

In this state of utter relaxation, I was so grateful for Mitchell's willingness to help, it was like a tidal wave inside of me. In fact, I was feeling so grateful for *everything*, that I silently reached over and placed my hand on his shoulder to express my gratitude.

When I did that, Allison jolted again.

This time I knew that her physical reaction was not a coincidence. Curiosity was once again jostling with relaxation to claim its spot as my dominant emotion, and it eventually won.

What in the world was happening? What was this? I could hardly wait to talk to Mitchell, but I remained silent.

Mitchell finally finished and Allison fell asleep without waking up for the rest of the night. Thanks to whatever energy that came from his hands, her headache had been subdued. After we left Allison to rest, he and I visited for a while, exchanging stories and notes.

I was quite surprised to hear this sincere and quiet man tell me about something disturbing he experienced while he was performing energy work on Allison. He described a clear vision that appeared out of nowhere. It was so real it seemed to be actually happening and it startled him greatly. He described seeing a large tree limb and a giant ant began rapidly crawling down the limb toward him. Just as quickly as it appeared, it disappeared.

How curious.

I told him about the mist and learned that he did not see what I saw.

We exchanged stories easily with each other that night, but we agreed we would not speak of this energy work openly or broadly amongst our circle of friends. We weren't comfortable doing so. On top of that, we were in agreement that this healing technique would never replace traditional medicine. We had both walked paths that taught us we are much more than just our physical bodies, we are also energy beings. Just as we seek the help of doctors to care for our physical bodies, we should also ensure we are taking good care of our energetic bodies through sessions such as this one.

We chatted for a short while longer and said goodbye. I immediately went to my computer to see what I could learn online about this vision he had.

Ants, I read, were voracious in nature—and strong! If ants were the size of a human being, we would be no match for them. They would devour everything in their path.

Looking back now, Mitchell's vision might have been a premonition, or maybe even a warning to us about the woman that was in my home. Was there a darkness inside this woman that would eventually devour everything in its path? Did I see that darkness in a mist near her head?

At the time, however, these thoughts did not cross my mind. Instead, what I understood this vision to be was in relation to the cancer. Cancer, as we know, can devour all the healthy cells in its path. It can destroy lives and we are sometimes no match for the voraciousness of the disease.

After he left that night, I began to get ready for bed. I was still trying to make sense of the mist I saw hovering so clearly over Allison. I thought of the dark mist by her head and wondered again if I had somehow been given the ability to see pain. I thought of the doctor who gave us the okay to do energy work and suddenly remembered his request for a report after we finished. I opened my laptop and shared the details of our session. I told him everything—including what I saw and the vision that Mitchell had. I hit 'send,' feeling confident it was going straight into his inbox and wondered how this man of science would respond to what he would read when he received it.

• • • • • • •

Allison awoke the next morning. No longer in pain and groggy from sleep, she told me that something frightening had happened while Mitchell was working on her. She said she had a vision of a giant ant on a limb—climbing rapidly down toward her. She said it scared her to death. I was completely stunned! They must have had some kind of strong connection to both have experienced the same vision.

The next e-mail that arrived from Dr. M. said, "Whatever you did, K, do it again. Only this time you should lead. I really believe the connection is through you, and that Mitchell had only been channeling your connection to Allison. Drink lots of water and incorporate prayer."

Wait, a minute. What?

What did he mean by 'this time I should lead?' What did he mean when he said the connection is through me? What does he mean by 'connection' period? Who is this doctor? And most of all, why is he telling me to incorporate prayer?

Prayer? What did I know about prayer?

What came to mind when I thought of prayer was a highly-formal ritual, using eloquent, meticulously-chosen, and non-fumbling words. I was certain I would fumble my words. Let's get real, I never talked to God in a formal way. You know, in that way that we are supposed to talk to Him. The rare occasion that I talked to Him was when I was super happy or excited. "Thank you God." Or when I wanted something. "Please dear God..." But I always did so informally and with the addendum... "I mean, if You are really out there, that is..."

But the inner voice nudged me, "Do as you have been requested. And trust."

Eventually, I pushed my trepidation aside and focused on my inner voice. I realized from somewhere deep inside of me that helping someone to believe they are able to source from the energy that is all around us is no different than accepting my long-held belief that we have the power to reverse the negative with positive thoughts. It was no different than balancing energy as I had done all my life. It was no different than what I suggested Allison do when the reports from "the doctor" got increasingly worse.

I knew I was going to do this prayer thing—but first, I had to do a little research to understand where to begin.

Everything from my Internet search came back with something similar to, "Prayer with God is simply having a conversation with God."

OK, easy enough. *But doesn't it have to be formal and filled with rituals?*

It appeared the answer was no, it did not. Speaking to the Creator of all could be like speaking to the earthly parent you love. It did not require ritual.

With more than a small amount of discomfort, I decided to do as had been requested. Not because of the doctor, not because of Allison, and not because of Mitchell. I did it because of the inner voice I had trusted all of my life.

I talked to Mitchell about a second session, and as usual his willingness to do what made me happy trumped all else. We repeated the energy session for Allison, but with me at the helm this time, incorporating silent prayer as best as I knew how.

It was *nothing* like I thought it would be, even with the perceived weirdness of it all. It felt natural to focus my energy and visualize. I had been doing that for much of my life upon choosing to become intentional in my thinking. My visualization was strong, I could see in my mind's eye the light pouring out of my hands. It was a beautiful stream of white light so pure that nothing unhealthy or negative could survive in its brilliance. I used both visualization and my belief in the power of what I was doing. It felt a lot more natural than I expected.

How interesting.

I modeled what I had seen Mitchell do just a few days earlier. I was sure my mind was more muddled than his, but I did it anyway. I visualized and I believed—that part was easy. There was no dancing mist this time, there were no ants on a limb. The only thing repeated from our previous session was the beautiful energy that filled the room, and the peace and gratitude that overtook me.

I stopped when prompted by the inner voice that delivered the message, "That is all."

I did it. I made it through my first energy healing session. *That was not so bad*, I said to myself as I reflected on the experience.

Then a little thought nudged my mind. It wasn't a clear thought, rather it was the inherent understanding that something needed to be tweaked.

But what was it?

I didn't know.

But, somehow, I knew the answer would come to me over time.

CHAPTER 17

Hungry for Hope

The things I had come to understand when I was a child, about those who were overlooked by society and about the importance of caring for those in need, never left me. It was always my desire to keep hope alive by inspiring others to see their own potential. And I had a special compassion for the homeless.

When I was working for the big global company in downtown Atlanta, my workload was at times so heavy that I often left the office late in the evening. I wanted more than anything to get home in time to spend pre-bedtime hours with my family, but it just wasn't possible every night. My former husband did his best to share those times equally. I would be home when he couldn't be and vice versa. But, more often than not, we worked really hard to be home together.

My office was in the corporate headquarters building, in an area of Atlanta that was considered, back then, to be in transition. On my way home from work I would drive past many men and women who had nowhere to be but on the streets at the end of the day. It always brought back memories of when I was a teenager leaving the fried chicken restaurant. Similarly, I would hear the whisper of my inner voice and would stop my car to see if I could be of some help. Just as before, they were mostly men. Unlike my teenage years, this city was much larger, and I wouldn't risk inviting these men into my car to go buy them a meal. First, I did not sense that pressing on my heart. Second, I didn't have that kind of disposable income because there were just too many.

At this phase of my life, when I would stop my car, it was for one purpose; that was to simply visit with these people in need of so much, and to share the love inside of my heart. I would sit down next to them on the sidewalk in my business suit just to talk, and surprisingly would experience some of the very best and real conversations I would ever have. These folks were eager to tell me their names and share their stories, to be seen and heard by someone other than those struggling with the same issues and circumstances. To be visible again in a world where many turned their heads away from them. Even if only for an hour. Even if only late at night. Even if only by one person.

When a person loses everything of a material nature—all their worldly possessions and comforts—they are left only with what they might discover about the spiritual aspect of themselves. The faith that many of these men and women had was truly pure and beautiful. Although I would caution anyone reading this who might be thinking this is something they should do, to be smart and be safe about it, I found enormous fulfillment in the time I spent during those evenings on the sidewalk. I never ever stopped without first feeling the pull from the inner voice at my command center, as I would not willingly put myself in a dangerous situation. If you cannot hear that inner voice clearly, or if you cannot discern that it belongs to God, I would recommend finding another way to help.

Interestingly, at that time I still was unaware that it was God I had been feeling during my interactions with them, but I had, for many years, trusted the inner-voice.

I truly loved visiting with the people I met. Back then when I would think about all the things I was achieving in my career—the major wins, my progressive ascension up the professional ladder and growing income—I would find that the time spent with these forgotten men and women filled something inside of me that the corporate and material worlds simply could not.

Years after I left my corporate job to launch my own business, the time I had available to make those sidewalk-talk visits became less and less. My business was very demanding. I was traveling three times as often as I had in my corporate role, and my new office was not nearby the areas where I would find men and women experiencing homelessness. I needed to find a new way to give back.

One afternoon, in 2012, weeks after the Mitchell-led energy session, I was given the opportunity to speak at a community center serving the homeless in that area. I shared with the audience about the power of positive thinking and the command we all have of our own inner strength. I talked about becoming bigger than our circumstances and environment. I shared how we all have the power to pull from the life-force energy that surrounds us, and that we all possess the ability to maintain a connection to this energy through our conscious thoughts and intentions. I explained that while I had inherently known these things nearly my entire life, I had only recently applied this knowledge in working with another person. This was a gift, not just within me, but within everyone.

"We are spirit beings." I told the group who gathered that night. "We go to our doctors when our bodies need care and psychiatrists to care for our minds. We must not neglect our personal energy channels." I discussed ways that we can strengthen the flow of our life-force energy in our daily lives through yoga, exercise, and even laughter, but that we must also learn to open the flow of our energy through conscious intent. I talked to them about mind-over-matter as a powerful companion to modern medicine.

I went on to offer, "Energy healing is a practice that has been around for ages, but it is not widely embraced in mainstream society. That is because we are skeptical of the things we struggle to understand. *Let your mind be curious for the duration of your life. And don't let the doubt of others stop you from exploring,"* I emphasized. "This is about setting your intent and controlling your thoughts. Mind over matter is about choosing to be positive above your current circumstance and allowing yourself to imagine, feel, *see, and be grateful* for the things you want before they come, so that they DO come. Let nothing but love and faith govern your hearts and become a warrior for the love already there."

I assured them they already had everything inside of them they needed to create the change they wanted to see for themselves, no matter the circumstances they were currently in.

From the results of that one speech, it became apparent how hungry this community was for someone to be bold in reminding them that they could find spiritual strength, and to be on a path that leads to hope. Many lined up to talk to me. Others left and shared my message with their loved ones. For the weeks to come, I was introduced to people they knew who were struggling with either physical or emotional issues and facing diminishing hope.

I met with them all; the willing who were eager and open to these messages, as well as those not so willing and skeptical, but who came out of curiosity or because they had been persuaded to by a loved one. They were all seeking something—to no longer feel alone in their personal, private struggles, to be reminded that they are not helpless and that they are strong, or to gain a clearer understanding of how they could connect with the Divine Energy around them to help them through their periods of difficulty.

Each session began with an easy exchange of stories and ended with visualization and energy work if they requested it. Oh, how far I'd come! I had gone from only using this knowledge for my own purposes to being able to share this gift with others. This tapped my innermost passion to help others.

It didn't take long for a pattern to emerge. The people who believed without doubt in the unseen healing power that exists in all around us, experienced monumentally positive results, while those who held onto skepticism experienced minimal results. They may have felt relaxed or inspired by my personal conviction, but they remained largely unchanged. What's more was that their individual results really had nothing to do with me. I gave everything I had to each person who came to me for guidance. Clearly, whatever had happened in their sessions was an exchange solely between them and God.

The great thing was, I immediately understood and saw the positive effects of sharing the beauty of our soul's wisdom and might with others. It just felt so natural, so right to be able to share love, encouragement, and hope this way. It was as though my own soul had released a huge sigh of relief that said "Yes, Keryl, finally!"

But even so, I still had that nagging feeling that something about the way I was approaching this needed to be modified.

I just didn't know yet what that meant.

There was no turning back now, though. I was not only a warrior for my own light, but I was now on a path to help others become a warrior for theirs.

CHAPTER 18

The Unwanted Guest

Still July 2012

For a rare two weeks at the end of July, my house was "mine again." Allison was summoned to the out-of-state hospital to Dr. M., for treatment and surgery to her leg. He suggested that I use this time to refuel. "Self-care," he said, "was critical for a caregiver who is a cancer fighter."

It had only been four months since Cancun, and I was not one to need breaks so closely spaced together, but the intensity of the days made each one feel like a month long. I needed a break.

I'm not ashamed to say that I was thankful she would be out of my house and that it would be mine again for a much-needed reprieve. I was looking forward to many things that fell by the wayside with the demands of care: quality time with my daughter, my family, and with Mitchell. I was eager to have a night of uninterrupted sleep without being awakened by her voice crying out for help. I was thankful there would also be less disruptions during the work day, and the social freedom to see my dear friends like Gary and others.

I could not stop my mind from once again going to the questions that surfaced repeatedly, *how did one small offer to*

help a near-stranger with her immediate treatment turn into
full-time caregiving? What did heeding the inner voice get me
into? And for what purpose?

By July 2012, Allison had been a part of my home for almost six months. Her family showed worry and concern, but they were not present, and the only friends that supported her were mine who came to support me. She appeared to have few friends of her own. Gary was becoming invaluable to me during that time—from bringing over dinners, to continuing to work from my home while she rested, and the ongoing task of driving her to appointments with her doctors. On top of that, he was becoming my primary caregiver in this situation, just as I was hers. A true and devoted friend.

My life had changed drastically. I no longer had my coveted quiet or alone time as the needs of this individual were great. Caregiving drained me emotionally, physically, and what was now becoming, financially.

Add to this, now her doctor wanted me to start doing energy work regularly. Although I liked the peace that filled my home when I connected to the energy surrounding me. I was still not comfortable with guiding another person by using the techniques I had used solely on me throughout my life.

What's more, I was encouraged to add *prayer,* and that made me extremely uncomfortable.

I had obliged the pressing of the inner-voice to do the things requested, but it was a lot to absorb, and by the time she was summoned by the doctor for these two weeks in late July, I was in desperate need of this break.

Mitchell and I planned a spontaneous overseas trip to visit his family and we brought Madeline with us. I fell in love with his family the first time I went to visit them a little more than a year earlier. We had gone on that trip without Madeline and had spent a week exploring the country, seeing old castles, and laughing at the stories his mother told about him as a young boy. Allison was not in my life and so it was vastly different than what it had become.

I could hardly be present with this trip in July. From the moment the plane touched down, my phone lit up nearly non-stop with messages from Allison, from the doctor, and now from the doctor's wife as well as Dr. M.'s colleague, Dr. Andrew—who in no time, would claim to be falling in love with Allison. There was no reprieve to the barrage that came night and day, and I allowed myself to miss a good portion of witnessing the experience of my daughter's first trip to this country.

Surgery, chemo, and super chemo—in that order—was the protocol dictated by Dr. M. and his team. She would have an irradiation treatment on the bone, which entailed the doctor applying radiation directly to the area that hosted the rapidly growing tumors, and then dousing the bone with a chemical to kill what was left. An easy procedure, he had said in one of his e-mails, nothing too invasive.

From there, she would go into recovery for 48 hours, followed by a round of chemotherapy and then 'super-chemo'—a stronger, more targeted dosage than its predecessor. The effects of super chemo were expected to be so violent, they would first coat her teeth with extra enamel to protect them.

Every bit of it sounded terrible to me, but the doctor was confident this would generate the results they were seeking— remission, God willing.

She was not in my hands. She was in the rightful hands of the doctor. And from everything I read online about Dr. M., plus what he revealed of himself throughout the six months we had exchanged messages, I knew she was in the best of care. I was not at all worried, and in fact, was feeling hopeful this would be the end.

That is, until the message arrived, informing me that something had gone terribly wrong.

In the midst of the surgery, her heart had an episode of atrial fibrillation that brought her dangerously close to a heart attack. She also spiked a fever that reached 105. I received a barrage of urgent messages telling me I had to decide NOW—as her medical proxy— if she should be kept on life support or not. *"NOW, Angel K, I need to know NOW. "*

Angel K was the latest nickname given to me by the doctor.

As Mitchell drove through the beautiful countryside on our way back to his parents' home, I was sitting silently in the car, my own heart mimicking a-fib with the rapid pace it began to beat, facing the most critical decision I had ever had to make. And I was doing so with very little knowledge of the person who was living in my home. What did I know about her except the tragic stories she told? Where was her family? How did it take only 6 months to come to this urgency?

Caregiving, I had read once, was a lot like stepping into the shallow end of a pool. Time passes for a caregiver and before they know it, they are in the deep end—often in over their heads.

That was where I was right then—in over my head.

My mind went back to an e-mail I received from Dr. M., almost immediately after receiving the signed medical proxy papers from Allison. In its original form, [name changes in brackets], the message read:

"[Allison] is a special patient for many reasons. One of the main ones being that I believe her genetic markings hold part of the answer to furthering my research dramatically in the field

of pediatric cancer. She is only one of several patients (really the main one) in the United States to have had the fastest type of aggressive pediatric bone cancer eradicated in the shortest amount of time by high levels of IMRT radiation. I need and will take very good care of her and even better care now that I know what has been going on in Atlanta at Emory. I promise Keryl. Please keep this information confidential. Our grant money for research demands it until we have enough evidence to support it. [Allison's] now our main source of initial evidence that we need to present at some point to the oncology medical review board.

"[Allison] is also a very special friend of mine and now of my family. We care for her deeply. Her capacity to give to others under cancer free circumstances blows most of the people that I have met in this life away. She gives selfishly, freely, and intelligently without asking. She is utterly amazing. I think in you she has met her match. I am thrilled that the two of you have connected.

"My most recent and best story of [her] was the last time she was in [city name] about three weeks ago. I wonder if she has shared this with you. I love this story. I share it with many of my patients when they are out of hope and have little forbearance.

"She had just spent a very painful night in bed after the spinal tap she had the evening before and was not in the best of places emotionally. It was a little bit before lunch and a father had come into one of the [Cancer Center] wings where she had to go for her next appointment with me post spinal tap. The man was a father to one of our patients and he had gone home for his guitar so that he could play for his young son hopefully getting him to sleep after 4 nights of no sleep. He was so upset and tired that he could not play and broke down in the hallway away from his son. I was walking down the hall towards him with [her] *and she went over and picked up the guitar and asked how she could help. The boy's father told her what he was going to do and she just went in the room and played for this boy until he went to sleep for the first time since the beginning of the week. It must have taken an hour. What is unbelievable is that I know she was in terrible pain. She gave 100% of herself to make sure that child had what he needed. To this day when I see him he asks me when the guitar lady is coming back to play for him.*

"This is the kind of person we are healing."

This was the same boy whom I learned, sitting in the pizza shop with Mitchell, had died.

I thought of this e-mail that night, 4000 miles away from Atlanta. I thought of the poems she liked to send, the cards she purchased and sent to people regularly to lift a spirit, and the little things that showed up when cancer wasn't in the forefront. Of course, one would want to keep a person like that alive, no matter what it took.

What do I do? Life support or no life support? The doctor was waiting. How can I make a decision so blindly? How could I be so far away while she was hanging onto her life by a thread? I needed to be there, providing the support that I delivered daily.

I recalled the instructions that were in the medical proxy paperwork that bore her signature. I had scanned all the documents into my digital archives for safe-keeping. I could see the docs in my mind. With that, I told the doctor, Do Not Resuscitate.

I was emotionally drained. Moreover, I was creating an energy of concern that began to seep to those around me. The gentle, beautiful woman that was Mitchell's mother was aware I needed to be somewhere with cellphone connection at all times. In this remote country, that requisite became a source of angst.

I found myself apologizing over and over, "I'm so sorry. I'm her primary caregiver and she really has no one else."

"She sounds so brave," said Mitchell's mother, "and you are so kind for what you are doing. God will surely bless you." The latter part of those words, delivered in her lovely accent, filled me with warmth. Although I didn't have a relationship with God, somewhere deep inside I knew my selflessness through this situation was pleasing to God.

But gosh, that was intense. And certainly not the break I was hoping to have. I was not feeling refreshed nor rejuvenated. In fact, I began feeling anxious to get home. Once again, the energy was permitted to permeate my reprieve.

Maybe I'm not supposed to be enjoying myself during this time. Maybe I'm supposed to give all of my focus to helping Allison heal. The rest of the trip was the same, minus the urgency—I received a nonstop barrage of communications.

The week flew by. Thankfully, Allison made it through this frightening scare that almost took her life. But she was not out of the woods yet, not by a long shot.

• • • • • •

We returned to our respective homes on a Sunday. I walked into my blissfully quiet home. Once again, I was looking forward to the caregiving break. There was still one more week without Allison.

On Monday, July 23, 2012, I met with my running club for a group run followed by dinner. It was hot that day, even after the sun went down. The daytime temperatures were in the 90s and there was not much difference by sunset. By the time I returned to my home later that night, I was overflowing with the after-effects of a wonderful evening filled with exercise and the post-run dinner with friends. My home was quiet and peaceful, and I looked forward to a hot shower and a good night's sleep.

Before I stepped into the shower, I checked in via chat window to see how things were progressing with treatment at the hospital. I chatted on one window with Dr. M. who told me she was in recovery and on the other window with the patient herself. She shared events of the super chemo treatment she was receiving, including intricate detail about its impact on her. Amid the barrage of details, came a note from the doctor to just spend a moment longer because she needed to rest. I retreated to bed and to the start of a night that I will remember for the rest of my life.

In the early morning hours, I was awakened from sleep by three things—an icy-cold air in my bedroom that seemed, at the time, to be blowing from my ceiling fan, the sound of loud noises coming from my hallway, and the strong smell of eucalyptus—an aromatherapy (or essential oil as it is now known) that I have used for years.

My bedroom was so frigid that I could see just a hint of my breath as I awakened further and began to get acclimated.

From the hallway, right outside of my bedroom, the noises sounded like a combination of the washing machine dial being played with and a large, plastic, machine being tinkered with. A clanging, if you will, but not metallic—rather it was like heavy plastic. "Oh no! My AC must be breaking down," was my first thought, followed immediately by "My bill is going to be through-the-roof if I don't get this temperature back up."

I got out of bed and walked into the hallway where the master controls were kept. The house had two units. The control in the master bedroom only controlled one. Without knowing which unit was broken, it made sense to go to the dial that was in the hallway.

The moment I stepped into the hallway, I was pummeled by a static electrical field that was so thick, it felt like it could physically knock me down. I felt like it had grabbed me and coiled itself around me like a snake. I was covered in it.

I had never felt anything like it in my life and I froze in my tracks. In this 'field' was the most insidious energy presence imaginable. Every feeling we dread was swirling within it. My entire body went on high alert and all of my senses became heightened. If I could see what I was standing in, I would not have been able to see through its thickness and density. It was palpable—the way my constant companion in my earlier years was palpable. But that is where the similarities ended. It felt *nothing* like the familiar energy of peace and love that was my constant companion, and this was many times more dense.

I was still frozen to the spot I was standing in, and I realized that a tidal wave of fear was rising up from within me. However, this thing, whatever it was, didn't create that fear; rather, it itself was fear. And it felt like it was trying to get inside of me.

I could feel the blood in my body get colder than the air, which was like a winter night already in my home.

I had an immediate understanding that what was in my home was the antithesis of light and love, but I had no understanding of what to do about it or why this was happening.

Without delay, the inner-voice took over, "Claim your house—forbid this intrusion."

Forbid this intrusion?

How does one forbid this intrusion? What does that look like? I didn't know. I didn't even have one idea of what to do to forbid this intrusion.

I chose a literal response to the instructions received by my inner voice; I stood taller, right there in my hallway, surrounded by the cacophony of noises, and this God-awful energy and said aloud to the invisible air, "This is MY house. YOU are not welcome here," I was so focused on the immediate task at hand, it didn't dawn on me that these were almost the exact words I used with the angels that had allegedly been sent to carry her soul home. Nor did I stop to imagine how crazy I must have appeared speaking aloud to nothing.

"You" are not welcome here. *Did I just I personify it?*

The return response was immediate. The noises increased —becoming louder and somehow more dense. I got the VERY distinct feeling that I was being laughed at. As though I was insignificant and small, an irrelevant pest to this energy. A gnat on a windshield.

Yet, at that precise moment, an understanding came upon me that I will never forget. *I was no stranger to this presence and it was somehow no stranger to me.* I didn't know what that meant either, but that was the thought that pressed on my heart.

Madeline! I turned toward the other side of the hallway and ran downstairs to check on my teen-aged daughter. When I reached her bedroom in the finished terrace level, I found her sound asleep. She was safe and completely unaware of what was occurring in our home. Her room felt peaceful. It could not have felt more different than what was upstairs. In fact, it felt more peaceful than I had ever felt it before—or perhaps that was just the law of relativity in action. This peace was in stark contrast to what was happening in the hallway directly above her.

I wondered, *do I wake her?* The inner voice answered "She is protected. God especially protects the children."

WHAT?

It was a monumental show of trust to leave my sleeping child in the bedroom downstairs. For a moment I envisioned those scenes from a horror film where a person is dragged up a wall and the room is terrifyingly possessed with evil spirits whose sole intent is to harm all in its path. What I felt in my home that evening certainly aligned to what the characters in those types of movies experienced when they were living it real-time. I had to literally shake my head to clear the vision and fight back the anxiety that was beginning to expand in the pit of my stomach.

The peace in her room was so reassuring, it made that task possible. Reminding myself that the powerful and wise inner voice had never failed me, I thought "I hope tonight is not the exception."

I hesitated only one more fraction of a second before hurrying back upstairs. I wanted my phone.

Somehow knowing that if I allowed fear to take over, it would exacerbate this situation, I remained intentional in my boldness. Peace and calm must surround me to face this. I also knew I needed to let my entire self connect to what came from the voice within.

My years of calling upon the energy of peace and love made this critical task achievable, even in this heightened state of alert. But my heart was beating louder than normal in my chest and I had to concentrate hard to quiet the brain so that I could hear the answers that I knew would come from inside.

I went back upstairs, trusting the message that God especially protects the children. *"Please dear God, if You exist, protect my child."* Would a God I didn't know be there for me?

My phone was still in my bedroom.

As I crossed back through the hallway, the noises escalated; and once again, the thought that I was being taunted came to mind.

What also came to mind was the understanding that we have the power to manifest the energy around us. This thought was followed immediately by the thought that somehow, in some way, this unwanted energy was coming from Allison—even though she was not in my house or, to my understanding, not even in the State of Georgia. I was positive she was somehow the cause.

My mind didn't go to her because of anything evil within her, it went to her because she seemed to evoke the opposite of what I was always surrounded by, and she seemed to exist perpetually in despair. So powerful was this thought inside of me that when I reached my phone, I didn't hesitate to send her a text message, nor did I bother to give my words the context they would need to even make sense to anyone who would receive them

"This thing that's happening in the house," I texted, "it's not wanted or welcome by me. Particularly not in the middle of the night. It's time for this to end. I know you'll agree...." I then shot a note to her doctor that basically said "Control your patient. Her emotions are wreaking havoc with the energy here."

Although by now it was well past two o'clock in the morning, she responded instantly from her remote location. "I am here," she typed, "Agree. It's here too. Nurse has been in twice. My fever is high."

Strange response.

There were so many things I realized much later as I looked back at this night. One of them was that bulk of my thoughts and actions were governed by my inner-voice which took the helm of my control center during this time. I relied heavily on

147

instinct and intuition in a near-disconnect from my brain and body. I willingly let the thoughts go dormant and the soul take command. Had I not, I would have been responding in fear, confusion, and the desperate desire to get my child and I out of that house. Like the characters in those movies.

It would be three years later before I would also think back on this night and realize that Allison didn't even ask what I was talking about when my text came in. She seemed to know exactly what I was referring to with my cryptic message. How was that possible? A more normal response would have been, "What are you talking about, Keryl?" Instead, she wrote, "I am here...It's here too."

These things didn't cross my mind in the midst of the chaos; they would come later. At that moment on July 23, 2012, even though her response hit me as odd, I could focus only on the utter shock of what I was facing at that moment, and more importantly, what do I do to return my home to its normal, peaceful state.

How does the mother warrior protect her child?

I placed a call to Mitchell, but he did not pick up. *What do I do? What do I do?*

The answer was hand-delivered to me at the very moment that I was silently asking the question. This would be yet another thing I would realize only when I looked back. In the throes of the chaos that night, I missed the massive beacon. God does not come to mind when He is not on your radar and you have not acknowledged that He is in your life.

Had I been aware of the Source of all protection, I would have realized that just as I had been wondering what I needed to do next, I received an incoming text message from Gary. He is a Christian man, with a faith that runs deep. His relationship with God spanned decades. "Keryl, I was woken up just now with a powerful urge to pray for your protection. Is everything OK there?" The time was nearing 3 a.m.

Never before had he or anyone else for that matter, sent a message to me like that one. Nor had he ever felt such a strong urge to write one. He had wanted to call, but immediately wondered if what he was feeling was even accurate, and didn't want to risk waking me in the middle of the night. He chose to text.

He later told me that the urge was so powerful, it almost jolted him out of bed. Another first. There were a lot of firsts lately, the mist, the energy healing, the noises, this presence—and now a supernatural push to offer protection through prayer

Like Allison to me, I responded in similar manner to Gary. I didn't have to ask the question, 'What are you talking about, Gary?' I knew precisely what his message meant. I responded, "There is something in my house that is not wanted—a presence of some kind."

He immediately wanted to drive over, but I told him it wasn't necessary as I had already called Mitchell who lived much closer; and although I had not been able to reach him, I was confident he would receive my message.

The events of the evening continued for the next few minutes. My gut instinct and inner voice told me to go back into the hallway and turn all the lights on. I obeyed. I stepped back into that force field of repulsive energy and turned on the hallway lights. I also turned on the light sconces in the great room right outside of the hallway. Finally, I opened the doors in the hallway where the washer and dryer were, almost expecting something terrifying to be lurking, and I turned the lights on there as well. Nothing was there—and anyway, the whole thing was terrifying.

With all of these lights on, the noises stopped. It was the most literal translation of 'only light can overcome the darkness,' I could receive, but as you can imagine, I did not catch the symbolism. There seemed to be a lot I wasn't seeing that night; even with my lifelong awareness of signs and the universal energy that surrounded us. I was still blind to so much.

Although the noises had stopped, my body, at its core, remained on high alert.

Time passed with no recurrence of whatever that was and by 4:30 a.m., all felt peaceful again. I quieted my mind, intentionally stopping its stream of thoughts, and settled back in to try to find rest.

This thing, whatever it was, had other plans.

Unfortunately, whatever charged the air in my home was not going to be thwarted with a few light bulbs, even with the silencing of the cacophony.

The peace was short-lived.

My phone, which I had plugged into the night-stand by my bed, began to buzz and power on by itself. It would start the moment I would begin to drift to sleep. The phone would first buzz and then immediately light up, like a message was being received. I'd reach for the phone to see if there was an incoming message and there would be nothing; so I'd put it down and moments later, it would buzz and light up again—as if a surge of power was flowing through it.

I finally yanked the plug out of the wall, intentionally took the time to fill myself with peace and love as I recognized that I was on a slippery slope to panic and what was beginning to feel like the start of anger. I used my lifelong practice to surround myself with calmness and at 5 a.m., Mitchell walked in. Twenty-to-thirty minutes later, after a very long night, no longer alone, and in a house that felt peaceful again, I finally fell asleep.

I wouldn't know it then, but this was day one of many to come. It never again manifested in my home in a way as powerful as its first entry, but even a small sliver of this darkness was unwelcome.

July 23, 2012: A night that is etched in my mind forever.

For the weeks that followed, the phone buzzed off and on through the night, the house was filled with electricity, a feeling of a presence, and a tingling (like hairs on end). One time, when the house was particularly charged, the faucet in the master bath turned on by itself. The noises never returned but overall the energy in the house felt awful—the opposite of the balance I always maintained. This went on until mid-October.

I will forever refer to those weeks as 'days of darkness.'

On July 23, 2012, I would realize that this other energy— this awful energy—was just as real as the other that I craved to have in my life. I also came to understand that it was the non-manifested version of the same energy that came through certain individuals. The very same energy that I had learned to keep out of my life years ago. Palpable, powerful, and repugnant. It too will surround you, if you let it.

I became a believer of the stories I had previously thought were the active imagination of the author or the creative minds of the screenplay writers in a movie. This was not my active imagination, this was happening. This was no movie set, this was in MY house! Nor was I drugged by this woman who was not even in my home when the first instance occurred, as has been suggested to me since then. Whatever was the opposite of that exquisite presence made itself at home in my home for the next six weeks.

• • • • • • •

In the years to come, I would face difficulty in finding a logical explanation for these events. I was careful whom I spoke with as I sought answers. I reached out to paranormal experts, I asked friends I had who led churches, I contacted mediums, and a myriad of other individuals to try to understand what had happened in my home.

The only explanation that resonated with me came from the Pastor of a non-denominational church. He said "There is an agreement between our souls and the universal energy that is God. This agreement is that our life's experiences are such that they are helping our souls remember that we are one with God. When you interrupt someone else's agreement, you are given a message from the universe. In essence, God says, 'You are disrupting this soul's karma.' I believe you were given a strong message that this person had to walk their path, whatever it was. Being in your home was a disruption to her path."

Disruption to *her* path? It felt to me that Allison being in my home had become a major disruption to my path!

I wondered for a moment, was that her purpose? To disrupt the path I set out on to teach others that they already have everything inside of them to live their best life? Are people here on this Earth for reasons such as that?

No. I refused to believe that.

CHAPTER 19

The Energy Shift

Late 2012 | Month 8 of Allison in my home.
On the brink of identifying God in my life

We had to get out of the house.

Despite the barrage of medical issues Allison had faced over the past recent weeks—from total amnesia, to temporary deafness and nearly everything in between—we needed a night out.

Madeline, Allison, and I went to a nearby Mexican restaurant.

As we waited on our meal, the two became engaged in conversation, allowing me a few moments of quiet to process some things in my head. I sat and reflected on the overall feel of my house. Something had changed and it was palpable. A strange energy seemed to now blanket my home—and the overall feeling was not one of safety and comfort to me. My surroundings felt colder and darker and became increasingly harder to rebalance.

I still had no answers and no clue as to where to go to get them, just as was the case in July when it began. It didn't help that I had no time either. I had a heavy task load and I could see that my current situation was having an impact on business, friends, family, and more.

I was deep in these thoughts and turned my eyes over to Allison, the nucleus of all this trouble. I observed her chatting away with my daughter, discussing things related to school. I felt a familiar twinge in my heart for the thoughts that I was having. Guilt. *Shame on me. I know better than to give power to those kinds of thoughts.*

At that moment, my phone, which was sitting on the table in front of me, buzzed. I glance at the screen and my blood ran cold. I looked at the name.

RWilde.

Impossible! He died months ago.

I grabbed the phone hastily off of the table and swiped open the message with hands that were starting to tremble.

The message was brief and ominous—seven words that packed a powerful punch: *"Keryl. Take extra, extra care. Robert Wilde"*

My face must have drained of all color because both of my table companions looked at me with curious expressions.

I manage what I hoped was a humorous smile, as though I realized how utterly ridiculous I must look. "Sorry. I got a weird text but it wasn't for me." I added a chuckle.

I didn't want my daughter to know what had just happened. *Robert Wilde? How is this possible?*

When I thought she wasn't looking, I discreetly handed the phone to Allison, who in turn did not have a subtle reaction. She almost dropped my phone. I snatched it back, which prompted yet another strange look from Madeline. A mixed expression that silently declared, "I know you're trying to keep something from me." I couldn't read how that made her feel.

So not cool, Allison. Nice subtlety.

Somehow, I managed to eat my food and stay present in conversation.

The moment I returned home, I sequestered myself away and contacted one of my sisters—the one whom, at the time, was most vocal about her faith. She did not easily limit the power of God.

"Sometimes when a person crosses over, there are still messages that need to be delivered. Ask what he wants to say."

HE'S DEAD! He is no longer living! Who is going to receive this message if I send it? Am I hearing that we can still text when we die?

The inner-voice said "Listen to her." But I could not. I could not send a note to a dead man. There must be some sick prankster who hacked into this account. I am not buying it.

I asked Allison if she had closed down all of his accounts when she closed his estate. I was assured she had.

Sick.

Someone has a sick, mentally ill mind.

I tried hard to shrug it off.

There I was, standing with my toes touching my own boundaries of faith. For all of my years of understanding that there was so much more to our world than what we could physically see, and for all of the years I spent practicing the manipulation of energy with the understanding that we are so much more powerful than we know. For all my love of quantum science and with all of the unexplainable things I had experienced throughout my life. And even as I had just been sitting at that table thinking over the energy shift that was happening in my home; when push came to shove, I was no different than anyone else.

I was limited. I was nothing like the disciple Peter.

The moment something was impossible to understand, when it was not normal, I blamed it on mental illness.

We live in a world of mystery, Keryl, open your mind. I was already scolding myself.

I was contemplating sending a text message to a dead man. Does that make ME mentally ill? I could not help but wonder.

Three days later another message arrived.

Robert Wilde <rwilde***@___.com>
9/29/12
to me

Take extra, extra care Keryl. I will be with you and I will hold your heart. When the time comes I will hold your heart. Take extra care until then.

Ok, what if this *is* real? What could be so big, it would prompt a transcendental message? Madeline? Was something going to happen to my daughter? It was then, because of that one thought, I responded.

9/29/12
to rwilde

Dear Robert,
Thank you so much for your constant love and protection. Can you tell me....is this for Madeline tonight?

Robert Wilde <rwilde***@___.com>
9/29/12
to me

your child is protected.

It did not go unnoticed that these words that were very similar to what I heard from my inner-voice on July 23, 2012 when I ran downstairs to check on my daughter. "God especially protects the children."

Once again, I made the list: Mists, noises, cold air, a palpable and unpleasant energy shift, Gary being jolted out of a deep sleep to pray for a dear one's protection, and now these phantom messages warning me that something was coming that required me to take extra, extra care.

I had lived decades and never experienced a multitude of things like this so closely knit together. What was happening?

I began to dread going home.

The Mama Bear sent Madeline to stay with her father because suddenly nothing felt good. He was more than happy to have her.

Just like the events of July 23, these messages would also taper to an end. But the feeling of dread did not. In fact, it increased exponentially until the energy of love and light that I had always been able to keep in my home could not be felt. It was as though all of the oxygen had been sucked out of my warm nest. I could not breathe in the oppressiveness of my home.

Once again, something in the deepest part of me knew that all of this was connected Allison.

I just didn't know how or why.

I still believed it was tied to her current state of mind— specifically her turbulent emotions. This thought pressed on my heart, over and over again.

My logical side always kicked in and I would tell myself that I was simply picking up on- and empathically feeling- the despair of a person whose body was invaded by one of the most dreaded diseases of all.

And just when I would find a moment of peace with that logic, the thought would return, *but what if she IS behind all of this?*

No, stop it Keryl. She was not the cause of the things that could not be humanly explained. How could she create cold air in my home? Or that energy field? Or the mist? Or turn on the faucet?

The energy of the disease was shifting the normal into the abnormal. That had to be it.

It was not lost on me that I blamed a lot of things on this disease.

Regardless of the cause, for the first time in as long as I could remember, I was unable to balance the energy in my home, nor discern the truth about someone's authentic nature.

Nothing felt the same.

Something had to change.

CHAPTER 20

A Place of Peace

October 2012

My day of awakening

Have you ever noticed how many homeless people you can find sleeping on the stoop of a church? Why?

A church is private property and authorities can ask them to move. The concrete of a church stoop is not any softer than the concrete outside a convenience store or gas station. It is still out in the elements. Why do you think they gravitate there? Why can they close their eyes and rest more easily there?

I believe it is because the love and light energy of God surrounds and protects sacred places of prayer, meditation, communion, and worship. These buildings house the energy of life, love, hope, and strength, and that energy is very palpable. Being in proximity to true places of worship that honor God can fuel the depleted spirits of those who are in need. To the displaced and discarded, a church stoop is like a welcome mat, a place they can find some comfort.

I found myself being pulled, as if I was metal and it was a magnet, to such a place for the first time in my life.

By the grace of God, the doors of a Catholic Church on the way home from my office were always open. I had driven past it countless times without hardly giving it a glance. But these days, I felt drawn to this church. Sometimes the pull was so strong for me to be there, I found myself turning into the parking lot regardless of the time. I just wanted to go sit inside.

Every now and then, I would arrive from work to my home, only to leave it again to sit in the strange, mostly empty church. Occasionally I would bring Allison, more often I would go alone. I would sit in blissful quiet with eyes closed. There in the empty chapel, I would clear my mind and find stillness.

I could breathe deeply and freely in there, inhaling the energy of peace. It felt like I had been handed an oxygen mask. I couldn't breathe this deeply in my beloved home where it felt like I was sucking in air through a coffee stirrer.

I was not a church goer, and in fact, wondered if someone who didn't practice the worship of God even belonged there. Somehow, that discomfort was trumped by something much bigger—this church felt familiar. It was so reminiscent of my time in the woods as a child when I was surrounded by what I thought were my angels.

It was uncanny how similar.

And in one flash moment, a realization hit me with such clarity it practically blinded me.

My mind was no longer silent. It began to process.

I thought about the feeling inside of the church and recalled the feeling of my constant companion. I placed these two feelings side-by-side in my mind and realized what I was detecting in this church was in fact my constant companion.

They were the same!

Could this be?

I dared to think 'yes,' and test it out like a new pair of running shoes.

Like a new heart.

Yes. They felt the same!

This foreign place felt so familiar because the energy that emanated from it was the same that had been my constant companion for the majority of my life.

And just like that, the exquisite presence I first noticed as a young child again surrounded me. I could hardly breathe from the beauty of it.

It was acknowledged. My eyes had been turned to it.

All along, the presence I had been detecting was God.

I sat in stunned, beautiful silence in a building that suddenly felt like my truest home and a movie began to play in my mind. Memories of the times in my life I had felt surrounded by something protective or guided by my inner voice. The memories were countless, the movie reel endless, and each scene brought me the same feeling of comfort and love.

I thought back to all of the times I would be doing something mundane, when suddenly, out of nowhere, I felt blanketed by serenity, like everything in the world was perfect and whole—and exactly as it was supposed to be.

Like a big hug from the purest form of love there is.

A hug from God.

For as long as I live, I will never forget those cherished moments of understanding that came to me in that empty church.

God—a presence I had never given an identity to, but had somehow always acknowledged, whether as a pressing on my heart or a companion that engulfed me.

God, whom I trusted and whose instructions I followed simply because it felt right in my soul to do so.

It was God that I had referred to most of my life as 'my spidey sense.'

GOD was my constant companion. The sovereign God that some look for all their lives is with us, right here and now—guiding, nudging, loving, and bringing key experiences into our life at just the right moment. Like that one in that empty church.

It was another monumental understanding in my life.

God doesn't need to be found, because the love and light that is this Divine Source is with us always. We need only to acknowledge it to know it and feel it. Seeing is not believing. Rather, *believing is seeing.*

It was suddenly simple and obvious.

And just like that, everything changed.

I realized that belief in God is not a matter of evidence, it is a matter of awareness and heart. Like everything else, it is a choice we make. It is a trust we choose to have.

When things became so out of balance in my home and in my life, God showed up for me. There may never be the words that can accurately describe this moment.

I had the same response with this understanding as I did during my first energy session, something deep within me breathed its own deep breath, filled to the capacity with God, and exhaled. "*Finally.*"

Nothing touched me more deeply.

● ● ● ● ● ● ●

If I had any inkling of what was to come, I didn't feel it in that moment. But in the months directly ahead of me, I would draw upon my newly-identified God with everything I had when an unimaginable truth began to emerge.

CHAPTER 21

Trinity Soul Sisters

October 2012

Once again, emotional and tearful, Allison was on the phone with me. This time, however, the tears were from joy.

"You have to come home, Keryl. You will not believe the beauty of what is here."

I no longer felt the urge to rush to where she was when she said it was urgent. Cancer was becoming secondary to a series of unexplainable circumstances that seemed to stem from that one fateful night in July. She was not in any apparent health danger, and besides, her doctor was always available to her when crisis hit.

Whatever this was could wait until I got home from the office.

Allison was still in my home by October 2012—in no time we will be at the one-year mark of the day I extended an offer to help and opened my home to her as a place she could rest after her treatments.

A year and a lifetime, it seemed.

A few weeks had passed since the original message came in from the late Robert Wilde. I had received a few more, each warning me to prepare myself for something that was coming. These few messages spoke of the omnipresent, non-bartering

163

power of our God, and the beauty that was found there in the place where God exists.

What was coming? Who was sending these messages, and why was I being warned?

There was very little that resembled normalcy in my life and my mind had begun to expand to accept things that I would have outright rejected just prior to all of this.

Nothing was small. Events were happening as though God had placed an upgraded lens over my eyes and I was seeing everything polarized.

Everything appeared bigger.

Identifying God did not change who I was. Rather, it enhanced it. And knowing that the Creator of all was always with me instilled a measuring rod in my life that made me want to be a better person.

I was filled with God.

I knew somehow that the extra energy I had felt in my home, that I once thought were God's angels coming to escort a soul home, was not about Allison but about me. A connection, a pull, a knowing that my soul was drawing closer to its Creator.

Or perhaps God did truly send His angels, not because someone was near death, but because God knew that a home belonging to an individual devoted to care and compassion, was about to be infiltrated by something that was not of His divine light.

Only our God can see what is coming.

That evening when I did return home, I knocked on Allison's bedroom door in the pretty guest room in my home. The words she had been holding inside, since sending the message to me to come home, began to tumble out. Emotionally.

I listened past the emotion and gleaned the following story.

A family had moved into Robert Wilde's home in Florida. The family had been painting, stripping wallpaper, and all of the things that new homeowners do. They had a grown niece who had come to help them, and they put her to work in the master bedroom walk-in closet. It had been wall-papered and her job was to strip it.

The young lady began her task. When she reached one particular wall she pulled down the wallpaper and was shocked to find a built-in storage hidden behind it. It appeared to be a small jewelry box, built right into the wall.

The niece excitedly opened the drawers, wondering what treasures she might find. She found only two things—a ring and a slip of note paper.

The ring was lovely. It was silver with a small cross.

Transfixed, she put it on her finger, but immediately yanked it off. She didn't like the way this ring felt on her. It was as though this lifeless piece of metal did not want to be on her finger. The feeling that washed over her was not a pleasant one.

This ring was not meant to stay with her.

Finding her Aunt and Uncle, she showed them what she found and asked what she should do with it, choosing not to tell them how she felt when she put it on. Instead she said, "I feel very strongly we should find who this rightfully belongs to."

They agreed—and contacted the realtor who then contacted the executor of Robert Wilde's will. He gave his address to the new homeowners so they could send him the ring.

When the ring arrived, it did so with the note that was in the hidden storage area.

Allison handed me a flat FedEx mailing envelope that felt practically empty to me. I took it and shook it over my hand. Out tumbled the companion ring that was identical to the one Allison wore. The other item flits out. It is a small note, on it is scribbled "For Karyl." My name is almost spelled correctly.

I look closely at the ring and see an inscription inside. It is hard to make out, but eventually I do, "Trinity of Souls."

A magnified photo of the ring shows an inscription inside. The inscription reads "Trinity of Souls."

Allison was crying again. "It's for you," she says. "Teresa left it, not for me, but for you. It had to wait until we found each other for it to make its way to you."

She was bawling.

I sat silently.

"Don't you see Keryl? She knew about you. Before she died, she was given the vision of you."

•　•　•　•　•　•

The letter arrived to Allison's home separately.

It read [cancer patient's name is changed, revelatory information removed, and misspellings are unchanged]:

"Keryl, my trinity soul sister,

166

We will never meet face to face in this lifetime...my sister, the privilege of knowing you for a short time is mine. I met you early this morning before the sun crested on the horizon and blazed into my windows on the east wall. My father, your grandfather, was sound asleep in the big couch chair in the corner – the one [Allison] always falls asleep in when she reads and studies. [Allison] was asleep in the bed with me – snoring. I know you will discover this joy all on your own. God brought me the image of you and described you to me. He showed me the beauty of your soul. [...]

He showed me you and said that you would be [Allison's] dearest friend for the rest of her life. When I was with our Father you would help [Allison] become what I could not. Your path was never to replace me, it was always your own path to be what I could not be. [...] You know by now that God does not bargain.

[Allison] was always the stronger of the two of us and I am told when she needs your strength you will be stronger. I can't imagine anyone stronger than my sister [Allison] so I am eternally in love with you.

At some time in your life my cross ring will make its way to you. It is the same one that I hope [Allison] still wears – silver with the holy cross. It will have traveled a great distance over a long time to get to you. It is already a powerful talisman and it will come to you when you need it the most. Wear it and know that I sent it to you to help and guide for the rest if your life. It will make its way to you for the next nine consecutive lifetimes. You will know its touch well. You will know it is your when you see the inscribstion "trinity of souls" on the inside. It is a saying of [Allison's]. She coined it for both of us when we bought our rings together at the university of the South.

I lost the original ring I purchased there and have replaced it. This one is just as powerful of a talisman as the one I lost. Wear it for love and protection.

You know by now that I will die of cancer in 6 short days. I miss my sister and I am not gone yet. I will miss her face and her laugh. Guard her and love her well Keryl. I know by the time you read this you will know why. You are his first love. She will give all of her love and trust to guide, follow, and protect you.

Loving you for lifetimes to come. I am at peace dear soul sister.

Your loving sister, Teresa"

"She even knew you liked butterflies," sniffled Allison.

I did indeed like butterflies. Their emergence mimicked life to me. A caterpillar went through extreme pain as it pushed through the confines of its cocoon to emerge on the other side transformed—beautiful and with wings to fly.

Most people would dismiss a letter like this, but I did not. I believed in its authenticity because I knew that God was sovereign above all time and dimension—and nothing was impossible for Him.

If that logic wasn't enough, I also asked myself, *why would a person who was brought into my home and was receiving night and day care, make this up?* I could not imagine a person would do such a thing; which added to my conviction. This letter astounded me. It made life seem even more beautiful and more mysterious.

Still, I didn't immediately wear the ring. In the beginning, I felt unworthy of such a gift. I rationalized that I was only doing what any compassionate soul would do upon learning that a cancer patient was battling the disease with no support network. In fact, if anything, it was Allison who was the worthy one, not me. After

168

all, she was the one donating her blood and tissue to science to help find a cure for childhood cancer.

On top of all this, the ring was the *one thing* she had asked for and did not receive when Teresa died. I urged her to keep it. However, Allison felt certain it was Teresa's dying wish that the ring go to me, and that I accept it for the gift that it is.

Eventually, I acquiesced. Over time, I put the ring on my finger and it was a perfect fit. "Teresa's fingers were the same size as yours," I was told.

But then something shifted inside of me. I couldn't identify what. After a few months of wearing it, a day came when the ring no longer felt good on my finger. I would recall the niece who found it in the hidden jewelry storage area and think to myself, "I now know how it felt when you first put it on."

One day, I took it off and although I still have it, I have never worn it again.

Keryl, my trinity Soul Sister,

We will never meet face to face in this lifetime.... my sister, the privilege of knowing you for a short time is mine. I met you early this morning before the sun crested on the horizon and blazed into my windows on the east wall. My father, your grandfather, was asleep in the big couch chair in the corner - the one [ ]. always falls asleep in when she reads and studies. [ ] was asleep in the bed with me - snoring. I know you will discover this Joy all on your own. God brought me the image of you and described you to me. He showed me the beauty of your Soul.

Content removed

He showed me you and said that you would be [ ]'s dearest friend for the rest of her life. when I was with our father you would help [ ] become what I could not. Your path was never to replace me, it was always your own path to be what I could not be.

My purpose here is long over. God told

. You know by how that God
does not bargain.

☐ was always the stronger of the
two of us and I am told when she
needs your strength you will be stronger
I cant imagine anyone stronger than
my sister ☐ So I am eternally
in love with you.

At some time in your life my cross
ring will make its way to you. It is
the same one that I hope ☐ still
wears — silver with the holy cross. It
will have traveled a great distance
over a long time to get to you. It
is already a powerful talisman and it
will come to you when you need it the
most. wear it and know that I sent
it to you to help and guide for the rest

of your life. It will make its way
to you for the next nine &
③
consecutive lifetimes. you will
know its touch well. You will know
it is your when you see the ins-
scribstion "trinity of Souls" on the
inside. It is a saying of [____]'s.
She coined it for both of us when
we bought our rings 2gether at
the university of the South. I
lost the original ring I purchased
there and have replaced it. This
one is just as powerful of a talisman
as the one I lost. wear it for love
and protection.
You know by how that I will die of
cancer in 6 short days. I miss my
sister and I am not done yet. I
will miss her face and her smile
and her laugh. Guard her and love
her well Kery! I know by the time
you read this you will know why. You
are his first love. She will give
all of her love and trust to guide,
follow, and protect you.
    Loving you for lifetimes to come. I
& am at peace dear Soul Sister.

CHAPTER 22
An Empath Dial Set to 'Off'

The word "empath" was not mainstream even a few years ago. Judith Orloff, MD, author of *The Empath's Survival Guide: Life's Lessons for Sensitive People*, describes an empath this way, "Empaths are highly sensitive, finely tuned instruments when it comes to emotions. They feel everything, sometimes to an extreme, and are less apt to intellectualize feelings. Intuition is the filter through which they experience the world. Empaths are naturally giving, spiritually attuned, and good listeners. If you want heart, empaths have got it. Through thick and thin, they're there for you, world-class nurturers."

One of the traits that an empath possesses is a high level of discernment, formed by their ability to intuitively read another person's energy. They can listen to what someone is saying while feeling the energy behind the delivery. Empaths, also referred to as Sensitives, know a person is lying when their words are not in alignment with their emotional energy.

They have the ability to feel the distress another person is feeling. They can often even feel another's illness or their judgments. They can feel their love and purity. An empath can feel something in the air prior to the world finding itself responding to a tragic event—it just feels like something big is on the brink of happening. They can sense the vibration of any place they walk into, whether it is a place of joy or sadness. They often hurt when someone else is hurting. Because they feel things so intensely, empaths make it their purpose in life to try and create a world that is good. Empaths love children and animals, and really want to help everyone who they see suffering. It is very difficult for an empath to look away from someone in need without feeling angst.

Empaths are highly-sensitive, but this does not mean they are weak or fragile. Vulnerabilities arise when an empath does not learn how to protect themselves, so that they do not absorb or take on the negative emotions they pick up from others.

Even though I am not fond of labels, I recognize that I have always been an empath. Yet, for whatever reason, it seems I kept my empath power switch turned off pretty much the entire sixteen months Allison was in my home.

Was that by choice? I don't believe it was. As I look back upon it now, I believe it was a subconscious decision made by the part of my highest self that sought lessons that serve to expand my spirituality. I believe the empath dial was turned to off because I knew I would learn something that I would otherwise not with my normal level of discernment. I believe it is why the inner voice prompted me to invite her in.

I had become aware of God, but I was on the brink of learning something else.

In April 2013, at long last, Allison's cancer had finally vanished and she moved back to her home. It was during this time, my family discovered something and tried to warn me. Something I refused to hear or believe.

She was a fraud, they said. "Honey, this woman is not mentally sound."

I was mortified by their words and disappointed they would even have this thought.

They were adamant. They took the stance of warrior for me and for my child and were confused as to why I could not see what they saw.

Their perspective mirrored that of the employees I kept onboard when I closed my lucrative business and opened a small consultancy that worked with nonprofit organizations. They too did not understand who or what this person was in my life. They trusted me, though. They trusted my inner voice.

My family, on the other hand, tried with everything they had and still I would not listen—breaking their hearts and temporarily tearing at the fabric of our strong relationship. Communication between us stopped and I felt the pain of that deeply.

I love my family with everything I have.

It was also in April 2013 that Mitchell and I would both receive the first phone call from an investigator, interrogating us to test our authenticity before informing us that Allison was not a patient of the hospital she claimed was treating her. This detective wanted to know, were we giving her money? Where was she getting the medicine? What kind of drugs were they? Were we supplying them? And a host of other questions.

Believing her story of a proprietary research study that few knew about, I refused to cooperate with this stranger on the phone. I had no idea who he was or what firm employed him. I wasn't about to betray this good doctor who was devoted to cancer fighting.

Although her presence in my life was disruptive and I did not feel drawn to the person she was, I refused to believe any of what I was told was true. I believed Allison had cancer. We witnessed a body that spiked fevers, had nosebleeds. She slept so much. I mean, look at chemo days, for heaven's sake. *Who on earth would make up such stories and live such lies?*

I didn't believe any of this. Warnings fell on deaf ears.

I would not know for another two and a half years, that on April 23, 2013, from a room within my home, Allison confessed the truth of who she was to this investigator to avoid being arrested for identity theft of a medical professional.

She was a fraud.

And in that same room that was provided to her with a heart of compassion for her plight, she had been sending me nonstop messages and e-mails—under the alias of a pediatric oncologist, his wife, his two sons, his colleagues, a broken man who lost his family, a childhood friend whose love spanned dimensions, and a host of other personalities—and had been doing so for the past 16 months.

CHAPTER 23

From the Broken Comes Beauty

2013

Maybe our Divine Creator uses the broken because God knows we can relate more easily to a person with obvious shortcomings.

In the *Holy Bible,* Abraham was an old man, Moses had a speech problem, Rahab was a prostitute, and David a murderer. Yet we find honor in these people's stories and we marvel at their faith. They remind us of the humanness of all of us. It brings comfort that we can be flawed and still loved.

Abraham took his long-awaited son to the top of a mountain to be sacrificed to God, when he heard God's voice command this to be done. Moses announced to people far and near that God spoke to him through a burning bush. He is also credited with giving us The Ten Commandments and being a channel for miracle after miracle when he was used by God to free the Jewish people from slavery.

Tying your child on a rock to kill them as an offering to God? And a talking bush? Really? Today Abraham would be spending life in prison and Moses would be on medication.

Today, it is our will that be done on Earth, not God's.

When did we start thinking we were smarter than God?

If, in 2013, when the first suspicion of Allison's deception was revealed, I over-rode that inner voice and listened to concerned loved ones, I would have launched my own investigation into her history to learn more about who I had brought into my home. I would have learned quite a lot. However, the well-intentioned warning fell on deaf ears.

Something—an intuition, a knowing—told me that our paths crossing was not without purpose. That same intuition also comforted me, telling me that all would be well again, especially with my family. *Just trust.*

Had I not walked this path, I would not have used my long-held belief that we have the power to aid in our body's physical and emotional healing with positive thoughts, to help another. I would never have done energy healing on a person.

I would not have experienced how my soul seemed to bask in the familiarity of connecting to energy in this manner with a breath that said "Finally! At long last," and how it felt so natural at the time.

I might not have discovered that the invisible presence I felt in the empty church where I went to desperately escape the oppressiveness in my home, was the same that I had felt from childhood through my mid-twenties. It may have been years before I recognized that God was with me always. The greatest gift I could receive, if not the greatest human achievement ever, came from this dark period in my life.

What's more, my unflappable new faith in the endless power we have with God in us, combined with my promise to not let my limitations get in my own way, paved the way for others to discover the same.

Who can measure the beauty of that?

What follows are a few of the touching stories that resulted from this. What is most remarkable about these immediate stories and the ones that follow later in the book is the diversity of the individuals. They include one person who had such a strict Catholic upbringing that she swore off of a relationship with God and to this day, can no longer eat fish. Because of what transpired, her heart returned to Him.

Another is a man living on our city's streets, overlooked by many, but not by God.

Later in the book you will meet a woman who has chosen an alternative lifestyle, yet still felt the hand of God in one of the most powerful stories—proving that our Creator loves every person equally.

And young Everett, who reminds us of the incredible, boundless faith that resides within a child.

From a period of deception and brokenness came beauty. Nothing less than God—the Source of love—could achieve this.

CHAPTER 24

Diane's Story

"...Do you believe that I am able to do this?" "Yes, Lord,"
[the blind men] replied. Then he touched their eyes and
said, "According to your faith will it be done to you."

Matthew 9: 28-30 NIV

By April 2014, Diane had worked for me for nearly a decade. She began as my Executive Assistant, later adding the responsibilities and title of Office Manager. Diane knew me better than I knew myself at times. She has such a generous heart that I once remarked 'only Diane's friends have a friend like Diane.' Although I was very fortunate to have her working for my company, I was even more fortunate to have her in my daily life. The bond of trust we formed was strong.

One day, I chose to work from home, rather than commute into the office. I called Diane and asked if she could please stop by the office supply store to pick up a few items I needed and drop them by my house. "Of course," she said.

At this time, Allison was no longer living with me.

Diane had a garage door opener to my home, and in no time, I heard its motor rumble, letting me know she had arrived. As she was climbing the two short steps from the garage into the front entry, her leg buckled. She grabbed it in pain, cursing at the iliotibial band syndrome (or IT band syndrome), she suffered, that physical therapy had not been able to heal. This issue inhibited her ability to walk her dogs, climb hills or stairs, and work out in the gym—all activities she loved to do.

"We should do energy healing on you." I said almost too casually.

"Okay," she responded without hesitation and just as casually.

Wow, this was something different! Normally, I would prep the space with meditative prayer focused on intent, and I would burn sage to purify the air. I would take an hour beforehand to quiet my mind and get centered in the light of God. But not this time. I simply looked at my watch, saw that it was 3:15 and said, "I have a phone call at 4:00, so we have to be done by 3:45."

"No problem," she responded.

"Let's do it, then."

I took her to a room in the back where I had her lie down. I told her that her only job was to relax, trust, and believe without any doubt that this would work, and that we were not alone.

I added, "When we finish, don't question me about if it worked or not, because there cannot be any doubt."

Fifteen minutes later, we said goodbye.

The next day, she made no mention of her leg and I wanted desperately to ask her about it. But I had to abide by my own advice, so I did not. Finally, after two hours, Diane exclaims, "Oh! How could I have forgotten to tell you? I have no pain! Nothing! Look, I can do this!" Full of excitement, she stands on the one formerly injured leg, then squats down on the one leg she is standing on. "There is no pain at all," she says, adding Please thank God for me."

182

I smile in the office and I feel utterly overwhelmed at the power that resides within us. A power that is ours simply by asking, and believing—one that never leaves us.

"You have access to Him. You thank Him yourself," I responded with a smile.

Total awe.

Four months later, on a Saturday evening, visiting with a friend, I received a text message from Diane. "I think my healing is wearing off. My leg has been hurting for the past few days," it read.

I laughed aloud at her choice of words, and playfully responded, "Wearing off? You do *know* you didn't buy the extended warranty, right?" We were bantering back and forth a bit as we would often do, when my inner voice spoke up unexpectedly, "I think we can take care of her pain," was the message received. I repeated it to her, which delighted her.

Again, she says, "Please say thank you for me."

Such trust.

Again, I say, "You have access to Him, YOU thank Him."

The next day I realized we didn't schedule a time for her to come over. As the day threatened to get away from me, I sent her a message asking for times that work for her. The message I receive in response, took me completely by surprise. "The pain is gone." It goes on to explain that it stopped while we were texting, and it never returned.

Diane believed. And because she believed, her results were one of the most incredible of all those who chose to embrace the power of this light within all of us.

What she would come to learn, was that she too, had the same access to God that she saw I had. We all do. She would eventually not need me to say thank you, or to channel the energy; she could do this herself. She would come to approach healing with the uninhibited faith of a child.

What I loved most about the whole thing is that when her pain returned, she did not say, "Well THAT didn't work—I need to go find a doctor." Rather, in her own way, she said, "My pain is returning, can we do another energy session?" In essence, she was saying, "I need more of God's light."

We all need more of God's light.

I am forever in awe of the power and the gifts to which we have access, should we choose to acknowledge and embrace them.

• • • • • • •

I saw Diane recently, almost three years after that day. She has retired and owns a second home in the mountains of North Carolina. I was invited to spend a weekend with Di and her husband—an invitation that is open to me any time, in typical Diane fashion. One day, I accepted and we spent a wonderful few days catching up. Their home is beautiful. It overlooks a noisy creek, and there are tons of nature trails on the property on which I could tromp around. Just like my childhood. I was so happy!

During one of our chats, Diane tells me she had not had any pain in her leg since we had exchanged those text messages a few years back. I marveled at this wonderful news. She then told me she did, however, have some pain in her arm and suggested maybe we could do some energy work on it.

"Whenever you're ready," I told her. "You know what to do."

The weekend did not permit us to work on her arm, but I thought long and hard about the miraculous results we had with her leg.

The Divine Source does not need my hands. Diane didn't need my hands. What Diane needed was to hear that it could be done. Hearing "I think we can take care of her pain," was all it took.

Everyone is different, and in no way would I ever suggest that anyone should forego traditional medical treatment. I just want to stress that I believe we should also look to the enormous power we all have within us to reverse deteriorating health issues with a powerful will to heal. One cannot separate the emotional (energy) body from the physical body.

Diane has been blessed with abundance in her retirement years. And as time passed, she has learned to take the faith and gratitude she directed toward me and rightfully give them to God—for much more than her leg, for everything in her life.

CHAPTER 25

Joshua's Story

May 2014

It was a spring evening in Atlanta, in 2014, when I first saw Joshua. I set out to deliver small meals and some comfort to the men and women on our streets with my friend who was the Program Director at a local shelter that rehabilitated men experiencing homelessness due to substance abuse. Joshua was lying on the sidewalk near the city medical center. He was highly agitated because moments before we arrived, he explained to us with animated gestures, a group of people had been hurling chunks of broken concrete at him, trying to get him to move from his spot. We could see the cement stones shattered around him. A modern day public stoning. *What a world.*

Josh was wrapped in a dirty red blanket, yelling almost incoherently from his spot on the sidewalk to get the attention of someone who could help him. To a person just passing by, he would have appeared erratic and irrational, perhaps even mentally unstable. It's so easy to form a completely inaccurate first impression of someone.

My friend and I spoke kind and gentle words, trying to calm him down as we offered him something to eat. We told him that they were gone now, and he was okay. We tossed the cement stones away from him and convinced him to take the food we offered. After a while, he calmed. There was not much more we could do for Josh that evening, so we wished him well, then returned to our goal of distributing the remaining thirty or more sack meals.

We met a great many people and heard a great many stories that evening, but for some reason Josh stayed in the forefront of my mind for the rest of the night. I wondered why.

The next evening, I called Allison. I didn't know who else would understand what I wanted to do that night, so I called her. I explained there was a man on the street I wanted to take care of and asked for her help with this task. This time, the items I packed were water, bandages, home-made first aid ointment, and of course, love. I always kept supplies at my home for the many times I visited our city's homeless. She arrived and we journeyed off into the night.

Just as I located Josh, who was lying in the same spot as the night before, the skies opened up and a torrential rain came pouring down. I could barely see through my windshield wipers, so I parked in the first spot I saw. We ran through the rain back to Joshua's spot and quickly helped to move him and his meager belongings to the underside of a MARTA bus-stop shelter before they became completely drenched. Of course, focused on all of this, I never noticed the parking meter...

A 66 year-old feisty veteran who was still very much a warrior, Joshua could barely walk. It took both of us holding him up on either side to move him out of the rain.

Josh was injured in two places, his knee and his foot, wounds he had gotten a few months earlier fighting off a group of men who mugged him and stole his belongings, which included his military duffel bag containing his ID. His wounds had been treated weeks prior, at the medical facility nearby where he slept, but they became grossly infected from living on the streets. His knee and shin area were many times the size they should have been. His foot was just as bad. "No matter what they do," he told us, referring to the medical facility, "this damn leg doesn't heal."

Every day our doctors perform modern day miracles. However, when a person's will-to-live is battered, it makes it much harder for their bodies to heal. Human beings are complex machinery. Do our thoughts block our ability to heal ourselves? Neuroscientists tend to think so. Unfortunately, we can stand in the way of our own healing.

I first treated Joshua's injuries with ointments and fresh bandages. I followed this with an energy healing session, focusing on opening up the channels in the impacted area of his leg and foot, and especially around his heart to get the energy flowing again. I was struck by something that stayed with me for a while. Each time when I would think of something I needed from my backpack, I would find Allison holding the exact item to me as though she could read my mind. I looked at her inquisitively one of those times with a facial expression that asked the question, 'How did you know?" She shrugged at me with a facial expression that said "I have no idea, I just do." We were in total synchronization and it was one of the few times of late that I felt not so frazzled by her seemingly constant presence.

Throughout this, Josh was remarkably calm—very different from the man I had encountered the night before. He showed himself to be a man of strong faith and integrity. A man who was very tired of living on the streets. His spirit was weary, like a soldier who needed rest from the war.

After treating his wounds and performing energy healing, there was nothing more I could do for Josh that evening. Allison and I returned to my car soaking wet. I removed the parking citation from the windshield with a loud groan, tore it in half in a moment of frustration, and departed for home.

The next day I returned alone, and at first, could not find Josh. I knew he couldn't have gone far unable to walk. I scanned the people hanging out near the bus stop where we had left him and it took a minute to realize that the man I saw standing tall and straight behind the MARTA bus stop bench, looking vastly different now, was him. He had relinquished his seat so that a woman who also lives on our city's streets could sit.

As I approached, in utter shock at his appearance, I told him I barely recognized him and had the hardest time finding him. "I wanted the lady to have the bench," he explained, revealing the gentleman inside of him. I felt like I was seeing more of this man's true self emerging. And as we talked, this feeling continued. Josh was strong and faithful, a gentleman with high-integrity. "I don't know what you did," he told me, "but so much fluid began to pour out of my leg that I had to change my socks and put on my other shoes!" He was still animated, but this time in a way that felt more positive. He lifted his pant leg to reveal a knee and shin that were now normal size and looked well on their way to recovery. For the first time in weeks, Josh was able to walk—less than 24 hours after believing in an energy healing session I performed right there on the streets.

"Thank you," he said with a rarely seen smile.

"Don't thank me," I told him, using words that were becoming familiar. He looked at me with total understanding. I always seem to find God in the spirit of our city's homeless, and I was reminded that God likes to show up in the most surprising of places.

Now that he was feeling much better, we found a place to sit and he told me his story.

Josh had family in Florida, but a series of events landed him on the streets of Atlanta separated from them. What followed was a perfect storm of occurrences that created a situation where a man with a family could not return home—assault, id theft, a 66 year-old mind that could not remember numbers, a daughter with a new last name that was not easily traced, and most of all, the inability to reach the right person who can help make a simple connection to his family.

I found it hard to believe that the man sitting beside me was the man who I had found lying on the sidewalk, unable to walk, yelling incoherently at the injustice of the actions of others. As he shared his story, it revealed his deep faith in the Lord. His reliance on God, he explained, sustained him in the moments when he didn't think he would survive the brutality of the streets. He finished, and we sat in reverent silence for a while.

Now Josh just needed a bus ticket home. Could changing his life for the better be that simple? Despite my dwindling savings account, I was happy to spring for his ticket.

I placed a call to the Program Director of the rehabilitative shelter, the man I was out delivering food with when I first met Josh. I knew that the shelter had resources that would make it possible for Josh to shower and get a change of clothing. All programs are different, and this was not what we call a night shelter. Men did not stand in line for a cot each night, and leave in the morning. To be admitted into this program required an arduous selection process and a battery of health tests to ensure the men were not carrying communicable diseases that could be spread to staff, volunteers, and other residents. The men who were admitted entry to this program stayed for a year. My hope, when I approached the program director, was that it would be possible for Josh to use the facility to shower and change clothes to prepare for his journey home. My friend could have said no. Instead he chose to bend the rules to help a deserving man in need. Josh was given a hot meal, a fresh change of clothes as well as a second set of travel clothes, and a hygiene kit. Staff members helped Josh contact his family. "We are not in the business of dumping people." I was told. "It is important that we know he has someone waiting for him when he arrives at his destination." They had access to the online resources that track our city's homeless; as well as national registries, and this made it much easier to help Josh find what he could not find on his own.

A week later, I received a text message. "Thank you for bringing my father home," read the text message on my phone. "He is living with my aunt, and he's doing really well."

Don't thank me, I think, and I feel the smile of gratitude gently come upon my face.

● ● ● ● ● ●

For a while Josh would call me regularly to keep in touch. He asked me to send him a picture, because he wanted a picture of the person who helped him. I smiled. I wished I could take a photograph of God, because it was all Him. But we see God at work in those who are obedient to His whisper like Josh, like my friend at the shelter, their staff who fed Josh, and the unknown person who delivered clothing to the shelter. It goes on and on.

Yet, it also makes one wonder: How many of the people we see bundled up in blankets and living on the streets, who sound mentally ill, appear frightening to approach, are our nation's soldiers, and faithful, loving, children of God like Josh? We will never know unless we actively choose to offer our hands and our hearts.

By the way, The City of Atlanta retracted the parking ticket when they were sent a summary of the story.

A happy ending for everyone involved.

CHAPTER 26
A Purpose Fulfilled

March 2015

The months were passing and I had returned my attention to the task I had initially set out to achieve when I chose to close my company—give my expertise to organizations whose missions were helping our community members. With everything that distracted me since my offer to help Allison through treatment that fateful day in 2012, the attention I paid to my company was almost nil.

I was intent on rebuilding and looking forward to ensuring I did so without checking my soul at the door when I stepped into my work persona. It was important to me that I create a career that is a blend of who I am on an intrinsic level with the expertise I have on a professional one.

It was a Friday morning in early 2015. I was preparing for a business meeting on the other side of town, when I received a phone call from my mother. "I know you've been trying to have me over to see you for several weeks now and I think I would like to come today, if that's okay." My mother lives approximately 120 miles from Atlanta in the North Georgia region. With traffic, the commute is two hours. Without traffic, it is 90 minutes. Relatively speaking, it was not a long distance, yet with busy schedules, it was not easy to come together for a visit. Although she could still not understand why Allison was in my life, she never stopped showing me love.

I missed my mother and had been asking if she wanted to have a mother-daughter weekend with me for the past few weeks. Was that okay? Are you kidding? "Yes, yes," I told her excitedly, "I'm leaving for a meeting in an hour, but will be back around 11:30. I'll leave a key, so you can let yourself in.

"Wonderful sweetheart, I will be there around 10:30. See you soon."

We said goodbye and I immediately thought, *oh my gosh, there's no food in the house.*

At that moment, Allison knocked on the door. She doesn't own a vehicle, and relied on bicycle, rapid transit, foot, or the grace of friends to get around. She was in the area, she said, and just wanted to say hello.

I explained that it was not a good time for an unexpected visit. I was preparing for a meeting and also I needed to quickly pick up a few items from the grocery store beforehand.

"How can I help?" She asked. "Do you want to give me a list and I'll pick those items up for you?"

"NO!" bellowed the inner voice.

"No," I said, much more calmly than what erupted inside, "That's okay. Thank you, though."

"Why not? It will take me 15 minutes. Let me take your car and I'll just run to murder Kroger up the street."

Murder Kroger was the horrible nickname given to the grocery store closest to my city apartment. Dubbed because of numerous murders that happened at the location. I preferred to call it Beltline Kroger, in homage of the ramp that led to the walk, bike, run path known as the Atlanta Beltline.

No matter what we called the store, another "NO!" came from my inner voice at the offer by Allison to take my car to it. This one with enough force that it caused me to furrow my brow.

"No, really, I will get it done," I said with more assurance than I felt. "And I'm not comfortable with you driving my car."

Normally, what belongs to me, belongs to anyone in my life. I have never been one to harbor material items. However, during the period when she lived in my home, Allison had access to a second vehicle I owned and she wrecked it. I had it repaired, but when it came time to sell, it was greatly depreciated, thus making it difficult to get what it was worth prior to her mishap. Both the repair and the loss of value impacted my wallet and not hers.

Allison had the tendency to draw a cloud of mishap. I recalled the many stories she told when I asked if there were unresolved issues in her life. And like that dark mist that hovered around her left frontal lobe, I sometimes felt that her mishaps were finding their way into my life.

But still, time was passing and I still had preparation to do for my meeting as well as my mom's visit.

When I went to visit my mother, her refrigerator was always stocked. Nor did she simply leave a key. She made sure she was home to greet me when I arrived for a visit.

As the thought of my mother letting herself in to an empty apartment with empty cupboards and not even anything to drink besides water, filled my mind, I could feel myself relenting on my hard stance with my car. I churned it over in my mind, over-riding the powerful inner-voice I had learned long ago was never wrong. *There were no more than 7 items on my list. This would be a huge help. What could go wrong? Why are you holding back?* I asked myself.

Human logic, one of the pillars of free-will, trumped all, and I gave in. I went into the other room where I had previously placed my purse and, putting down the phone that I still held since my mother's call, grabbed pen and paper to hastily write out a list. I came back with the list, the remote fob for my car, and handed Allison some cash. She took these things from me and said, "I will be back in 15 minutes."

"I leave in 45 minutes, don't be late!" I said, and as the words echoed in my ears, I knew I sounded harsh. I was becoming tired of being so interwoven with this person who has now been cancer-free for two years. She showed up at my city apartment day and night. I had even instructed the neighbors not to give her the new front door code, but she still managed to show up at my door. It seemed like the dependency that she had on me as a former caregiver was still as strong as when she was in my home. I needed her to clip that umbilical cord and re-gain entry into a life that was separate from mine. The chaos that her presence brought to my life kept me battling for my emotional health through the two years of her alleged return to health.

I returned to the front of my apartment where my office was set up and resumed my preparation.

I didn't notice when 15 minutes passed as I was deeply focused on refining the pitch I was preparing to make. The person with whom I was meeting was one who was a mover and shaker in the nonprofit arena. A mutual business peer had introduced us, and today's meeting was about sharing my vision of the idea that was forming that would hopefully become my own nonprofit. I had been looking forward to this meeting for a week.

After what felt like only a few minutes since Allison left, I glanced at my watch. 30 minutes had passed! *Where was she?* I looked around for my phone but didn't see it near me. Remembering the list and my wallet, I went to the room where my purse was and found the phone sitting next to it.

7 missed calls from Allison. "Please tell me this is not about an item she can't find," I thought with a little irritation. As I prepared to call her, I received an incoming call from my former husband. *What on Earth?*

"Hi there," I answer, my inflection hinting at my surprise and curiosity.

"Oh, thank God, you're okay," came the relieved response.

"What? Why would I not be okay?"

"BMW called and said the impact sensor went off in your car. They can hear someone in the car, but the two-way assist is disabled so they can't communicate with them. They still have me listed as your emergency contact, so they called me. The GPS is saying that the car is in midtown."

I had one fraction of a second to process the words he had just spoken, when my phone buzzed with an incoming call.

Allison.

I thank him and hastily push to activate the next call, already anticipating that my response for what was coming next was not going to be one of grace. I could feel something churning up inside of me that was adding to the compounding feelings of frustration. When one gets to the point I was finding myself nearing, there is little that can be done except to let it course through you.

Now, I was heading toward a scenario that would, as the saying goes, be the final straw to break the camel's back.

"Ms. Oliver?" The male voice on the phone took me by surprise. "I am a paramedic at the scene of an accident that involves your vehicle." I could hear Allison in the background, in between deep guttural screams of pain, she was yelling "Tell her I'm hurt. Tell her I'm hurt."

I close my eyes, for one eternal second, and let the true emotion wash over me. I was right—it was the farthest thing from grace. With the paramedic in my ear saying something about 'injuries, and in front of the Kroger on Ponce de Leon Ave,' and the screams in the background, the thought that raged up like a tidal wave was "You have got to be [expletive] kidding me." IF there was a morsel of grace within me, it manifested in the fact that I didn't verbalize my initial thought. Grace commanded me to bite my tongue and let my true response stay inside of me. I knew at that moment the camel's back was broken.

She had officially impacted every area of my life in a negative way: family, career, friends, social, finances, community, and now the last asset from my former life as the owner of a thriving company.

To the man on the phone I asked, "Where are you taking her?" He confirmed what the BMW tracking system had told my former husband and gave me the name of the closest hospital to that location. "The ambulance is here and we will be transporting her in a few minutes. You are welcome to ride in the ambulance."

How lovely. The snarky side that appears when one is totally devoid of grace had full control of my command center now and I had no desire to take it back. *This is precisely what I want to be doing instead of preparing for an important meeting that I have been looking forward to all week.*

I told him that since my vehicle was at the scene, I would have to find my way there and that if I don't make it in time, I will go to the hospital.

With methodical clarity, I made two other calls. One to cancel my meeting, another to cancel my mother-daughter weekend. Both of those calls broke my heart, the latter more than the former. I had not yet started to think of the mountain of tasks that would be thrust on me with this latest Allison mishap.

I then sent an "all-points-bulletin" text message to my friends and neighbors that shared the pretty nine unit building that was my city apartment. "If anyone is going toward the Beltline Kroger, I could use a ride." The responses were instant "I'm at work, sorry," and "I'm going later, what can I pick up for you?"

I texted all, "It is the site of an accident involving my car. I need to get to the site."

"I was just heading that way," came a text. "I'm in the parking lot. I'll wait for you." *Great!* In my heels, in my business dress, grabbing my phone and my purse, I bolted to the parking lot.

We crawled to the accident site as we got caught in the traffic that was caused by the accident. I sat in the front seat of my friend and neighbor's car. She was telling me how she would have already left but something odd had happened this morning for the first time ever in the years she had lived there. Her windshield was so heavily covered in bird droppings that her wipers alone could not clean it. She had to manually clean it, which caused the delay that allowed her to see my text.

God was amazing, I thought. I will never get over that. Plus He has a sense of humor. Aren't bird droppings the symbol of bad luck?

As we neared the scene, we could see up the street to where the flashing lights were. I got the first glimpse of my car. It was in the opposite lane of traffic and it was facing us. Why? I thought. The grocery store is to the right. The car is past the grocery store, coming from the other direction. *Where did she go?* I wondered suspiciously. Intolerance is an ugly creature.

I could also see from the front of the car that there was barely any damage. I was relieved.

Traffic was not moving, so I hopped out of my friend's car, with the intent to run (heels and dress) the remaining half block to the heart of the scene. Before getting out, I turned to her. "You are helping so much, but I need to ask you one more favor. I'm sure there are groceries in the car that need to be put in my apartment. Can you make your way to the scene and tell the police officer you are removing items from my car per the request of Ms. Oliver, the car's owner?"

"Of course," my God-delivered helper replied.

The screams of pain increased in volume the closer I got to the accident scene. I was confused, the car didn't look so bad. Why so much pain? When I approached from the right side of the street—the same side as the grocery store, I could see what couldn't be seen from the front. The entire driver side was demolished. The vehicle was t-boned. One didn't have to be an expert assessor to see that the car was totaled.

The last time my brain experienced a numb zone was as it processed the disappearance of my bicycle from Sherry's hitch-mounted bicycle rack all those years ago. Until now. I felt the fog of numbness tap on my exhausted brain cells. As was the case with the bicycle, even in the numb zone, I could hear every word from the voices that were speaking around me.

The police officer on the scene was compassionate and kind. Simultaneously, he was authoritatively keeping the accident scene safe, as he bellowed fiercely at drivers who tried to penetrate the scene. A gentle warrior. My favorite balance. "The person who hit your vehicle is a young man," he said, nodding toward a large, barely dinged, pick-up truck where another officer was speaking to a young man. "He feels terrible for what happened," the officer tells me in one breath, then yells to a car trying to get into the accident scene to move their vehicle AWAY from the scene, in the next. He turns his eyes to me again, kindness replaces the fierceness I saw a moment ago. I think not of Allison at that very moment, but of my friend I asked to place herself in the midst of the accident scene. I don't want her facing the fierceness I just saw. I point out her car and explain what I have asked her to do. He assures me he will help her. "Take everything out of your glove box and car that you don't want going to the impound lot. Put your registration and insurance in your wallet, if they are in there. You will need them. Your friend can take the rest. I'm sorry for your trouble ma'am."

You have no idea, I think. I still haven't even looked in the direction of Allison, but I could see her peripherally through the open doors of the ambulance.

The shock of the car, the screams from Allison as they work on her in the ambulance, the despondent look of the other driver, the inconvenience I heaped on my friend, the people stuck in traffic, the frustration I had for not listening to the inner-voice when it bellowed NO to handing over the fob to my car—all of these did nothing to remove the irritation I felt. I was a little unnerved by my total lack of compassion for the pain that Allison seemed to be suffering. That was so unlike me, I realized, but I was so done. The only remorse I felt was to the God I loved because I knew that not one iota of these thoughts and responses were sourced from Him.

●　●　●　●　●　●　●

I never knew that there was an intercom from the back of an ambulance to the driver. Why would I not have thought of that before? It made perfect sense for the ambulance driver, who is also a paramedic, to know what was happening with his or her colleagues and the patient being transported. Each little bump triggered a howl. They almost didn't sound human to me and it gave me an eerie feeling.

A voice came from the back and into the front cab. "Slow it down, we have some rib injuries," it says. *Slow it down*, I think. This tells me the injuries are not life threatening.

It took a long time to go the short distance to the hospital and she was wheeled into ICU.

It occurred to me, that in the 16 months that this cancer patient was in my home, this is the first time I have been in a medical facility with her. *Interesting.*

She disappeared behind a curtain that was a make-shift exam room and I had nothing to do but wait and continue my dark thoughts.

I will need a temporary vehicle is the first thought that comes to me. I had sold the second vehicle not long after moving into the city because it was too hard to find parking for it and had become a hassle to manage.

So, I called my insurance company to begin the arduous process of reporting a claim. It's a well-reputed company, and I have had the same agent for more than 25 years. I went almost 20 years without a phone call and now, since Allison, I was making my second call to them about an accident. They will gently advise me that I might want to consider not letting her drive my cars.

Ya think? Says the dark, snarky new Keryl

We'll cover a portion of your rental car costs, I'm informed.

I begin the automated task of calling rental car places nearby, beginning with the ones that advertise delivery.

Atlanta's Hartsfield-Jackson airport is the world's busiest airport. It is the hub of many connections, both national and international. Earlier in the week, the northern part of the country was crippled with winter weather that caused hundreds of flight cancellations at Atlanta's airport. Thousands were stranded. As such, I heard the same story from each rental car company I called "Stranded travelers rented cars to drive home. All one-way trips. We have nothing." Over and over. "No cars, sorry."

I thought of my car. It was a rare indulgence, purchased in my past life, when I was the President and CEO of a highly-successful firm. It was not like me at all to invest so much in something tangible, but I set my eyes on that car one day and my heart was gone. I had to have it. Like the bike that vanished, it had been impeccably cared for. I had planned to drive this investment until it was old and worn out and could no longer be driven. I would not have known that the latter part of that would occur with less than 60,000 miles on the odometer. On this day, as the crew was undoubtedly sweeping its fragments out of that intersection, it was on the very end of its financing, and it was pristine on the side that didn't play host to Allison's driving. I began to process the situation I was in and knew that there would be no way to find its equal with the methods an insurance company uses to assess value and reimbursement costs.

I will never learn.

I didn't soften my position with Allison, which was a huge indicator of how deep my negative feelings were that were pooling inside of me. When they wheeled her to her room and I sat there with her, I felt nothing but impatience.

We have 12 ribs in our rib cage. Ribs 3-12 were fractured in one place, I was told. Ribs 3,7,8,9, and 12 in multiple. It would be weeks before she could move around unimpeded by pain, and much longer than that before she was back to whatever activities were in her life. It occurred to me, I really didn't know what she did with her days. Nor did I care.

The doctors were amazed that a lung wasn't punctured with the severity of her wounds. She was lucky to have escaped that. The door was pushed two feet into the driver side of the car, I would learn from the insurance assessor in a few days. They called that the intrusion level. She was lucky to be alive.

Maybe Allison's luck was turning around. Sitting in the hospital that day, I wasn't feeling so lucky. What I was feeling was a deep fatigue. I decided I needed someone by my side. I texted a very dear friend—the same one that told Allison years earlier, she should tell me about her diagnosis.

My friend used Uber to come to the hospital. This person was one of the many who had doubts about Allison's stories over the years, particularly the part regarding her loss of hearing. It seemed a little too far-fetched to be believable. *Master at lip-reading? Even when the line of vision Allison had on a person was from the side?* My friend didn't buy into that. I thought of these things as this dear friend made his way to the hospital to offer me support.

Later, as we sat in a waiting area down the hall, so we could visit in private, I was shown great compassion for everything I had endured with the convergence of my path and Allison's. I confessed that I was at the end of my rope. "No one would blame you for feeling that way. You have been through so much." I was assured, "I'm calling for my Uber driver in a minute, can I have them drive you home?"

"YES!" Home!

It was a long day and the thought of going home was a comforting one. I needed that more than ever.

I had made a mental list of the people who were in Allison's life that would assist her with recovery and the list was nearly nonexistent. Ever-the-sucker for compassion, ever-the-heart that can't turn away a person in need, ever-the-empath with its inability to bear the thought that there is suffering anywhere, I knew I would be caregiver to this woman again. Even with my hardened heart.

Together we walked into Allison's room and I told her I was leaving. I reminded her that she would be surrounded by medical personnel and that I have many things I to take care of before she was brought to my place.

My needs did not matter.

She begged me to stay. Pleading with such fervor that its memory stayed with my friend, the witness to it, for a long time. I thought of the doctor who told me that it was normal for a cancer patient to become attached to their caregiver.

I still believed she was a two-time survivor.

My friend got into the Uber car alone.

* * * * * * *

The next morning, I was in the car with another friend and neighbor, Breanne. I was finally going home. Breanne had come to pick me up from the hospital and I was updating her on the events.

"So you ended up staying. How did the evening go?" she asked.

"I slept on the recliner chair in her room," I answered. "She woke me up in the middle of the night and begged me to do energy work on her."

"Did you?"

"No. I told her 'no.' The thought of helping her made me shudder. I was too annoyed still. Plus, my thoughts are not connected to God right now. There was no way I could be a channel for healing energy."

"How did she respond to that?"

"She begged me but I held my ground."

We were silent for a moment.

"But then," I break the silence, "Around three in the morning, I felt stirred awake. No one was there but the pressing on my heart began. 'You are much more than this. You are much bigger than this. The gift is Mine and it is a sacred one.' And the disappointment I felt with my actions overtook me. I felt terrible about what's been forming inside of me, but good god it's so hard! I had to fight every part of me that is human to heed that inner voice and make my way over to her." I paused as I saw the scene in my mind.

"She was so relieved. She closed her eyes as I went through the process of faith and connection and gave everything I had to rebalancing the energy to help with the pain. I only got as far as the upper side of the rib cage when a nurse came in.

"'Hi, don't mind me. I'm just doing energy healing. I'll be done in a minute.'" I say to Breanne in a mocking tone, "Yeah, I'm sure that would have gone over like a lead balloon. I just went back to the recliner while the nurse checked on all of the things that nurses check."

"Did it work?"

I smile at the question. "I didn't question it," I respond, seeing the scene continue in my tired mind. Allison had opened her eyes when the overhead light was turned on by the nurse. "But I overheard her telling the nurse that there was a lot less pain in the top part of the rib cage."

"That's so awesome," Breanne smiles. "I love it." She reminded me that there are many who believe in the quantum sciences that are a part of our world. The awesome power known as God.

Just as suspected, I brought Allison to my place because she had no other options.

Despite my obedience to the voice within, I didn't soften my stance.

Allison could not sleep lying down so I created a comfortable setup using the futon in my front office and a footstool. I piled pillows so she could sleep comfortably sitting up, brought a large table as a night stand, and laid post-it notes with dosages and times across it. On the post-its I placed the pills she would take for pain. Water was placed so she could independently take her pills. She was set.

Bedtime for me.

I was exhausted from a night nearly devoid of rest at the hospital, the hassle of the tasks that came from the accident, and the endlessness of wondering how to replace my vehicle. I was no longer commanding the salary from my business, and the nonprofit work I was doing was paying only a fraction of my overhead, so I was drawing heavily from savings.

And now, I was a caregiver to this former cancer patient who I should never have given over my car to use, once again berating myself for not listening to the inner-voice.

Bedtime.

The first phone call woke me up in the middle of the night. Nothing is scarier than a phone that rings in the middle of the night. I looked at the screen. Allison.

"WHAT?!"

"I'm in pain."

"Your pain meds are there."

"It's not time to take them yet and I'm in a lot of pain."

"I can't help you. What do you want me to do?"

"I want you to please come and do some energy work. Please Keryl. I need it. I'm in so much pain."

For some reason my siblings came to mind. If this call was coming from one of my siblings, I would have bolted down those stairs, taking them two at a time. And I would have planted myself at their side to give them whatever emotional comfort I could give them, for as long as they needed it, without any hesitation. There was no doubt that would have been my response and the tug of regret I felt in my heart was awful. It gave me a feeling of anxiety to know that I was going against what is my true spirit.

God's will, not mine be done.

But non-grace still had my command center. It had only been one day.

"No." I responded without hesitation, "I don't feel the call to do that. Go back to sleep."

The next day I received the same request. The next night I was woken again. The next day the same request. I refused each time.

Word had gotten out and she had some visitors to the house. They came to offer support and to relieve me of caregiving, but instead I found myself hosting with snack and drink. Extra work.

I will never learn.

We had many more mutual friends back then than we do now. One mutual friend called me and asked what I needed. "Someone to come and be here so I can go to the gym." I replied. I was desperate for the endorphins of exercise. Like an angel, this friend arrived.

Allison once again loved the attention given by these friends. It was like I had hit rewind on a film watched in 2012.

Day three. "Please Keryl. Please. I am in so much pain. Please do energy work," she pleaded.

I believe my venomous response was the truest indication that I was on the brink of no return. That line would be crossed just a few short weeks from that day, but it was already manifesting in the total lack of compassion I was feeling for the situation Allison was in. My response to this latest pleading was to bundle up her things, help her into my rental car, and callously dropped her off at her house.

Looking back I still can't tell you who was more surprised.

I *can* tell you that today, I feel awful about doing that. Back then I did not.

Days 4-7 post incident were filled with a blessed return to normalcy. I was never able to reconnect with the person whose meeting I missed, and it would be some time before my calendar and my mother's coordinated, but I was free of care giving. When the waves of remorse for my behavior hit me, I pushed them away. "No one would blame you for feeling that way. You have been through so much." The words from my friend whose Uber I rejected were a source of comfort to me as I replayed them over and over in my head.

Day 8. The pressing on my heart was overwhelming. "This gift is Mine to be offered with MY heart not yours. You are bigger than this. You are bigger than this disdain in your heart."

Love your enemies. She was not my enemy—my responses to her were.

God was relentless and I couldn't fight against the tidal wave that was rising within me. I have never won a battle where I stand in opposition to the light and love that fuels all there is in our universe.

So, on the eighth day, I stopped trying and got into my rental car.

I drove the short distance to her home where she was laid up in bed recovering from the rib fractures. I shrug off the feeling I always got when I walked in. If she was willing, I told her, I would offer an energy session. She was only 8 days into her pain meds and I was certain this would help offer her relief. One thing I knew about Allison, she was a believer in this.

Of course she was willing. She was grateful beyond words.

Using the same technique that closely mirrors Therapeutic Touch, but without the touch, I began. I felt the little knives in my hands that tell me there is pain in a body, and the cold that signified the areas where the energy was not flowing. I visualized light and heat from Source—from God—pouring into her body and rebalancing what was injured. I visualized the pain diminishing to nothing and total healing occurring.

I swear I could almost feel God's pleasure that I had put aside everything I was feeling to be obedient to His will and not mine.

I spent 30 minutes until I no longer felt a fluctuation in the energy field and when I heard the familiar inner-voice press, "That is all."

I left her sleeping and walked out the door.

I was certain that I too would sleep better at night. My soul was not designed to carry this frustration I had been feeling. I know too that the message from God was right, I was bigger than what I was allowing to build in my heart.

"You're human," has never been a valid excuse to me. We are here to learn how to become bigger than our limited human self.

A text two days later from Allison confirmed what I never wanted to ask after a session, "did it work?" She had joined the local track club and was encouraging me to come check it out. "They do a lot of community things, Keryl, you would love it. Right up your alley."

The local track club. 10 days after a car accident that fractured her ribs. Good stuff.

I was 100 percent certain at this point that whatever purpose Allison had in my life was now fulfilled. I was certain that it culminated to that moment when I gave myself completely to God's will–His and not mine. I was certain this was the moment when the paths would separate again. I could live my life, and she would live hers with her new community.

However, like every single assumption I made during this period of my life, I was wrong.

The impact created a two-foot intrusion into the driver's seat of my car, which was driven by Allison.

CHAPTER 27
Not This Time

June 2015

It was just like the days when she was in my home. The phone call came in and the voice on the other end was distressed.

Cancer had come back. This time it was in her brain. "Please come over," she pleaded, "I need to see you."

It would seem from an outsider viewing the scene without hearing the accompanying audio portion that I was once again the compassionate friend of the past, the one that eventually became the accidental caregiver to a cancer patient.

I drove to the house that I never liked being in and found her sitting in her room, rallying against a God that would take the illness from her only to bring it back two years later—again. Just like round 1, which showed up in 2007 and was defeated two years later in 2009. And round 2, in 2011, which was defeated in 2013. Here we were, 2015. The tick marks were equally spaced. Two year battle, two year reprieve. Round 3 was right on queue. "Three dots a trend makes," as we say in the business world.

She had found a doctor in Atlanta. No more long-distance doctor. No more communication only by e-mail or messenger. No more of the caregiver not having face-to-face meetings with those who were treating her. She wanted this one to be different, and she was positive she can't do it without me. Will I please help her again?

Now, turn on the audio track to the current scene, and recognize that there is very little that is the same with this one. There is no inner-voice nudging me to help a person in need. There is no compassion on my part for someone who looks robustly healthy and had been unfortunately dealt a tough card. No urge to open my home to her as a place of rest for treatment.

The collateral damage from the things I endured with this person in my life was what was on my mind. But that wasn't even at the forefront. What was at the forefront was the energy read that I was receiving. *She was lying.*

I sat stiffly in the guest chair of her bedroom, looking across to her sitting on her bed. *Let's see where this goes.*

"I'll help you, but let me make myself clear. I expect full visibility. If I am not present in the first meeting you have with your doctor, I am out. You will get nothing from me. Is that understood?"

She promised. Nothing is hidden this time.

She informed me that she had an appointment in the cancer ward of a local hospital the next day, and asked me if I could be there with her. She had found a doctor fascinated by her case, who is willing to take this on.

●　●　●　●　●　●

I looked around the waiting room of the cancer ward. The people in the room were sitting either in pairs or in groups of three. Nothing on their physical body reflected any of the signs of a progressive battle with cancer. Hair was intact and skin was glowing. *This is step one on their path*, I thought.

It occurred to me that it was my first time ever in a cancer ward. The energy was oppressively heartbreaking. I felt it blanket me like sadness.

I looked closer. Using the same discretion I did as a teenager sitting across from the man in the tattered clothes, I discreetly scanned their faces. My own face must have shown a look of concentration, as though I was an X-ray machine intent on seeing past the exterior and into their souls.

I didn't have to look that deeply, it turned out.

Cancer was not revealed in a full head of hair that had yet to succumb to the treatment they would inevitable endure. Rather, cancer showed up in their eyes. It was right there, on the window to the soul.

I saw reflecting from their eyes, something that I never once saw in Allison's—fear. Profound fear. Terror, even. And utter fatigue.

I didn't have to spot the purple wristband that was the hospital-assigned mark to know which of these individuals were the patient and which were the supporters. I only had to see the fear in their eyes.

One by one they were called up to a door that led into the mysterious room where their fates would be determined and their future mapped out. As each name was called, I was able to affirm my accuracy. Yes, that was the patient and yes, that was the supporter. Each time.

More arrived. More with the same marks of fear on their faces, and more with their same army of supporters. They checked in, were given a wristband, and like the others before them, they too were called up and eventually disappeared through the door. I looked at my watch and then over to my left where Allison sat with the familiar computer that had delivered the message from her childhood friend. "Why are those who came after you being called before you?" I asked, intentionally not mentioning her empty wrists.

Because her appointment was last-minute, she explained. This was a squeeze-in from her new doctor.

"Why don't I ask the receptionist how much longer she thinks before you're called," I helpfully volunteered.

No need, she tells me, adding that she had to run to the restroom so she'll just inquire at the same time, and would I mind watching her things. "Of course not."

I resume my discreet study of the room and I am so filled with compassion, I find myself silently sending prayers to each person. I try to direct energy to them—the light of God's love that is so abundant in me. I want them to have the health I have. To use it for their healing. It matters to me. It matters so much to me that I find myself toying with the idea of asking whoever is willing to answer, what else they are doing besides medical to help win this battle. I want to know if they know how much more powerful they would be if they also pulled from the endless Source that is God's light. I daydream that they choose to believe this with a total abandonment of fear, and that an energy session is performed right then and there. I can see the scene play out in my mind, when that person goes in to receive their diagnosis and the doctors are SHOCKED that what was certain to have been cancer was actually nothing. A clean bill of health.

Stop, Keryl. You sound crazy! says the logical, human, cautious part of me.

But you're not, says that wiser part.

Let me tell you, if I was wearing a purple wristband and waiting to walk through those doors, there is nothing I would not try to eradicate a disease like cancer from my body.

I could temper my message, I think. *Your career was spent in strategic communications. Meet them where they are.* I can simply inject them with hope. Empower them. Give them the sunshine that Teresa asked Allison for.

But I stay seated in my chair across the room. I rationalize that a stranger talking to them is the last thing they need right now and I hold back.

Coward. Who wouldn't want words of comfort and faith at this time?

The internal battle ends when Allison comes from a place that is behind me; her voice breaks me from my reverie. I don't know who is on the other end of the phone she is holding to her ear, but she is saying thank you with such gratitude and warmth—such deep sincerity and authenticity in her inflection—and I am reminded that for all of her emotions and the chaos that swirls with her, she comes off as exceedingly polite and authentic. She wraps up her phone call as she nears me, saying again that she understands and please don't apologize, they will try again.

To me, she says "That was my doctor. We are going to do this differently. I will see her tomorrow instead. She was unable to make it here, after all. Her schedule got away from her. The nurse was supposed to call and inform the hospital, but she did not." Her sentences are short and equally spaced, like the tick marks on the calendar of her three dances with cancer.

The sincere authenticity is now directed to me. "I am so sorry for this time that I wasted in your day. We can go now. Thank you so much Keryl. "

As she begins to gather her things and pack her computer into a backpack, I was fully aware that she never went up to the receptionist to inquire why others were being called before her. Once again, there is a wall that separates me from the doctor who is treating her. In the 16 months that she was in my home, I never once saw a medical professional, or heard her name called into a room. Nor did Gary. Nor did, I would eventually learn, the person who first began to drive her to her radiation appointments.

At that moment, walking out of the cancer ward and away from the many who were sitting there, the feeling inside of me that something was very wrong began to grow stronger.

We walked toward the exit, then through the walkway that connects the building to the parking deck, and out into the garage where I have parked my car.

With that feeling expanding within me I turned my head to Allison. "Good luck," I say and began to make my way toward my car.

"Keryl?" The voice reached me easily. I stopped my trek and looked back at her. The expression on her face matched its tone. Confusion. I had seen that look more times over the past years since we met than I cared to ever count. It covered her face each time I caught her in a blatant discrepancy. Confusion.

I can't look at her right now. I just can't.

Furthermore, I felt a coldness begin to descend on me as I realized she had naturally expected me to drive her home, since she didn't own a vehicle. *Of course she has that expectation. I did everything for her when she was in my home allegedly fighting for her life.*

I took the few steps back to where I had stood next to her when we reached the parking deck. I am standing in front of her now, looking at her face so there is no misunderstanding my next words. "FULL visibility or nothing." I say with emphasis on each word. "Those terms are non-negotiable. I am not doing this again with you." I turned away once more, walk to my car and drive off without one morsel of regret that I may have just left a brain cancer victim stranded at the cancer ward.

●   ●   ●   ●   ●   ●   ●

The following day the opening scene of the next act was nearly identical to the opening scene that ended in the parking deck. A phone call. A distressed voice.

"I need you, Keryl, please. I can't do this without you."

And just like the day before, I drove to her house. Once again, I sat in her room with that feeling of dread that came over me every time I was there.

Immediately I noticed the purple wristband she was wearing. She was sitting on the bed with a stainless steel cooking pot in front of her, and once again she was crying and rallying against a God who was unfair.

She told me that she had gotten so sick in the middle of the night that she checked herself into the hospital and the doctor performed emergency chemotherapy.

I assumed then that the pot was so she didn't have to hang her head over her commode. With it, she could be sick without leaving her bed. I also assumed it was unused—a prop that was to strengthen the validity of her chemo treatment—just like the band on her wrist.

Chemotherapy in the middle of the night?

I stared at the woman on the bed, my empath dial was back to its rightful position.

Her cats were distressed, she told me. They knew something was happening. They knew she was sick.

She was in full storytelling mode now.

With the same concentration I had studied the patients in the cancer ward the day before, I studied her face. I looked deep into her soul and didn't like what I saw there.

My position was unchanged—full visibility or nothing. So far we were oh-for-three. A name not called by the receptionist, a phone call that took place in another room, a chemo treatment in the middle of the night.

She gets nothing from me.

I left.

It was Friday night and I had plans that evening. I didn't need to spend another moment in this oppressive place with what I was now starting to realize was a person whom I was never qualified to help.

* * * * * * *

The next day was Saturday.

The running group with which I was once active planned a few activities outside of running. On this beautiful spring Saturday, the activity was river rafting. I didn't go, but Gary did.

"Check out my cliff jump," his text message to me read, and included a link to a video.

The cliff on this particular stretch of river meant a leap from a height of more than 20 feet. It was a popular spot for kayakers and rafters. To get to the top, a person had to tether their raft or boat to a place where it was away from the jumpers, swim to the cliffs, and then climb the steep incline to reach the jumping spot.

Once the jump was over, the jumper then had to swim back to their boat or raft. The jump only lasted seconds, which was a much shorter duration than the effort required to enjoy those few seconds. But the exhilaration of the jump made it worthwhile.

I looked at the link sent to me, feeling happy that this deserving soul who had become my dearest friend was having fun with the gang—and I clicked it.

The link took me to a Facebook post filled with small videos that were uploaded by the person who captured each jumper. I scanned the names and saw "Allison jumps."

The smile disappeared.

With a feeling of dread, I opened the 'Allison jumps' link. It was taken from a close enough distance that there was no mistaking the identity of the jumper. Even if it was taken from twice the distance, there would be no mistaking the broad shoulders and heavier form.

Later that evening, with her voice reaching my eardrum through the phone, I felt the beginning of what would eventually broil over to a full-fledged rage and disdain. I was querying her, "How does someone with brain cancer who had just had chemotherapy 24 hours ago, jump 23 feet into the water and swim to their kayak?" I asked. Before she could answer I continued, "What are you doing Allison? What game is this?" I had thought about the hours I had spent sitting in that cancer ward, the purple wristband, silver pot, and tears from the previous day.

As though she came pre-programmed with an 'instant tears' setting and an answer to everything, she emotionally responded that she just wanted to feel normal. She asked,"What was so wrong about wanting to feel normal?"

In full drama, she tells me that she had flushed the chemo pills in the toilet that morning and told herself that she was not going to have cancer. She was adamant to not go through this again!

I had made a promise to God not too long prior to this moment, to open myself beyond my perceived limitations. To trust in Him and to keep my eyes on love. Looking back now, it appears that at that moment, I had already turned my eyes from Him.

Had I not, I would have seen something that I didn't see until much later. I would have seen that before me stood a woman who was battling something that was creating within her the desperate need to have attention and exist in victim mentality. Had I viewed this scene with love and not disgust, I might have applauded the words that she was speaking to me because I would have understood that her flushing these pills down the toilet and saying "No more will cancer claim me," was symbolism for her attempt to become bigger than this inner-demon. I would have recognized the deficiency in love that existed within her and I would have given her mine as a friend—just as I wanted to give those cancer patients my health and my inner light.

I might have understood that this may just be the first step toward her own healing, and perhaps I would have celebrated this with her.

Although I had practiced for years how to respond in love, I could not. This scenario took that ability to a whole new level and I was not there yet—not with her. I was still eyebrow deep in the lesson and not yet adept at how to deploy what I would eventually learn was grace. All I knew, was that the person in front of me, who had lived in my home for months, allegedly battling a cancer that appeared every two years, was once again claiming the same. I had watched this same movie in 2013.

A feeling began to coil its dark self around me, in a near-identical manner to a day nearly three years ago in July 2012, when an unwanted energy penetrated the safety of my haven, and wreaked havoc for weeks. An unwanted energy that the voice inside had tried to warn me was somehow coming from Allison.

A truth was beginning to emerge that I didn't want to face.

"You do remember that Allison has brain cancer?" was practically my only response to Gary's cliff jumping video. "How does a person with brain cancer cliff dive?" I asked him.

He couldn't answer.

"She not only cliff-dived, Keryl, but when rafts needed towing in the river, she tethered her kayak to them and towed them through currents," eluding to the strength it took to perform this feat. "Repeatedly," he adds.

His mind was where my mind was.

She was a fraud.

So disgusted was I by Allison that I wanted my every action to her to show how much she was the bane of my existence. I made it clear that I wanted nothing to do with her in my life. I was anything but grace. I did not overcome darkness with light.

Time passed and cancer did not return to the brain of Allison. But my own brain felt filled with something equally destructive. I replayed scene after scene in my mind of events that took place over the past years.

My mind didn't go to the enormous beauty of this season.

I didn't think of my day of discovery in that empty church. I didn't think of the lives irreversibly touched by the fact that I now shared my conviction in our ability to draw from beyond us when needed. Nor did I think of the return of my constant companion and a host of other positive events that happened.

Instead I saw everything that was dark. This person was a fraud. In fact, I couldn't even begin to try to see anything but that.

Everything pertaining to the days since I was introduced to Allison was like those optical illusions—are there two faces or is it a vase? When you look at the white, you see the vase, when you look at the dark, you see the two faces. Whichever you focus on is what you see.

For the duration of Allison's time in my home, I had been so focused on the light, I did not see the two-faces. I could not see the dark. Even when others tried to show me, I could not see anything but the vase.

I didn't stop to think that because I dismissed the darker side, I was embraced by the brightest, most divine light. It didn't matter that I discovered God or that I was given many signs that I was never alone. Or that "God especially protects the children."

At this moment where the truth of her was beginning to become clear to me, all I saw were the two faces, I could only see the darkness in the scene that was playing out before me.

If there was a pressing on my heart attempting to guide me in a different way, I could not feel it. Nor would I feel the presence of comfort and peace that I loved so much.

It would be months before I would once again listened to or felt the presence of God.

CHAPTER 28
On the Brink of Truth

October 2015

I had taken the call in another room but my tonality was heard in the room next door. The call ended and I made my way back to the room where my childhood friend and I had sat talking just moments earlier. I had stepped out of that room a friend and re-emerged a stranger. She was looking at me like I was someone she had never seen in her life before now. "In all the years I have known you, I have never heard you speak to anyone with such disdain, Keryl."

We have been friends since 6th grade.

Her tone is deeply troubled. She needs an explanation, but how do I do that? What words can I possibly use that could even come close to explaining why I sounded the way I did.

"That disdain you heard is the reason I'm here with you in New Jersey," I respond.

I had needed a change of scenery. Not for a day, not for a weekend, but for however long it took for me to rebalance. I had never driven to New York before, I had always flown. But the road began to beckon to me and I packed up my office equipment alongside a large suitcase with a separate bag for my running gear and I hit the road. I barely mapped out the route to get there. All I knew was I wanted to get out of Atlanta.

The friendship that Stacy and I shared resembled family more than it did friends. We connected in 6th grade and have been an increasingly important part of each other's lives as the years passed. We frequently said we should never be living in different states.

If my sudden intrusion into her busy life was an inconvenience, she hid it with a mastery that could win her an Academy Award.

I loved being back in the part of the country where I started my life. We took trips into New York, back to the old hometown, we talked, we drank wine. We walked. I filled myself with her life and her children, I saw my cousins, I met their babies. And I geared up for runs every chance I could get. I ran and ran, yet no matter how much I ran, my thoughts kept up. I couldn't outrun them.

Eventually I made my way back to Atlanta.

Gary and I arranged to have the items removed that I had stored in Allison's basement when I had moved into my city apartment. He made most of the arrangements because the thought of my doing so filled me with the same feeling of dread' that came over me now every time she came into my mind.

The home she claimed to own was a duplex. She lived on one side and a young couple lived on the other. They shared the basement and the backyard. The exit from the basement to the backyard was luckily on the side that was occupied by Allison. We would not have to disrupt the young couple whom we both barely knew.

Allison was informed on which day I would be moving my things into storage and was asked if she would kindly be out of her home that day. We really had no desire to see her. She told me she would be in England, as a matter of fact. She had landed a job involving the overseas schools that followed a

U.S.-developed curriculum and her new job would be to assess the efficacy of each.

Fine.

I could care less where she would be as long as she wasn't there.

In the backyard, Allison's tenants sometimes used the shared clothesline for those times when they preferred to air dry their clothes. This early evening was one of those times.

"I heard you moved to New York," said the young neighbor. I was confused. "Where did you hear that?" The look on her face spoke a message in a volume that had nothing to do with my one simple response. At that exact moment, her eyes also looked beyond me. "Never mind," she mumbled and turned away.

I looked behind me. There stood Allison. I looked at the neighbor who had begun to hastily hang clothes again—her mannerisms made it very clear she wanted nothing more to do with anything regarding the start of the confusing exchange.

Allison answered her question, " I might have said something before I knew."

"Before you knew what? And what are you doing here?"

Gary came and stood by my side, echoing the question,'what are you doing here?'

It seemed that Allison had another tragedy in her family.

Her cousin's one month old baby died suddenly, almost immediately upon her arrival to the UK, and she quickly boarded a flight back so that she could fly out to the funeral to be with her cousin. *A day trip to England?*

Her cousin lived in another state. She informed us that she was waiting for the person who would drive her to the airport to arrive, explaining that she could not put her suitcase on her scooter. She assured us she would stay out of our way unless there was something she could do to help. She would be happy to help.

With my new dark lenses and the coldness inside, I told her that staying out of the way, as she had promised to do, would be the greatest help we could have.

She stepped away but not too far, and we resumed.

Reaching for her phone as though it had just buzzed in her pocket, she spoke into it, confirming the time and meeting place with her ride to the airport. She went up to her room to pack. Her room overlooked the backyard of her home which meant that our activities could be watched from there. That didn't phase us as we continued to load up the rest of the items that had been stored in her basement. They were primarily office-related from the closing of my agency.

But then at one point, Gary and I experienced the same sensation. Both of us, in near synchronization stopped what we were doing. Both of our eyes traveled to the same spot on the back of her house. Both of our bloods ran cold as we saw her standing away from the window, looking into the backyard at us. As dramatic as it may sound, the look on her face was burned into our memory. It was a look that was purely the opposite of light.

Fifteen minutes after that blood-chilling experience, she strapped a duffle bag to her scooter, said something about meeting her airport ride somewhere and left.

As short as the trip to England was, the funeral for the one-month old baby was even shorter, Allison returned later that night.

This experience was validation of the growing and nagging thought that we were on the brink of learning something very disturbing about this woman.

And she was about to misstep greatly.

CHAPTER 29
And Then Came The Rage

Remember and know this…There will always be energies
that try to take you from the pureness of Me. You have
control over all of these things. Don't let anything take
that from you.

A pressing on my heart

December 8, 2015

I stood outside my car in a parking lot face to face with Allison. We were meeting in a public place at the advice of a good friend who recommended that I pick a place that would not impact me if it became tarnished forever. I chose the parking lot of a nearby Home Depot. We were there because Allison was providing an audio confession—spawned by her panic when I informed her of my plans to launch a formal investigation to understand the depth of her lies and deceptions.

She was speaking into the recorder I held in my hand.

"Well, first of all," she stammered then paused. "I think you had to get to the point that you did…uhhmmm…with your anger…and the frustration… uhmmmm… to get to the point where I really had a chance to get some help.

"It...I...I don't know what you'll believe, and I can't worry about that...I just have to tell you...y'know, first of all...that I'm really sorry...and...and that doesn't cover anything...."

Allison had eventually become sloppy, almost blatant, like she was living her fabricated life in a manner that had her desperate to finally be caught. Her misstep occurred during the period I had left Atlanta to fuel myself in my old hometown with family and friends. It was not enough, in June 2015, when she again claimed to me that cancer was growing in her body, but she later tried to share her fake sob story with a family who had actually, in real life, already suffered a great loss to the disease. It was November when I learned that this family who had lost their loved one was considering helping Allison. I found out when I was contacted by someone they knew who was aware that Allison had lived with me during her illness. When I heard that she was trying to convince another group of people that she was sick, I knew I had to do something.

I drove to Allison's house and with an unexplainable calmness, asked her a simple question. "If I contact the hospital you said treated you, what will I learn?" She didn't answer the question, but her emotional response gave me the information I was seeking. She became hysterical and questioned why I would do such a thing. I began to feel my calm slide off, replaced by horror, then disgust, then horror again.

As her desperation grew before my eyes, she promised me she would give me more evidence in the form of additional medical records, all the while questioning repeatedly why I would think she was lying. She said that the person who contacted me was the one who was lying.

I looked hard at Allison, finally seeing her for what she was. And I left. But not before I dialed the phone number of her mother, in Allison's presence, and left a voice-mail revealing the truth of the enormous deception that was played by her daughter. *This poor mother*, that ever-compassionate part of me thought, *so close on the heels of her husband's death.*

However, that sliver of compassion slipped away in my desperate need to immediately get as far away from Allison as I could.

The next day, in complete terror, she changed her phone number and proceeded to tell the person who contacted me, plus numerous others we knew, "Keryl is threatening me; don't give her my new number."

I too was busy the next day. I contacted Dr. M.'s assistant by phone and told her I was e-mailing to her a scanned copy of medical records including a document showing that I was granted medical proxy to a patient I was calling to question her on. She received the documents while I was on the phone and I was immediately rerouted to the Director of Investigations, through whom the truth about Allison was fully revealed to me.

"Did we speak in 2013 or 2014?" I asked, dreading the answer. Gosh, I didn't even know what year all that happened.

"We did, Keryl."

I was besides myself. The investigator who tried to warn me all of those years ago, thanks to the diligence of my family, was not some random, shady private eye hired by them. He was the head of all investigations at this leading medical facility. "Why didn't you tell me you were with [hospital name]? Why didn't you identify yourself as such? Oh my god, my family! Oh my god." I was so grateful to be sitting when the tidal wave of grief washed over me.

He was patient and gentle. He was heartbroken to know all this time had passed without a full reconnect with my family. He

230

remembered everything. He had investigated both of us, he told me. "Two vastly different stories emerged in my investigation. You—a caregiver for the homeless, a successful business owner, a compassionate friend. Keryl, I remember thinking back then 'I would like a friend like this in my corner.'" His words did not bring me the comfort he clearly intended. I was too devastated. But I was also glad that he seemed to be a decent and compassionate man, and not some hardened law enforcement agent. He continued, "Allison's story was a different one." He listed some of the things he discovered, adding that even her LinkedIn profile was largely made up.

He continued to show concern that I had not, at that time, reconnected with my family, telling me that he had been certain this had been resolved. He was exceedingly patient even when the thought began to enter my mind, *how can I believe anything that is no longer face to face? How can I know this man is not making this up?*

I couldn't believe anyone. I no longer could believe anyone ever again, is what I thought, and I began to become increasingly skeptical to anything he was saying on the phone—a mirror of my response in the past.

I didn't want it to be true.

He was unflappable. To prove he was not lying, he promised he would mail me a formal affidavit regarding Allison that would include her extensive list of infractions. He said he would have it notarized and officially filed with the hospital.

When the document arrived, I scanned its contents.

And then came the rage.

I felt it begin to build inside me. It came with such force that I better understood those many stories we read of a normally rational person committing a heinous, violent crime in the heat of a moment.

At long last, the Director of Investigations was able to pierce the armor that he had been unable to pierce when he tried to warn me years earlier. April 23, 2013 was the date of her confession according to this affidavit that I now held in my hands. 2013. It was two and a half years ago that my family made the medical facility aware that a person had fraudulently used the identity of the doctor—and out of love for me, had tried to intervene on my behalf. They had tried valiantly, but futilely, to tell me the truth and I would not listen. My empath dial was turned to off. They left it in God's hands and trusted that in the end, truth and love will prevail. My wise, beautiful family.

Days before the meeting in the parking lot, immediately after I learned the truth, and in the midst of my shock and rage, I had somehow managed to keep my composure intact enough to make only one request of her: "Gather my friends who worked so hard to support me while I supported you and tell them the truth. I want the truth out there and not the lie." There were so many who, like me, believed they were helping a person in need. They were the ones who were close to the situation.

She promised that she would.

I was rightfully skeptical.

Her mother had received my voice-mail message and drove the nearly two hours into Atlanta to plead with me not to contact authorities. "She doesn't need that. She needs mental help," her mother implored. "I'm going to see that she gets help."

A week later, nothing had changed.

So, on that day, December 8, 2015, I delivered an ultimatum—either tell the truth or I will engage an investigative reporter to uncover it for me. She begged me not to expose her in that way, promising she would do it. She even stated that she knew it was the right thing to do for the people who cared for her through me.

I gave her one week.

"In addition," I told her, "I want an audio confession to keep in my records."

And that is how we found ourselves in the parking lot at The Home Depot. Her mother was with her, promising again, she would get her daughter the mental help she believed her daughter needed.

Neither mother nor daughter kept their promises.

I could tell that her mother was trying to be gentle and light, but she interrupted constantly, and I had no patience for her. After one too many interruption, I looked at Allison and said "Control your mother." An echo of an afternoon three years prior when this same woman screamed into my phone that if her daughter died, it would be my fault.

Allison sent her mother inside the store to give us time to talk uninterrupted.

It was just us now.

I looked at Allison standing there before me—my eyes traveling from her worried face, down her body, to her feet, then back again, as if I wanted to remember forever what the face and body of deception looked like. As I did so, I felt repulsion shudder through me so intensely that I cannot find words to describe it. Even if I had wanted to execute my well-practiced response of focusing only on the light, I would fail. I could not yet find a sliver of it as I stood before her. It was too soon. The rage and repulsiveness I felt at that moment needed to run its course before I would be able to deal with it effectively and do my best to let it go.

This miserable day in December was not the day.

All I knew in that moment was that this person who lived in my home for 16 months, was a fraud who had faked having the most heart-wrenching disease a person could face. She happily ate the food I and others prepared for her, relaxed and enjoyed the comfort offered, receiving care night and day from me and many close to me, and hid behind me as I defended her from those who believed she was a fraud.

Everything large and small was flying through my mind. No wonder she and the doctor used the same words and phrases. No wonder she knew Mitchell's vision of the ant that I reported to the doctor. No wonder Robert Wilde contacted her the very next day. It was all her. This and so many other lies, it was impossible to count.

"Do you know Teresa Wilde?" I asked her mother before she was sent away. She looked at Allison. "Isn't Teresa Wilde the one whose wedding we went to years ago?"

I felt sick to my stomach.

I would learn through her audio confession that almost every single thing she said had been a lie. And she continued to lie throughout her panic of being discovered.

She didn't look the least bit contrite. She looked scared. She showed no remorse that her deception had impacted my familial relations, friendships, and business. She lied easily about the people she called friends, and that too without remorse. It was nothing to her—unimportant. What was important to her was that nobody finds out who she really was.

Standing in front of her on this day, it was not lost on me that I handed her a foundation on which to carry out this insidious deception and invasion of my life. I let it happen.

"WHY?" I asked, with the recording on, "WHY would you do something like this?"

"I wanted another life," she said. "I hated mine."

"And THIS was your solution?" I asked incredulously. I could not comprehend what I was hearing.

I had asked the same question to the Director of Investigations on the phone a week before. "Why would anyone do this?"

"I am not a psychiatrist," he said, "but I suggest you read a book called *The Sociopath Next Door* to understand who you had living in your house."

My God, what was inside all those syringes I injected into her body? And in front of friends and witnesses? How could I have been so careless, so trusting?

I was sloppy and could have severely endangered myself and my child. I was seriously considering pressing charges.

I held up the audio recorder and she confessed into it that she lied about cancer, had opened numerous e-mail accounts in the names of the doctor and other individuals, impersonated a doctor, forged medical records, adding boastfully, "It only took me five minutes to do that." *Was she proud of that?* She confessed that she fabricated romantic relationships, places of employment, her education and the degrees she claimed to hold. Almost every story, the hours and hours of them, were made up. Andrew, Jenna, Dr. M., the surgeries, the little boy and his guitar, the times in the home with the doctor, the hearing loss, the memory loss, the urgent decision to resuscitate or not, Teresa, her cancer, the ring. What about my car? Was that intentional? Were the rib injuries faked? All the screaming in the ambulance, was that part of the act? How could I tell what was real now and what wasn't? Everything was a lie.

I thought about how I didn't want her to read Teresa's letter aloud for the first time in case there was something in it that was private. *She wrote that letter. She knew exactly what was in it. And the second letter, the one written to me."* She even knew you liked butterflies," she had sniffled.

And Robert Wilde. It was all her.

The file cabinet of my mind was wide open now and I was mentally staring at all the contents inside. There were mountains in there. She had presented me with a copy of countless medical records, with her signature on them! How foolish does one get? She had sent letters written to me from her father, Robert Wilde's Last Will and Testament—all of these and much more were her doing. There was no way I could get my arms around it right then and there. It would take months to sort through all of it. I would learn about the depths of this deception for months to come.

For instance, I would eventually Google the name of the notary public stamped on Robert Wilde's Will and it would come up in a stock photo site. The name was used as a stock photo notary stamp by this image-provider, the same name appearing across many states in this piece of artwork. She downloaded and inserted a stock image into a make-believe Will.

I would also notice that the notarized document was dated April 1, April Fool's Day—*well, I was certainly the fool, wasn't I*—as was his last e-mail to me.

No, I absolutely could not get my head around any of this. What sane person could?

She used her dying father! How could she use him in this scheme? The letter she claimed had come from her father was left in his Will. In it was stated that, like Teresa, he too had known our paths were supposed to cross. When I showed it to Allison and her mother, they both cried and cried. *My gosh.* Was her mother in on this? Something told me 'no.' But please tell me she could now see how *wrong* this is. The lengths Allison went through. Why? What was the purpose in all of this? What was her end-game? *What was this?*

It was too big to comprehend. I thought of all of the things that she did, all of the things not listed in this book, and felt like I was a central character in a horror film. One of those who are so immobilized with the horror they are witnessing, they can't will themselves to move. That was me. Paralyzed with the horror of what stood before me.

I felt at that moment that she has no conscience at all.

She continued confessing into my recorder, listing some of the mutual friends she had lied to in the final days before the truth was revealed, in fear that others would know what she did. She told me she was so afraid they would find out. I bet I could name them based on either their response to me when they saw me or the very blatant un-friending by one or two.

I couldn't think about what others thought. What mattered right now was knowing the truth. From 2012 to 2013, my life had been a lie. I had not been a caregiver, devoting my time to helping a person in need. I had been the engine that gave something far more insidious than cancer, the chance to take flight.

"Yes, almost everything was a lie..." she said into the recorder, "I lied about so much to you. I lied about...just during that time period, I lied about so much...I became so narcissistic about everything. I became narcissistic because I wanted a different life."

I looked at her as she desperately tried to communicate with me and I continued to see the history of her in my mind. I recalled everything: The barrage of messages from the doctor that arrived to my phone and inbox night and day were actually her, sitting in the next room, typing them all. When I was out with Mitchell, she sat in my home and bombarded my precious few moments of time away with e-mails posing as the doctor. She wrote—as the doctor—of her strength and her beauty and selflessness. Of the doctor who fell in love with her. Of tragedy in her life. Of childhood friends and an educational path that were nonexistent. She invested 16 months in my home, night and day to this deception; and kept it going for the years following my family's alert to the hospital.

Allison continued to confess in the miserable parking lot of The Home Depot.

And then out of nowhere she tells me that despite everything she had done, she did not and would not admit to being responsible for the message from the doctor I had received while Mitchell and I were performing the first of our energy sessions on her. She said she was so scared when it happened she didn't know what to do—she wondered at the time, how could she tell me she didn't know who sent the e-mails from the doctor without disclosing that *she* was in fact the fictitious doctor, and this illness was a scenario that only existed in her mind?

I stood before this self-proclaimed liar, and detested sharing a space with her. Also, for the first time, I resented the familiar pressing on my heart that I have known all of my life; it was saying, "I am here. Trust," which created an inner-conflict that raged against my human mind.

If You had been with me, I would not be standing in this parking lot, I raged against that inner voice I now knew was God. *Go away.*

But its presence was like a band-aid on my heart. I let it engulf me. Eventually, my trust in that voice won and I let her words sink in "I don't know who sent those messages." Is this yet another lie? I replay that evening in my head as I stand across from her. She had been laying on the bed with her eyes closed when I got the first message. "Energy work is fine, K. Just do not put any pressure on the left frontal lobe. Find me when you are finished and send me a report."

How did that text come in when she was laying there right in front of me? There are apps that can delay the delivery of a text message but this one was a direct answer to a question I had just sent the so-called doctor.

I then recalled the mysterious grey mist.

Allison also said she did not send the second message that said to do it again but add prayer.

So, who did?

I don't have any idea why I should believe an individual who confessed to lying compulsively, but something in the deepest part of me believed there was truth spoken—but only with those words.

CHAPTER 30
Falling on the Sword

December 12, 2015

Less than one week had passed since the long-winded audio confession in The Home Depot parking lot. If anything had changed, it was only the behavior toward me of those few friends she confessed lying to after the truth emerged. I don't know what they were told, but there was visible shock when I ran into two of them at a social function. I could only imagine what story she conjured up. Lying was her mastery, it was who she was at her core.

Other than that, nothing seems to be different. I wondered if she was getting the help she needed. That part of me that belongs so completely to God hoped she was, but I was still too filled with poison to feel anything that resembled a morsel of a softening heart toward her.

I was also tired of fielding the calls of those who believed with everything they had that this new community she was inserting herself into needed to know who was amongst them.

I retreated. Away from social, away from anything that crossed lines with wherever she was. It was easy enough to do, given that it was only one community group that brought us together. She was not a part of any of my other circles of friends.

On December 12, 2015, I saw her name in an e-mail message to me. The subject line read "Falling on the Sword."

I had been told by my neighbor that she was standing outside the gated door of my city apartment the night before, and I sent her a note telling her that I had had enough and she was never to come to my home again. She was *not* welcome there.

Perhaps it was an apology.

I read the contents. I could not have been more wrong.

"No Keryl. I HAVE HAD IT and it is time for me to take a HUGE risk and tell you what you have missed in the truth. I am not afraid of the truth. I have never been. All along. I am afraid of what has threatened to snuff out the truth. On the contrary I am angry. Seethingly angry and not with you. And the truth is far greater than you know. And I am no creature and never was. I stopped by your house to have a conversation and that is it and I was gone in 5 min. I would have told you the following last night.

There is much more seriousness in 'play' here than you know and I have been protecting you for a long, long, long time. Yes, protecting you and not from the supernatural. I fell on the sword in FULL for you - in FULL and you have no idea even what I have done - FOR YOU! I do it everyday now. And the burden of it grows heavier by the minute. I was sure you who are so tactical and strategic would have figured it out long before now. You say SHOW me what you are doing for me. I have been doing exactly what we spoke of. Meeting with a doctor who could help but not for me. I never have. I did it for you and what I agreed to do. I have been living on a fallen sword for you to not get involved in anything past what you know.

I have been hung out to dry with you thinking I am the enemy and the creature and the bane of your existence. I have never been

*and never will. In your own rage and anger and assuredness that I
am exactly what you think I am you have missed the actual truth. I
kept it from you or more correctly I was threatened to keep it from
you. Still am. And I am far from paranoid. Far from it.*

*Why am I standing up now? Why am I telling you the above?
Because you need all the information before you move forward
for yourself. And because I am supremely fatigued in an entirely
different way than you think I am. I need a different kind of help
or assistance and I need to know which way to go next. I need to
know who to go to.*

*I am no saint or martyr. I am someone who cared for another
and risked my entire life - ALL OF IT to make sure that she could
live hers. I played the meek, weak friend thought to be damaged
these weeks so you could show disdain openly with your friend,
family, and even your messages. I fell hard. Maybe then you would
stay SAFE.*

*I would never hurt you or myself or anyone. Legal advice for
that? I could never do these things even with the burden I carry.*

*I thought I could keep up this pretense and continue to do
this - continue to fall on this sword and not have you know anything
- do what is asked and move on out of your life, but I can't anymore
without you knowing. And you need to know what you don't. And
you are the only one I can talk to. NO one else. Period. NO one.*

*Meet me today. I will come alone to the [city store] parking lot
by Binders book store. Come by yourself. I will come on my scooter.
And come without your recorder or I won't come at all. If I am scared
of one thing I am scared of what has threatened me these years
and I will never have it recorded - not right now. After these weeks
I trust your spidey senses and your gut and your instincts enough
to talk with you. How ironic that in all of this you are the one I turn
to now. I knew the public humiliation would come. I prepared for it.*

If you have any small doubt or inkling and possibly know of what I am talking about then you will come. If you have any small inclination that I have taken my life - all of it - to fall on a public sword - which I have done then come. And the things is - I will stay on this sword for you. Willingly. But I can't shoulder this burden anymore without your knowledge. I have trusted you all these years. I will trust you will all that I have of me - of you - of my family. I take even a risk now in just writing this.

Binders. Tell me what time and I will be there. You will find a very different person than you have seen these past weeks and you will know the reasons why.

I ask for this time. You have already built your case against me. Hear me out Keryl. You can decide what to do from there. There is nothing left to lose and only the truth to gain.

Allison"

Numerous times she insinuated that I should have a clue as to what she was trying to say. I had none. I read and reread the e-mail but it spoke in cryptic circles. A lot of words for very little message. What did she mean she has been protecting me for a long, long, long time?

The idea of seeing her again made my stomach curl. I didn't have a nudge from my inner-voice on which way I should respond to this—ignore it or meet her.

I finally agreed. I wanted to know if she had kept any of her promises to come clean with friends.

She arrived on her scooter and climbed into the car I had purchased on May 5, 2015. A replacement to the one she totaled.

The moment she sat back in the passenger seat, my car shrunk down to the size of a sugar cube with the oppressiveness of her proximity to me. Like sucking air through a coffee stirrer once again. I am reminded of days of darkness.

She cuts to the chase The words coming out of her mouth are now telling me that she was not the one who was lying, after all. She said what she needed to in the confession to stop me from contacting an investigative reporter. Rather, it was the hospital who was not telling the truth.

This well-reputed hospital was *illegally* conducting research using the blood and tissue samples they took from her, and now were threatening her because of my interference.

Her brother, through a text message sent directly to me, corroborated her story.

This had to stop.

I push a button on my phone and through the speaker system comes the voice of the investigator. Allison looks mortified.

"Detective, I have Allison in the car with me and she wants to inform you of something I think you should know." She looks at me with a face that is saying "What are you doing?" Pure panic.

Well practiced in the art of deception and storytelling, she recovered well.

Leaning into the phone she tells him that the hospital is conducting secret research and they are threatening her, me and our families.

He interrupts her.

"*Stop this NOW,* Allison. It is time to stop. You have hurt many people with this charade. You have upset a doctor who is a good man, who has dedicated his life to cancer research, you have hurt a good person who believed she was helping you during a time in need."

"Keryl," he interrupts himself, "Connect with your family. Do that today." To her he continues, "It is time to stop now. You have never been a patient of Dr. M., or of [medical facility]."

She gives me a look that says "See? What did you really expect?" and gestures with her hand to my phone with a second expression that says, "Can you believe this guy?"

Then something happens that I wished hadn't. In the ensuing brief exchange between Allison and the investigator she learns that the statutes of limitation for identity theft have passed since she was caught in 2013. She learns that the hospital is not going to pursue a criminal investigation, primarily because Allison had stopped using the e-mail accounts back in April, when her cancer vanished and she no longer needed the doctor.

I wanted to groan as the words came through the phone. I knew at that moment she would never gather the good souls that supported her and tell them the truth. Somehow I know I would not either. Our reasons could not have been more different.

For now, I am not happy with this investigators non-strategic slip.

I inwardly cringe again, not at his words, but this time because I have to look at her face to see what is reflected there. So intense is my dislike for the person next to me during this period so shortly after learning the truth of her, that even her face utterly repulsed me. *I had to get her out of my car.* The feeling is amplified when I glance over and see by the expression on her face that the need to make up stories about this no longer existed as of that moment—thanks to the investigator. Will this nightmare never end?

"Give a person like her enough rope and they will hang themselves," the wise friend in the justice department had said when The Home Depot parking lot was suggested.

What if she doesn't? I wondered at that moment in the car. The inner war raged on.

Let it go, said the part that kept its eyes turned to God. His word says, *Do not take revenge, my dear friends, but leave room for God's wrath, for it is written: "It is mine to avenge; I will repay," says the Lord.* (Romans 12:19, NIV)

The human part could not let it go.

It took only two phone calls to authorities to learn that there were other charges that carried a much stiffer penalty than identity theft with a much longer statutes of limitation. This scenario qualified for them.

Good. I could use that if I had to. Sorry God, I thought, tempted to use the age-old excuse, "I am only human."

That afternoon, she got out of my car and she walked back to her scooter. Before she reached it, she said "I still believe you are who God says you are."

I didn't respond.

I drove away and no words have been exchanged since that day.

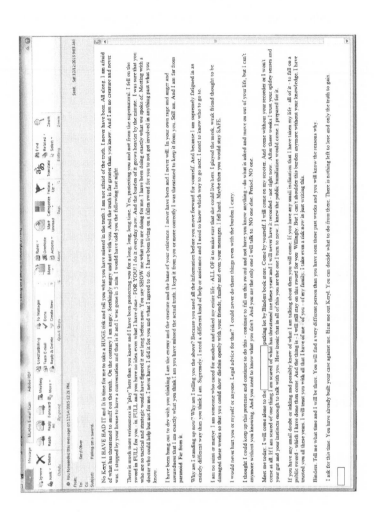

No Keryl. I HAVE HAD IT and it is time for me to take a HUGE risk and tell you what you have missed in the truth. I am not afraid of the truth. I never have been. All alone. I am afraid of what has threatened to snuff out the truth. On the contrary: I am angry. Seethingly angry and not with you. And the truth is far greater than you know. And I am no creature and never was. I stopped by your house to have a conversation and that is it and I was gone in 5 min. I would have told you the following last night

There is much more seriousness in "play" here than you know and I have been protecting you for a long, long time. Yes, protecting you and not from the supernatural. I fell on the sword in FULL for you. in FULL, and you have no idea even what I have done - FOR YOU! I do it everyday now. And the burden of it grows heavier by the minute. I was sure that you who are so tactical and strategic would have figured it out long before now. You say SHOW me what you are doing for me. I have been doing exactly what we spoke of. Meeting with a doctor who could help but not for me. I never have. I did it for you and what I agreed to do. I have been living on a fallen sword for you to not get involved in anything past what you know.

I have been hung out to dry with you thinking I am the enemy and the creature and the bane of your existence. I never have been and I never will. In your own rage and anger and assuredness that I am exactly what you think I am you have missed the actual truth. I kept it from you or more correctly I was threatened to keep it from you. Still am. And I am far from paranoid. Far from it.

Why am I standing up now? Why am I telling you the above? Because you need all the information before you move forward for yourself. And because I am supremely fatigued in an entirely different way than you think I am. Supremely. I need a different kind of help or assistance and I need to know which way to go next. I need to know who to go to.

I am no saint or martyr. I am someone who cared for another and risked my entire life - ALL OF it to make sure that she could live here. I played the meek, weak friend thought to be damaged these weeks so that you could show disdain openly with your friends, family and even your messages. I fell hard. Maybe then you would stay SAFE.

I would never hurt you or myself or anyone. Legal advice for that? I could never do these things even with the burden I carry.

I thought I could keep up this pretense and continue to do this - continue to fail on this sword and not have you know anything - do what is asked and move me out of your life, but i can't anymore without you knowing. And you need to know what you don't. And you are the only one I will talk to. NO one else. Period. NO one.

Meet me today: I will come alone to the _____ parking lot by Binders book store. Come by yourself I will come on my scooter. And come without your recorder or I won't come at all. If I am scared of one thing I am scared of what has threatened me these years and I will never have it recorded - not right now. After these weeks I trust your spidey senses and your gut and your instincts enough to talk with you. How ironic that in all of this you are the one I turn to now. I know the public humiliation would come. I prepared for it.

If you have any small doubt or inkling and possibly know of what I am talking about then you will come. If you have any small inclination that I have taken my life - all of it - to fall on a public sword - which I have done then come. And the thing is - I will still stay on this sword for you. Willingly. But I can't shoulder this burden anymore without your knowledge. I have trusted you all these years. I will trust you with all that I have of me - of you - of my family. I take even a risk now in just writing this.

Binders. Tell me what time and I will be there. You will find a very different person than you have seen these past weeks and you will know the reasons why.

I ask for this time. You have already built your case against me. Hear me out Keryl. You can decide what to do from there. There is nothing left to lose and only the truth to gain.

The original e-mail, name hidden.

247

CHAPTER 31
It Was Time to Heal

December 22, 2015

I had the archives of the messages that arrived to me from the doctor, his fabricated family, and business colleagues, as well as from Allison and her numerous identities. I had also made numerous copies of the audio confession. For the next two weeks, I spent the majority of my day resisting the urge to release them.

Keryl versus God.

I still never win when I go against God. There is too much beauty when I honor His way.

I promised Him and I promised myself that I would only tell this story if it was to show the power of God's presence in the darkest of times. I promised I would use it to bring hope to those who become so mired in their challenges that they forget they are never alone.

Then I locked everything away safely and proceeded with the task of putting back together the pieces of my life.

Part 3

Heal to Lead
Heal to Love
Heal to Forgive

A pressing on my heart

CHAPTER 32

Always With Us

January 2016

Three weeks after Allison's confession.

For the first time in as many years as I could remember, I got sick.

I couldn't fight what was attacking my body. What churned inside of me, utter disgust and repulsion for the woman who had been so selflessly cared for by me and my loving friends and so deeply deceived us, stirred up an inner hornet's nest that impacted my health. It was flu season, and the mental, emotional, and spiritually exhaustion from living the past three weeks with the foreign energy of hatred raging inside of me, took a major toll on my normally healthy body. I was completely out of balance and my body succumbed to a flu that lasted for days.

I finally overcame it, had a very brief respite, and then out of nowhere, it returned.

I was sicker than a dog.

Somewhere deep down, I knew that this extra dosage of illness was the poison and rage I had been holding onto that eventually manifested into physical illness—*where the mind goes, the body follows..*

Thank God for the friends I had that brought me electrolyte drinks and soup.

Thank God for the friends who surrounded me with so much love and compassion during my days of rage.

Thank God for my dear friend Gary whose head I had filled with so much of this, it is any wonder how he did not go insane. Thank God for his patience and his willingness to just let me get it all out of my system.

I was still in battle about releasing the evidence, but this time the battle was not within me. As word began to slowly seep out, there were many people who insisted that everyone needed to know the truth. They felt strongly that I had an obligation to warn the new circle she had gravitated to, so that this wouldn't happen again. On the flip side, the word of God tells us to turn the other cheek. Admittedly, I was conflicted as I believed there was truth to both of these perspectives. In the end, I didn't believe that Allison needed to endure any more misery than what she inflicted upon herself with her feelings of self-loathing.

Thank God for God. It was because my constant companion still pressed on my heart, telling me 'at this moment, everything is okay,' that the true healing process began. I used everything I had learned in the seasons of my life to bring my thoughts to the now, and to say "I AM intact." *Right here, right now, I am no longer involved in that mess. I am grateful for this moment, and this day.*

Between my family, my friends, and my faith, I was able to begin purging the toxic thoughts and emotions that had accumulated during this unprecedented period of my life. I could also not deny the insistent thought that somehow, I called upon this situation subconsciously for lessons I desired to learn.

As I began to heal my emotional body and battered spirit, my physical illness finally relented for the first time in nearly two weeks. My bed and sofa were no longer the center of my universe. On my first day of feeling better, I did what I have always done— pushed my own boundaries. I made the rather unwise decision of driving to one of my favorite parks to run, hoping to get the blood pumping through my body again. Luckily when I arrived, I chose to just walk the five-mile path instead of attempt to run it. Unfortunately, I had not been wise enough to give myself enough recovery time before attempting even this down-graded feat.

It felt so good to be outside. It was January, but I bundled myself up, and it was not a blustery evening. The cool air felt good on my skin after being stuck inside with a hot fever for days. The direction I chose to go on the five-mile loop began with a downhill section, so my body wasn't doing as much work as gravity was. I felt okay. A little shaky, but okay. I was so happy just to be breathing the fresh air and listening to the sounds of nature.

As soon as I hit the first uphill portion, I began to feel winded, but that was to be expected. I slowed my pace down a bit, trying not to feel jealous of the strong joggers as they whizzed past me. The sky was beginning to hint of the darkness just around the corner, and at mile marker 1.75 I started to feel the weight of my legs and arms increase.

"Uh-oh. This might not end well," a part of me thought. But the part that remains strong during life's trials whispered "you'll be just fine." I tuned in to the stubbornness that live in the depths of our spirit and decided to aim for mile two. "Then," I told myself, "instead of finishing the loop, I will just turn around and go back the way I had come. This will shorten the trip from 5 miles to 4." So I trekked with arms and legs that felt like lead, the rest of the way to the mile marker two. By the time I got there I was so exhausted, I wanted to curl up into a ball on the cold ground and fall asleep. It felt like the flu was fully upon me again.

ALL THE LIGHT INSIDE OF YOU

Not good.

This had clearly not been one of my brighter moments—
but the part of me that got me in a situation where I overstepped
my physical limitations, had shown itself many times before. I
specifically recalled another event where my mind desired to be
in the nature that I love so much, but my body could not endure it.

When I was married to my former husband I suffered a
terrible miscarriage. It took nearly a full year to recover physically.

On the first days after returning home from the hospital,
I slept for nearly three days. My then-husband was so worried,
but the hospital personnel assured him my body just needed
enormous rest. When I finally woke up, he was there by my side
with scruffy facial hair and a look of utter worry on his face. The
worry was replaced with joy when he looked over and realized I
was awake. I looked up at him from the pillow and the first words
to come out of my mouth were, "I want to go for a run. Can you
bring my running gear?" I was almost slurring my words from
days of not speaking.

He didn't push back. Instead he simply said, "yes, of course,"
as he went to the closet to get my shoes. I felt like I was lifting a
sack of concrete as I sat up, and scooted over to the side of the
bed. I was dressed in long, comfy drawstring pants and a T-shirt.
"Can you help me put them on?" I asked him as he returned to
my side. After he helped me with my shoes he had to practically
carry me to the front door.

Dependent on him to hold me upright, we shuffled to the
mailbox at the bottom of our steep driveway. When we finally
got down there I turned to him and said, "That's good. I'm good
now. Thank you. We can go back inside." He smiled kindly as he
helped me turn around and walk back up the mountain disguised
as our driveway.

For as long as I live, I will never forget him doing that for me. He had clearly been aware that it was wiser to feed my spirit than to push against it and force me to stay in bed. From where did this awareness come? How do we inherently know there is power in healing when our spirits are lifted? Just like the scene on the streets that would come years later, where Josh had been given hope and love, I too was delivered hope and love that day— the greatest miracles, the greatest healers.

The same part of my spirit that made me think I could go for a run after being semi-conscious for three days, now had me two miles from my car as temperatures began to drop, on that night in January 2016, my first day upright after a flu. It wasn't an option for me to curl up on the frozen ground, and this time I didn't have another person to lean on.

I sat there on a retaining wall as it continued to get darker and said a simple prayer. "God, I need You. I know You know that I needed to be out here, to feel You in Your garden, but now I really need to get back to my car. I'm so tired." I said. "Please give me the strength to get to my car."

To the people who walked by, I just looked like someone resting on the wall. Conversations like this with my constant companion have always been silent, spirit-to-spirit. But my body language must have shown some serious fatigue, because at the very moment I asked God for help, a park ranger driving past slowed down and asked me if I was okay. For a moment I wanted to request a ride to my car, but something held me back. Instead I told him I was recovering from a few days of not feeling well, and that I was just resting for a bit before heading back.

"Are you sure?" he asks with some concern. I nod yes, and he leaves.

What the heck? Why did I say that? His vehicle was already completely gone from my view.

That scene then reminded me of another story: The Parable of the Flood, where a man trapped in his house during a flood sends a prayer to God asking God to save him. He has this vision in his mind of God reaching down His hand to rescue him. When the man's neighbor urges him to leave and offers him a ride in his truck, the man refuses saying, "God will save me." He does the same for a boat and then a helicopter trying to rescue him from the roof of his house where he had climbed to escape the rising floodwater. The water continued to rise, sweeping away the man who eventually drowns in the raging currents. When he reaches heaven he asks God, "Why did you let me drown? I believed with all of my heart that you would save me!" God replies, "I sent you a truck, a boat, and a helicopter. What more could I have done?"

In this case, I had been sent a park ranger.

I got up and I started shuffling the two miles back, mostly uphill.

"I have to do this, even this sick," I told myself.

I realized that during my two weeks of rage, I had stopped connecting with my constant companion because my ability to trust in what I believed to be true had impacted my new faith. It had been shaken to the core. That silent prayer had been the first time I had spoken to God in a while.

As I continued walking up the trail, I realized what I really needed. So, I dug in deep and drew strength from the Source of All, as I have done all of my life. "I need You. You're still my oxygen," I silently state as a wave of emotion suddenly washes over me.

Just then I spotted some movement in the woods to my right, and right there, less than a stone's throw away I see three beautiful deer! I am instantly filled with joy and reverence. I didn't want to move because I wanted to savor the moment without scaring them away. To my utter delight I watch as two more deer join them. There were five beautiful deer right there in front of me. I could feel a smile touch my lips for the first time in a while.

These majestic creatures didn't seem nervous that I was so close to them. Perhaps they could sense that I was totally depleted and harmless. They stayed alongside the wooded path heading in the same direction I was as I shuffled slowly along the sidewalk. They occasionally darted back into the woods, but they kept coming back out.

"This is incredible. What a gift," I thought as I walked along. They stayed with me like we were family. The joggers dwindled as the day got darker and colder. I took dozens of pictures, careful not to turn on the flash as I didn't want to scare them. I was enjoying them too much.

Time passed quickly with my enchanting deer entourage staying close, all of us seemingly embracing the beauty and wonder of nature. As I continued along the sidewalk, getting closer to the parking lot where my car was, they all darted off into the woods like they had been beckoned to return home. It was so sudden, I looked around half-expecting to see another animal or something else that unnerved them, but I saw nothing there. *Maybe they make their home in this part of the woods*, I thought, *Thank you, beautiful creatures. I think I'll try to paint you when I can find some spare time.*

After the deer vanished, I checked a nearby point marker to see how far along I had gotten. Turns out I was less than a half mile from my car. My furry woodland friends had stayed with me for an entire mile and a half. I was stunned to discover I hardly even felt the physical exertion. The last half-mile was actually easy as I had been so energized by the power of their gentle spirit and immense beauty.

When I am finally called home at the end of this life, will I reminisce this day with God? Maybe God will whisper in my ear, "Yes, My child. I sent you a park ranger and a few gentle forest creatures to assist you that night, just as I had done many other things like that for you in your life."

The thought fills me with love and hope—the greatest healers.

* * * * * * *

I recently told the story of the deer at a social gathering I attended. The listeners were captivated and enchanted with the beauty of the story. Many of them had stories that were similar. As we listened and shared with each other, the common thread within all of the stories told under the stars of the sky that night was our choice to believe what we experienced. In my case, being escorted almost all the way to my car by these beautiful, normally-skittish forest creatures at a time I needed help from above, was not just coincidence but a sign from God that we are never alone. The group stated that we needed to see more signs we come across as gifts from God.

Yes, we do.

Then, someone asked me if I knew what the symbolic meaning of deer was as a spirit animal. Admittedly, I hadn't even thought about it. There are many who attach themselves to a spirit animal, I am not one of those people. But curiosity got the better of me because the experience was so profound.

"I'll have to look that up when I get home," I thought.

Here is what I found:

*[10]Deer symbolism. When you have the deer as a spirit
animal, you are highly sensitive and have a strong intuition. By
affinity with this animal, you have the power to deal with challenges
with grace. You master the art of being both determined and
gentle in your approach. The deer totem wisdom imparts those
with a special connection with this animal with the ability to be
vigilant, move quickly, and trust their instincts to get out of the
trickiest situations.*

*When you have the deer as spirit animal, you are able to
bring gentleness and grace into every aspect of your life, even
in the most challenging moments. By inspiration from the
deer's qualities, you can achieve ambitious goals and tackle
difficult situations smoothly and with a touch of gentleness
and grace.*

I still don't attach myself to a spirit animal, but I believe that
we would all create a better world around us if we were to bring
gentleness and grace into every situation we faced. We can learn
a lot from our forest friends—that much I did attach myself to.

As the beauty of those creatures put the first light back
inside of me, the turmoil inside began to decrease. I realized that
what I called my new faith, was actually my old relationship with
my constant companion. I knew that this new thing called prayer
was what I had done all of my life, simply by communing with
this unseen presence that I had felt since childhood, and that the
connection had not broken. I knew I was not alone. I know still
that I am *never alone.* And I now know that all creatures—big
and small—are God's instruments when needed.

10 www.spiritanimal.info

I began to work on forgiveness in earnest. I began first with me. Pamela Meyer, a self-proclaimed human lie detector, says "Lying is a cooperative act. Think about it, a lie has no power whatsoever by its mere utterance. Its power emerges when someone else agrees to believe the lie." I had to forgive myself for giving the endless stream of Allison's lies their power to exist. I had to forgive myself for being the observer that made her fantasy world a reality.

I had to forgive the part of her that is so broken, it formed the person she was.

These things did not happen overnight. Nor was it a one-time-only effort. It was an every day, every minute effort. Eventually, I was able to begin to forgive Allison, although I will never condone lying or deception.

I also knew I never wanted to experience that kind of energy in my life again. I never wanted to feel that sense of imbalance or sickness in my home.

I also made a decision, as I reflected on the incredible gift of those forest escorts that reminded me at that moment how beautiful God's animal creatures are. Animals love unconditionally. Dog owners can attest to the well-known, and heartwarming fact, that a dog who loves his owner will greet him or her like the greatest thing has just walked in the door, each and every time it sees its owner. So too is God's love unconditional.

I can reflect on the past five decades, and see all the times I was guided by God, throughout all of the years of my life since childhood. The perfection of God is in His love. We are forgiven for the endless number of things we do imperfectly, on a daily basis.

I knew that moment that my desire to honor that love, would be the catalyst for my own healing. Allison was out of my life. The greatest thing I could do at that moment was pray she finds the help she needs, keep myself rooted in the now, and draw on the many lessons brought forth from the experience.

For longer than a mile, these gentle forest creatures and their friends provided the energy boost I needed to get back to my car.

CHAPTER 33

His Mysterious Ways

An atheist looks around and says, "I see no evidence of God." A believer looks around and says, "ALL I see is evidence of God."

Unknown

Plucked from the news in 2016

In early 2016, media outlets broadcast a story about a young mother from Utah and her 18 month-old baby whose car careened off the road into a river. The car was partially submerged for fourteen hours before rescue units eventually arrived at the scene. Four first responders made their way down to the car and all they could see at first was the mother. As they got closer, the rescue team heard the young mother calling to them to help her baby. *A baby?* They had no idea there was a baby in the car.

Actual video footage shows these men yelling back to the mother telling her they were doing everything they could to help. But when they were finally able to enter the vehicle, they soon realized the mother was deceased. They were extremely perplexed. What did they hear? Could it really have been her voice they heard?

The baby was rescued, and the heroic men who saved her all said they believed someone was keeping watch over the baby to save her life.

The world reacted as it always does, many believing it was nothing more than the overactive imagination of the first responders. Sadly, many in our society dismiss the possibility of a miracle quite easily

Fortunately, not everyone chose to doubt. Many were equally certain it was the voice of a mother whose love transcended dimensions to save her child. Others believed it was the voice of God's angels. Personally, I know there is nothing stronger than love, and believe that love has the power to transcend our physical dimension.

We have free will and can choose our responses, yet I will never understand why one would choose to doubt something so beautiful and wonderful simply because it cannot be explained

People are going to do what they do. When it comes to anything outside our physical world, we are a society divided. We take a diverse and colorful world full of every shape you can imagine, and we try to fit it into a one-color, one shape box. When the circle refuses to think and act like a square, we judge, we condemn, and we separate. Life is a canvas, God is the artist, and I think He would not be the God He is if He created a one-dimensional, one-color, fully revelatory world that lacked mystery.

God is mysterious, likewise so is His world. What a gift that is. There is no denying that there are many mysteries in this world that cannot be scientifically explained and remain beyond human comprehension. There are countless numbers of highly intelligent people who claim to have received transcendental messages in the form of dreams, visions, and intuition,

We all can connect and receive messages from Divine Source in many ways as depicted in stories going back to ancient times. That has not changed one bit since then. We are still given the same choice when it occurs—believe or don't believe. I believe. With all my heart, I do. I conduct my life following my own beliefs.

Although I have never felt my purpose in life is to convert a non-believer to a believer, I will never deny that there is enormous joy in watching belief wash over a person when it happens.

CHAPTER 34

Everett's Mother

Spring 2016
Four months before I met Everett

Everett's mother is a three-dimensional example of the word jovial. Kindness and goodness emanate from her like rays of sunshine. She storehouses these in such abundance that everyone who meets her feels them, every time she is near. Even her speaking voice is upbeat and musical. Just a few words from her and your spirits are lifted.

By the Spring of 2016, I had taken the position of Executive Director for a struggling homeless shelter for men in Atlanta. I desired to continue my near-lifelong quest to uncover the deeply hidden or frequently ignored light I know is inside all of us—the same light I discovered as a teenager when I purchased that meal for the homeless man who touched my soul. I will never forget the impact he had on me, and I made it my silent mission to find it in each man who walked through the doors of the shelter. Some of the men revealed their light with ease, while others made me work to find it. But I would say the percentage of men who eventually discovered the Divinity inside of them was in the high nineties.

I came to love these men and I desperately wanted them to discover the potential they had inside of them, waiting to be acknowledged. I just wanted them to see how beautiful they were despite their external circumstances, and to help them dispose of old habits and negative thinking that was not serving them. I was confident in how powerful they could be with positive thinking and intent.

Everett's mother is active in nonprofit organizations and our paths crossed at the shelter. We clicked immediately.

● ● ● ● ● ● ●

Before I continue with this part of the story, let me tell you about a special place in Atlanta called Stone Mountain.

Stone Mountain is often called the world's largest piece of exposed granite. Geologists say that it is actually quartz-monzonite, which is often mistaken for granite. Regardless, even the Stone Mountain website refers to it as the largest piece of exposed granite. Whatever the case, no one can dispute its size. The circumference of the rock is 5 miles at the base, and to hike to the top you will climb 1.25 miles at an elevation of 1,686 feet.

It's really big—in fact, it's bigger than Mount Rushmore, and can be seen for miles and miles.

However, the most remarkable thing about this mammoth rock is that the majority of it is hidden beneath the ground. Only one-third of its actual surface area is exposed. It is estimated to extend 7-9 miles down, with a portion of it reaching as far as the neighboring state of North Carolina.

So where am I going with this?

• • • • • • •

Back to Everett's mom.

Four years had passed since I had first brought Allison, the supposed cancer patient, into my home, and three years since I finally asked her to leave. I no longer wanted her in my life. On this spring day in 2016, four months after learning the truth about her, I sat in my office with the exquisite soul that is Everett's mother and for the first time in many months, I found myself unexpectedly sharing a small part of my spiritual journey with her, including finding myself in that empty church. However, like Stone Mountain, I knew that the bulk of Allison's story would remain hidden underground.

Nothing had changed since childhood, my choice to listen to the voice within had little to do with my own desires and everything to do with the love I have for what I now understood was God. My choosing to tell her this small part of my story was in no way random, rather it was directly because that inner-voice once again pressed on my heart to do so. I tried with futility, to over-ride that voice, but as always, I could not.

I have never forgotten since I had begun to hear my inner voice, that when I do receive its instruction, I may not immediately understand the why behind it, but that somehow, its purpose will eventually reveal itself.

This moment with Everett's mom was no exception. When I acquiesced and shared a bit of my story to her in April of 2016, I could not have known that it would be the reason she would come to me four months later in tears over what was happening regarding the health of her young son and his debilitating migraines.

And I could never have known the beauty of the experience that was in store for all of us, or just how special Everett was.

However, the incredible force behind the entire universe, our God, knows all, and is endlessly at work pressing on us to listen for His whisper—and to trust. We don't have the ability to see past today, but we have eternal guidance from a Source who does. To have a connection to this infinite intelligence is an immeasurable gift.

We are wise to listen. Intuition is spiritual intelligence. When that intuition is steeped in love, and honored, it can move mountains.

It is a question that is worth repeating: Have you thought about how many times you might have heard your inner voice tell you to do something that made no sense to you at the time? Maybe even something you desperately didn't want to do? Do we get in the way of the will of the Divine?

As I sat in my office telling Everett's mother things I didn't speak of openly, I would not know it was a question whose answer, for me, was a short four months away.

CHAPTER 35

The Flame of Hope

August 2016

The day after meeting eight-year-old Everett for the first time, he returned to my city apartment with his mother. He was more relaxed on this day than he had been the previous day. There was no apparent sign of a headache, nor did his arm hurt where the IV had been inserted. His mother and I happily chose not to mention the pain he had experienced the day before.

I sat down, eye level with the sweet boy and said, "Everett, during my quiet time with God this morning, I felt a pressing on my heart to tell you about the candle you see burning here." As I pointed to the soft light glowing inside the lantern he whipped his head around, looking at his mother with wide eyes. She smiled at him and with her musical voice, said, "Oh my goodness, Everett. *This is something,*" placing heavy emphasis on the last three words.

I was really curious. "What is something?" I asked.

It was then that she told me how Everett had absolutely insisted they needed to get a candle for their house just like the one in mine.

Incredible.

I have noticed something, when one starts to recognize the ways in which God speaks to them, they begin to see that there is very little about God that is subtle. God's messages are usually fairly blatant.

To think that it was pressed on Everett's heart that there was something about this candle that he needed to know goes beyond a simple intuition. To dissect this is to understand something quite beautiful—that the same Divine Energy that fuels the evolution of galaxies, created the world and everything in it, knows that a little flame burns in Its honor inside an Atlanta apartment which is hardly a blip on the screen when compared to the massive size of the universe. The Divine knowledge is then passed on to an eight-year-old boy, that this little flame will bring comfort to him in the same way it does to the one who keeps it burning.

There is indescribable beauty in that and it generates the understanding, once again, that we are never alone.

I continued my conversation with Everett and was very careful with my words. He was at that critical age where if he were to share too much of what I was saying with friends who don't have the level of discernment he has, he might face being ridiculed. It would be a travesty for such a special child to lose his spiritual connection before it has a chance to really take hold.

I proceed with caution.

"Everett, have you ever gotten mad at your mom? Maybe you wanted something from her and she wouldn't give it to you? Or maybe she asked you to do something you didn't want to do?" He thinks for just a moment, and replies, "Not so often."

"Good answer," I say, "because 'not so often' is the same answer I get when I ask myself if I ever get mad at God. But sometimes I do, Everett. Sometimes I can feel God pressing on my heart to do something I don't think I'm prepared to do." I recall in my mind the pressing to tell his mother about my belief in supplementing medical treatment with energy healing four months earlier. I continue, "And sometimes I want something to happen that I believe God can make happen and He doesn't." He is listening intently.

"It doesn't happen very often, but it does happen every once in a while. When you get mad at your mom, you still love her, and you know she still loves you, right?" He nods his head vigorously. "It is the same with me and God. Sometimes I get upset with God, but I still love Him —and I have felt the love of God since waaayyyy back when I was a little girl, younger than you are now. Even before I knew that what I was feeling was the energy of God."

I watch to make sure he understands, then go on to tell him, "This is a very special candle. It burns in my home to honor God as the source of all the love that fills my house. I also keep it lit to demonstrate my faith in God." I tell Everett that I had been doing this for many years and I start a new candle right when the one that is burning is preparing to burn out.

"Actually, Everett, there was one day that I stood in front of this candle, watching it get very close to burning out, but I didn't prepare a new one. It was a day that I could just not make peace with the things I knew God wanted me to do. I was very tired, and I simply could not bring myself to light the next candle before the other burned out. So, I said out loud to God, 'If you want this candle lit, come light it Yourself.'"

I smiled at Everett. "Can you imagine that? Can you imagine me telling God to come light this candle Himself? Stomping my feet and acting like a child? Can you imagine our All Mighty and All-Powerful God actually coming to my home to light my candle?" He smiled at the question and I continued, "What do you think we would see? Would we see the lighter floating over to the candle? Would the candle just go POOF and light itself?" We laughed together for a moment, and then I got serious again. "But I really meant what I said. I spoke those words only to God at first and to no one else. That night my dear friend and neighbor came over. Her name is Breanne and she loves my candle. She noticed that it was not lit and asked me why. I told her what I told God, 'I am not lighting it. If God wants it lit, He can come light it Himself.'

For a moment, I am in my mind and no longer with Everett. I am seeing that night in my head as if it was a scene that was unfolding in the present moment. Breanne is sitting on the sofa to the right of me. The darkened candle is on the top of the bookshelf to her right. I had told her that I felt like I'd been pulled out of my old life and put in this new one, and I no longer knew what I was supposed to be doing or what God was trying to show me. I confessed, that at that moment, I was feeling very, *very* tired. If I was in the throes of lessons, I didn't want them anymore. She is surprised to hear my words, and it makes her a little bit sad. In her gentle, beautiful way, she asks me if I wanted her to light it for me. Returning her gentleness, I said "No, it doesn't work that way."

I look at my cherished friend and remember how incredibly fortunate I am to have the people in my life that I have. I love my friends.

I continue to remember the events of that evening. Even though it hurt my heart to see the candle dark, I was stubborn and refused to light it. I foolishly held my ground.

Two days later, I was coming home from a long day of meeting with clients, followed by volunteering at a long-term disability facility, and then helping a young man stranded in the torrential rain. Just like my teen years, when I spotted this drenched man, my inner voice spoke up and said 'Put him in your car and help him reach his destination. You are safe.' I did as my inner-voice instructed, and was indeed safe. Subsequently, now so was this young man, who as it turns out, was the sole provider for a brother who was only a few years younger than him.

When I finally walked into my apartment two hours later than expected, something immediately felt different. You know those movie scenes where someone walks into an apartment and the eerie music starts to play, telling you that something is not right, something is going to happen? There was no music but it felt like I was walking into a scene out of a movie. I cautiously step inside and look around. Every little thing looks in place. I wonder if perhaps the building owner had come while I was gone, which would have been unusual. He had a policy of notifying his tenants when a service call was going to take place and he was historically good at following that policy.

There was no denying the energy shift. It was not subtle at all.

Because everything was in place, I forced myself to relax, and after a few minutes, walked over to the television to listen to news while I prepared dinner. It was then I immediately noticed that the candle was no longer where it usually sits on the top bookshelf. The space once reserved for it was completely empty. My candle that honors God was *gone*! I stood for a moment and stared at the empty space on the bookshelf in mild shock.

Only one person had a key to my place besides me, Breanne. I called her and asked if she might have come over and moved my candle for some reason. She reminded me that she was in

Philadelphia at a writing conference, and then asks "Why?" I
told her my candle was missing.

I hung up the phone, completely and utterly perplexed.

Yet, given all that I have experienced throughout my life,
unexplainable things were becoming the new normal. I no
longer tried to explain certain peculiar things that just seem to
happen in my life. Still, I hunted for that candle in all the places
that I might have absentmindedly moved it, and did not find it.
Plopping on the sofa across from the bookshelf, I accepted the
fact that it was gone.

What more could I do?

That night I proceeded to prepare several meals for the
week, trying to get my mind off the missing candle. But I found
myself tracing and retracing my steps. No matter how things
played out in my mind, the candle should have been where I left
it. Not only was I puzzled, but I was a little irked that someone
might have been in my home.

Much later that evening, I retreated to my bedroom upstairs.

When I got up there, I was immediately hit by an electrical
field that stopped me dead in my tracks! The energy was thick
and palpable, and seemed to be contained to my room. It was
the same beautiful Presence that had surrounded me as a child,
multiplied a million times. And it filled me with so much love
that tears uncontrollably streamed down my face. I wasn't even
aware until I felt one drip, so riveted was I to what engulfed me
in that energy. It was a familiar presence that my soul responded
to like a child returning home.

I wanted to stay engulfed in this feeling forever.

I looked over at the window seat from across the room,
and there was my candle, burning in all its glory. It was almost
too much for my heart to take.

Somewhere deep inside were the questions, "Why is this happening?" and "Why is this happening to me?" When I ask that latter question, it is not to insinuate that there is something about me that stands above all others. No. I ask that question because if I could find the answer, I would reveal its secret to the world, so everyone could experience the utter magnificence of this. And so that those who are also experiencing these incredible moments, would share it, thus creating a wider sense of wonder and love for the Divine Energy, the relentlessly beautiful love of God.

Sitting beside the candle were two items. On the left sat a little plaque that I had actually not even unpacked since moving into my in-town apartment. How in the world did it get there? "You never know how strong you can be until being strong is your only option," it read. To the right of the candle I found my book, *Love Poems for God,* with a page marked by a sliver of paper with a heart on it. The poem on that page read:

WHEN SOMEONE I LOVE IS NEAR

I know the vows the sun and the moon took;
they are in love
but they don't touch.
But why should I not let My face become
lit before this earth
when someone I cherish is near?
St. Catherine of Siena

Although the details of that night are burned in my memory, I only shared a high-level with Everett, telling him about leaving the apartment and finding the candle lit upstairs. I turn to the wide-eyed eight-year-old next to me. "I don't know how it happened, Everett, but I know somehow, I was supposed to understand that my request had been heard and answered by a God who loves us, and is with us always. I believe that God knew I needed to feel His love so very much at this time. Even if someone came in to light my candle, I know that no human being could have created that energy that was felt upstairs in my room. I believe that was God's way of saying '*Thank you for letting Me use you to spread My love. I know it's been hard but I am always with you.*'"

Just like the story of the mother whose car careened into the ravine, I know there will be many people who read this and will choose to think it is ridiculous, maybe even impossible, but I stopped listening long ago to the doubters and the skeptics.

He has the power to do whatever He wants at any time He wishes.

I say to Everett, "It is as He teaches us in his word "Everything is possible for one who believes."" (Mark 9:23)

. . . .

So much time has passed since that event occurred, and I still marvel that it happened. The memory of that energetic presence still washes over me from time to time. I think again, *even if someone had broken into my apartment to light the candle, there is still no way that the energy field could have been placed by them.* It makes me think about how God knows our thoughts even before we have them. I believe his energy was present in the room to say to me, "Child. Believe that I AM here."

Can we even begin to fathom the mysteries of God?

We can study His words and abide by His laws, but not one soul can say they fully understand how, why, and in what way God will choose to reveal the awesome wonder of His love. But I do believe the greatest thing we can teach our little ones is the miracle of God's unwavering love and presence in our lives.

CHAPTER 36
Kassie's Story

April 2016

Tara was a woman I met in 2014. Our paths crossed through a business transaction and we enjoyed each other's company well enough to promise to stay in touch long after our business dealings were completed. We kept that promise through the social mediums, but had not seen each other in person.

On a Friday afternoon in April 2016, I felt a familiar pressing on my heart from my inner-voice, "Tell the story of healing to the men [in the shelter where I held the role of Executive Director]." My reaction at the time was, "No way." As much as I strived to abide by the loving commands of this voice, energy healing was very private to me. Absolutely not. Besides, I had not felt the pull to engage in energy healing since Josh.

On that very same April day, located hours away on the Georgia coast, I popped into Tara's mind while she was at the beach with her family and her life partner, Kassie.

Kassie had been having health problems. She was finding herself in constant pain with back problems, and the traditional treatment was not fully working. The thought had entered Tara's mind that Kassie should meet me, as they both believe in supplementing traditional medicine with energy work. Tara grappled for a while with the idea of bringing up my energy work because she was afraid it might give Kassie false hope regarding her condition. As she watched her nephew on his surfboard in the waves, she decided to leave it to fate. "If he catches the best wave ever, I will make the introduction," she thought, mildly amusing herself. A coin toss to Heaven.

A memory from my teen-aged years came flooding back to me: I was on the fence about whether or not I should break up with a particular boy. We had been experiencing a little bit of turbulence in our relationship, and lacked the maturity to work things out properly. So, we decided to execute our own coin toss to Heaven. One of our favorite things to do together was watch the sun as it set for the night. We agreed that evening that if the sunset was beautiful, we would stay together. If it wasn't, we'd say goodbye.

Tara watched her nephew in anticipation, but as wave after wave rolled by it became clear he wasn't going to catch anything. Tara eventually retreated to the beach house.

Meanwhile, back in Atlanta, by the end of the night I had finally lost the stare-down with God. Okay. I will talk to the men. We held our community meetings on Monday evenings, which was a few days away. It was an opportunity for the men and the staff to gather round and share whatever was on their hearts in an open forum. We celebrated wins and shared our grievances. Sometimes I would bring in a guest speaker to help inspire the men. To oblige my inner voice, I decided for the next meeting that I would be the one talking to them. I would talk about the power we all have available to us as children of God.

Around the same time, Tara's excited nephew runs into the beach house and exclaims, "Aunt Tara! You missed it! I just caught the best wave ever!"

●　●　●　●　●　●　●

Monday evening came, and I stood before the circle of men as their guest speaker. "Forget that I am your Director," I told them, "No bantering like we usually do. No comments or questions until I am finished." I proceeded for the next thirty minutes to tell them my life story. I told them about my constant companion that remained unidentified for years. I told them about the homeless man who gave me the pendant. I told them about discovering the ability to draw upon and tap into the energy of light and love, helping me thwart illness and keep the energy in my home balanced, positive, and loving. I told them the stories of Allison, Diane, Josh, and the others before them. I shared the mysterious experience involving my vanishing bike. I used all these experiences as examples of how each and every one of us holds the same divine light inside and that it doesn't matter what their childhoods were like, or what mistakes they've made along the way. They have the exact same ability to draw upon a divine, endless source of strength, love, and grace.

After my lecture the men were silent and wide-eyed. Some asked me to please write a book. Others, a movie. How I loved these men, who were always moved by matters of the spirit.

According to the on-site shelter manager, they remained very quiet and reflective that evening. Many of them pulled out books and read, or wrote in their journals before going to sleep. It is amazing what a little bit of hope can do. It seems that evening, God whispered to these souls in need of His grace.

As I drove home after our meeting, recalling details and moments from the evening, feeling so filled with love for our Divine God, I noticed a voice-mail from Tara on my cellphone. It had been two years almost to the day since I spoke to her last, and assumed it was a business check-in call. I was tired, my mind was filled with the thoughts of the evening, and I came very close to not playing the voice-mail that night. However, my inner voice pressed strongly, *"Listen to the message."*

"Hi, it's Tara," played through the speaker in her effusive, exuberant voice. "Listen, I don't know if you are still doing energy work, but there is someone I would like to bring to you."

I was not expecting that message. I was stunned by both the message and the timing. It took me five days and a lot of prayerful meditation to finally return her call.

• • • • • • •

Three weeks later, Kassie made her way, slowly, gingerly, up the stairs to my in-town apartment with Tara at her side. I liked her from the moment we were introduced, and I especially liked the two of them together. We talked for a full hour. Kassie was open, ready, and receptive to supplementing her current medical treatment with an energy session on that same day.

When a person is skeptical, there is no point in moving forward. There is an agreement made between the energy recipient and the life force energy that is God. Our success is based on the belief that our intentions will manifest. As was the case with every person before Kassie, I knew my role was simply to be a willing instrument and lend my hands and heart to the process. We are all called to be instruments at different times, in different ways, each with the gifts we have been given in this lifetime. The gifts we choose to receive and access.

We finally begin our work. I quietly focused my intention on getting healthy energy flowing in order to open Kassie's channels. I could soon feel her body begin to relax more deeply. I had refined my ability to sense the Human Energy Field surrounding the body over the years, and eventually had come to understand the meaning of many of the sensations I would feel in my hands when I tuned into a person's energy field. A cold sensation lets me know where a body's energy is stuck and not flowing properly. Tingling (like when your hand falls asleep) alerts me to where the body is battling something such as inflammation or infection, while a needle sensation indicates pain. I must stress, however, that I would never, ever diagnose anyone's medical condition. That is strictly for medical professionals, and I always encouraged those who came to me to be sure to also seek and heed the advice of their doctors. My role was simply to help their energy to flow as it should by reopening and balancing their energetic channels, increasing the body's natural ability to heal.

I could feel the fluctuation in Kassie's energy field, or aura. Certain areas were cold where the energy was blocked, and others tingled, like the energy channels were fractured. At one point, I saw movement on her shirt near the right shoulder, like she had a muscle spasm in that spot. I made note of the spasm. As I did so, it happened a second time, only not so severe. I wondered what was going on with her shoulder, because I could feel the energy flowing there with no impediments. After 20 minutes, the energy in all areas of her body was flowing with no cold or tingling spots. I sent out into God's universe one final prayer of gratitude, and we were finished.

I went downstairs to visit with Tara, telling Kassie to come down whenever she was ready.

As the three of us came together after the session, we talked about what each of us could feel from our own unique perspectives. Kassie said she felt like there was something gently holding her down on the bed, and described a feeling of relaxation like she had not felt in a long time. "Then, on my shoulder..." she began before I interrupted. "Oh yes. I saw your sleeve move two times, with what looked like muscle spasms. I meant to ask what was going on with that shoulder." She turned to me and said, "That wasn't a spasm. I felt something that felt like a hand touch my shoulder and my entire body filled with such peace, I never wanted it to end. When the hand released me, I mentally called it back. I wanted it back. I felt a second, lighter touch and then it lifted away."

I sat there stunned.

After they left I still sat in utter amazement for well over an hour, and absorbed what I heard and witnessed. To see her shirt move and to hear her describe feeling something touch her shoulder was as close to seeing with my physical eyes the incredible and wondrous beauty of God's Hand as I have ever gotten. I felt the gift of love from this incredible Source in yet another way. This is the same love I would talk to Everett about four months from that April, not knowing he would use the exact same words to express how he felt when he would say, "I never wanted it to end."

Kassie's pain diminished greatly after the energy healing session. The two women invited me to dinner one night where Kassie presented me with a beautiful ring designed and crafted by her. A hobby she allows herself to indulge in periodically. Incredibly, she chose a stone that was my favorite color and sized the ring perfectly to my finger. God definitely works in big ways and small.

• • • • • • •

By the way, would you like to know what happened with my own coin toss to Heaven when I was young and in love? We had promised each other that if the sunset was beautiful, we would stay together, and if not, we would break up.

In the Western part of the United States, the sunsets are always beautiful. However, on this particular night, it was fairly drab. In fact, there was nothing about it that was beautiful at all. Yet, we both looked at it for a while, then we looked at each other. As we both turned our faces back toward the setting sun we agreed it was the most exquisite sunset we had ever seen in our lives.

We are two for two on those coin tosses to Heaven.

CHAPTER 37

The Church Leader

I had no intention of going to church on that particular Sunday morning in February 2017. I had finally found a church I loved in Atlanta, where I really enjoyed attending service, but that morning I had already spent two hours communing with God and meditating, so I didn't feel the need to additionally attend a formal service. Plus, I had errands I needed to run.

I threw on jeans, short boots, a long sweater and a fashion scarf, and headed out the door. It was ten minutes 'til eleven as I drove past a church on my right. I had never noticed it before, but all of a sudden I found my car parked in a spot in the church parking lot.

I walked in.

The first congregation members I met were instantly warm and welcoming to me, a newcomer in their midst. They introduced me around to others and shared stories about their experiences at the church as we waited for the service to begin. I loved the energy of the place and even wondered if I might like it better than the church I was currently attending.

The Pastor was powerful with his messaging. He spoke of the importance of being bold in our faith and being at the ready with the armor of God (Love, Life) against doubt and fear. When things seem hopeless, God is our hope. When we must endure hardship, God is our strength. If we are walking a path that leads to God, there will always be challenges to overcome, but through God, we can overcome anything. God is limitless and there is nothing too big for our Creator.

He was so right! Hadn't I learned that firsthand? I loved his message. What I loved most was how he took the messages found in scripture and related them to modern day. Too often I would feel that a church sermon was more of a history lesson. This was really different. *Hm, Maybe I will come back,* I thought.

A few days later, I found myself at the church again.

The Pastor asked if I would like some water. "No thank you," I said as we settled into the conference room where the administrative offices are, and began with some chit chat.

Before too long I decided to take things deeper. "May I ask you a question?" I said

"Of course," He said with a nod and a smile.

"Does your church believe in or offer to its members the kind of healing Jesus teaches about in the Bible?"

"No, we don't offer healing," he said almost dismissively.

"Why not?"

"I don't know. I suppose modern medicine has taken over and society believes less and less in that kind of healing."

I feel a sadness in my heart. This was the same man who stood in front of his congregation and spoke of being bold in our faith?

"I see." I said. Although I really didn't see. What does it really mean to have boldness in faith? I thought to myself of the words of Jesus who encouraged us to exceed our limitations and do greater works.

I thought again of how we wait on God—and God waits on us.

It's not enough to merely talk or learn about the enormity of our potentiality, and it's certainly not enough to learn the stories and history of others who have overcome their limitations. We must step into that role ourselves, experientially, with the kind of conviction that Jesus had when he walked among the people of Earth.

We must find faith to overcome our limitations.

CHAPTER 38

Everett's Story

August 2016

The day after meeting Everett for the first time

"I am ready when you are," I say to Everett.

Everett's mother permitted me to be in a room with just him—upon his request. It was something we had spoken about the day before. Given his age, I felt it was appropriate for me to give his mother the option to be in the room with us. I wasn't sure how that was going to work. Not since Mitchell had someone been in the room, and I knew that Mitchell had no skepticism in his heart.

"I feel like it's supposed to be just us," Everett had said. His inner voice was powerful. In my quiet, I had the same thought. Special child.

I had explained earlier what we would do. "I am only going to touch you one time, Everett. I will put one hand on your heart and one hand on your forehead where we have our strongest pull—heart and head. After that, you will not feel anything at all, except hopefully relaxed.

"What you must do is to focus your mind and visualize God's light coming to you. Remember how I taught you to think of the pain from your headache like a shadow? Well, I want you to see God's light in your mind, filling your body so completely that it covers the shadows until they disappear." Just as I did the day before, I spoke at his level and I was very careful not to use words he might carry to his schoolmates and risk being taunted. "Push the shadow into the light until you cannot see the shadow anymore and believe that the light and love of God is with us just as we are promised it always is.

"My job will be to let my hands be a channel for that light." I pause. "Everett, I want you to know that God's energy is so powerful, my hands are not needed. Your trust and faith can do this alone, but God loves to use His children because it helps us get closer to Him.

"Do you understand?" I ask gently before continuing. "And He needs my mouth to teach you what we have learned since we met."

He understands and he is ready.

"Are you comfortable? I ask him.

"Yes."

I place an eye mask over his eyes to relax him and we begin.

The pressing on my heart is instant as I stand before this little boy who has given complete faith to this day. A child. Still innocent and not jaded. Still trusting and not skeptical. The enormity of the oneness I feel with this child cannot be overstated. I think of Dr. Bolte-Taylor.

The incoming message that presses on my heart translates to words and comes packaged with such an overwhelming surge of love, it's as though I have been doused with stardust. It says. "He is like you. He has the same gifts you have embraced."

The message, the love it spawns, that moment when you know you cannot control the tears that spring. *Careful, careful... you will sniffle and Everett will know,* I caution myself.

But this dousing of love from God is relentless, and the pressing on my heart continues, "I will use him to do My work. He is Mine."

I am right where I am supposed to be.

I turn my hands over to this incredible life force with complete abandonment of doubt and a total faith. I am so honored to be right here. I am so honored to be so trusted, to be the channel of God's miracles. I am so grateful.

It's the same feeling I have had since that first session where I sat next to Mitchell.

I love the feeling of being a direct channel for love. Why do I ever hesitate? The journey that brought me here was paved with a faith that transcended human understanding, every step of the way — trials, storms, and pain. And yet here I am—a willing instrument who did not turn her back on the God of all.

I would do it all over again if I had the choice.

I turn to this trusting, completely relaxed child and simply remove myself from the equation. More specifically, I remove the human limitations from my mind and let my spirit reign.

I am given the sensory of the pain in Everett's head. I, just like the doctors, don't know the source—but that is not necessary for me. What is necessary is to rebalance the energy until I can no longer feel a difference in the areas that surrounds his head than I do around the parts of him that are pain-free. To get the energy of health flowing unimpeded.

But the energy would not balance. I would feel the warmth of flow for a while, then it would return to tingling and cold. Over and over.

Stubborn.

What was I not doing? Was it Everett?

I quietly re-center myself and reconnect to the unseen. I feel the pressing on my heart, "Remove what is in there first-- pull what is there before putting what is needed."

What? I had never heard that thought before. Pull out before putting in. This was a first.

I contemplate and process what just pressed on my heart.

Nothing breaks a spirit like relentless and perpetual pain; and there's no faster way to lose faith and hope than to be in constant pain that is not diagnosable. The absence of hope is despair. Yes, it's time to pull out what is unwanted and refill with the purest source of healing in the universe.

It takes twenty full minutes before I feel the rebalancing. I think those twenty minutes were *my* lessons, and *my* chance to fully reconnect to a gift that was revealed to me that I had not been using. I think those twenty minutes healed me as much as they did anything else in that they reminded me to fully remove all that was not needed within me as well.

Brilliant God. Always the Healer.

I quietly said to the resting child "We're done. Come downstairs when you are ready." I then bolted downstairs to have a private moment with his mother to share the beautiful messages I received about this little boy whom I already knew was special. But Everett doesn't give us any private moments. He made his way downstairs right on my heels.

"I'll call you," I said to his mother. I remind Everett that he has everything already inside of him to keep his headaches away and we say goodbye.

CHAPTER 39

The Mother Warrior

While Everett's mother waited downstairs in my apartment where Everett and I would be having our session, she reached for the Bible I had placed earlier on the table in front of her, opening it to a random page.

Ephesians 6: 16-18. *In addition to all this, take up the shield of faith, with which you can extinguish all the flaming arrows of the evil one. [17]And take the helmet of salvation and the sword of the Spirit, which is the word of God. [18]Pray in the Spirit at all times, with every kind of prayer and petition. To this end, stay alert with all perseverance in your prayers for all the saints....*

At the time, Everett's mother thought nothing of it.

After the session, they went home.

Almost as soon as they leave, I sent her a text message prefaced boldly with, For your eyes only. It said, "Please do something for me and I know it will sound strange. Please take some oil and with mindful intention, ask for it to be blessed. Then use the oil to anoint the tops of the doorways and windows in your home. It might feel awkward, but please do it to seal your home with love."

She agreed that it would feel really awkward, as she had never done that before, but said she would. Faith that transcends human understanding.

I received a text from her later on that day. It read, "He is at zero for pain. He said it was like something was trying to stop him from entering the room while he was walking up the stairs. Then when you started your work, he felt hands on his head and heart and a jolt of lightning down his spine. He said the healing felt so good that he never wanted it to end. He must be able to feel energy like you can."

I stopped at that line. I had not yet told her about the messages that pressed on my heart, that said "He is like you." I had not had the time. Her text continued, "He said it was like Christmas and his birthday all in one it felt so good. Thank you so very much, Keryl!"

Don't thank me, I thought to myself.

I reread her text several times, relishing its many wonderful and inspiring messages.

I love how my home feels, even hours after an energy session.

Back at home, Everett went to work immediately on his insistence that they must have a candle like mine. This time his effort was directed as his father. So, the two embark on a quest to find one that would satisfy this determined young man. Meanwhile, Everett's mother was at home alone. Deep in thought, she reached for her Bible as she sat back in her favorite chair and opened it to a random page.

Ephesians 6: 16-18. *In addition to all this, take up the shield of faith, with which you can extinguish all the flaming arrows of the evil one. [17]And take the helmet of salvation and the sword of the Spirit, which is the word of God. [18]Pray in the*

Spirit at all times, with every kind of prayer and petition. To this end, stay alert with all perseverance in your prayers for all the saints....

The very same scripture she randomly turned to as she waited in my home.

She sits up straighter in her chair, staring at the book in her hands. This time she doesn't just think nothing of it. She says aloud to the empty room, "OK, God. I get it. I am supposed to protect him."

With this, she remembers my text message, and while no one else was home, she anointed the doorways and windows as I had instructed her. Just as I had expected, she did feel uncomfortable doing it. It was such an unfamiliar feeling and awkward action for her, particularly as it was not something she had ever considered doing before. Yet, she trusted in what she felt called to do.

Everett and his father returned home. Full of excitement, Everett wants to show his mother the candle they found. He ran inside and stopped dead in his tracks. Standing still, he looked around the living room and with wide eyes, he says, "Mom, it feels safe in here."

His mother was alarmed. "What do you mean it feels safe?"

He responded, "Remember how I always told you and dad it doesn't feel safe in here? It feels safe now."

Her mind is blown. Or maybe it's that her pineal gland is activated. Maybe it's both.

Whichever it is, another set of eyes have been opened to the world we cannot see.

CHAPTER 40
One with God

June 2017 | Age 50

Somehow, I knew the powerful *being* of shimmering, radiant light standing atop the high mountain in the distance was me, even without being able to discern a gender. The luminescent figure was tall and strong, glowing like millions of tiny stars had combined to form a unified whole—joyful to be in that moment, fulfilling their purpose of embodying and fortifying this awesome presence. It exuded a tranquility that seemed to swirl about with unbridled power and wisdom as it stared out into the vast and magnificent beauty of the universe. I could see exactly what it saw—an endless canvas of color and infinite glory; the likes of which cannot be compared to anything on Earth. I was utterly captivated and could not turn my eyes away. This being appeared to be silently sourcing from the All That Is, Was, and Ever Shall Be, with a reverent whisper, "I am one with You because of You—and I honor You."

Spirit to spirit.

Glory to glory.

Its countenance was awe of that with which it communed, as though it was experiencing this Divine Source for the first time and had not done so continually since the start of its own existence.

As it fueled, I fueled.

I could not see my own physical body as I watched this radiant being that was also me. It was as if I had been given special lenses to peer into another dimension that we cannot currently see.

From behind me, to the left of me, to the right of me, and above me, I felt engulfed by an unseen presence, wrapped in love, serenity, and the feeling of total rest. *Bliss.* There was a true sense of belonging, of being home, of perfect love. *Let me stay in this moment forever,* my heart pleaded. Everything about it felt complete as it swaddled me like a baby in a blanket that had no beginning and no end.

It communicated to me by pressing on my heart. I was inherently able to understand the messages I was being sent. "Look over there, child," I was instructed, indicating the shimmering figure in the distance, "That is who you are. It is who you are *in Me.* It is your *true* essence." The messages hit my spirit like sound waves do an ear drum, reverberated in my heart, and became an inherent understanding that required no audible words. I felt such immense love in them—pure and selfless. The messages continued, "Now, go forth. Know that you are well, and you are loved."

The next morning, I woke feeling completely replenished and refueled. A feeling that, to this day as I write these words, has not faded. The memory and the messages are forever stamped in my heart.

●　●　●　●　●　●　●

This was the incredible gift I received when I called upon God for the extra strength I needed to get through the nightmare and horror of the situation that had been thrust upon me days earlier when my world went dark.

Holding the phone to my ear even after the call ended, I tried to make sense of the words still ringing in them. I had just been informed that my 22 year-old daughter was the victim of a crime. The moment my brain could process this information, I felt something shift inside of me like a train changing tracks. It was the awakening of a primal animal that raged to life from deep within. I wanted to forget all the rules of human decency and restraint and let it loose.

I had to fight hard against the overwhelming urge to give the animal the freedom to tear a path of destruction somewhere... anywhere... immediately...because I knew this action was not possible. Somewhere in the rational part of my spirit, I knew that my sole purpose at that moment—and for as long as needed—was to be a soothing, stabilizing, unflappable pillar of strength to my only child. She had a long road of healing ahead for her. So, I restrained the animal and turned my focus to sourcing forgiveness and peace from the endless supply that is God—a choice that was incredibly difficult in the heat of my raging turmoil.

Despite the many sleepless nights that followed, I maintained my role as a Mother Warrior who loves her child beyond expression.

The days were filled with raw emotion watching her suffer. Each time I witnessed it, I thought, "Give it to me. Give me your pain. Let it be mine instead." That would have been much easier for me. I wanted to extract her pain as tenderly as I would have pulled a splinter from her finger when she was a little girl. There are no words to properly describe the grip her pain had on my heart.

Even with my ability to draw strength from a source that transcends me, by the end of the week I was so exhausted, that sleep, if I even got any, could not remedy it. Thus, the evening before my transformative dream experience, I sat alone and silent in the presence of God and asked for the fuel to see me through just one more day. Just one.

The next morning, I awoke from a deeply restful night with a clear recollection of the vision of the bright light being. With it came a sense of refueling, a renewed understanding of our true essence, and a surge of love and gratitude so intense it was physical. We are graced with the ability to access what our spirits need to regain strength when it's needed. How does anyone survive in this crazy world without a connection to a source much greater than oneself? Where does one otherwise go to find constant strength when they themselves are feeling powerless? I cannot fathom it.

If I had any lingering doubt about who we are at our purest core, it would have disappeared the morning after that amazing experience when I woke up renewed.

Experience. Yes. I can't call it just a dream. I am unaware of any dream that allows you to fall asleep depleted and desperate for strength, only to wake up relaxed and rested, feeling profoundly at peace. We are part of everything that comprises everything. We get our strength of spirit from refueling through a Source we are eternally connected to.

Dr. Jill Bolte Taylor saw this connection when the part of our brain that grounds us in our physical world was temporarily deactivated. The image in her mirror was flipped and she saw all that can be sensed and not seen.

On a day that I needed it the most, and in more ways than I will ever be able to count throughout my life, that connection was and has always been apparent. With it comes the powerful message from our Creator, "*I am ALWAYS with you.*"

God never fails to show up.

I believe our true essence is one with God.

I will remember the feeling in my dream experience for the remaining days of my life, and until I am called home, where I will exist in that feeling eternally.

CHAPTER 41

All the Light Inside of You

What if we have it backwards? What if the things we can see, measure, touch, or change are an illusion? What if the only things that are real are those which cannot be measured, touched, or changed? That which never perishes and is eternal.

What if we began to make this shift in perspective today and we started seeing everything in our world as sourced from the divine energy that is God? What if we stopped believing that we are separate from this Source and instead believed in the power this connection gives us to our full potentiality?

What if we chose to see the people all around us as a part of ourselves? What if we understood that the bad behaviors we witness are areas deficient in love, and instead of responding in like manner, we chose instead to feed those deficient areas with our own love?

What if we based *every* response from the perfect love from which our soul draws and understood that it heals everything in its path? It heals in ways we may never see and supplies us with the fortitude to endure anything we face. It wishes the very best for ourselves and for those around us. It is the nucleus of hope and an endless source of grace and forgiveness.

What if we recognized that the more a person is filled with this Source, the less likely he or she will be to respond with behavior that goes against love? He or she becomes formidable in the face of adversity and desires a world that is harmonious and tolerant. A person filled with this kind of love wants it to radiate first from within their souls and then outward.

Perhaps we might find that it is not upon the physical passing of our body in death that we have access to all that Adam and Eve experienced before their lives changed and when they could see God with their eyes, but rather it will be upon our own spiritual awakening that will bring forth the glory of Eden—allegorical or otherwise. When we stop listening to the serpent (ego and fear) and we allow the divinity of our spirit to govern our actions.

When we choose to feel the joy of living our lives, striving to be the very best versions of ourselves. When we choose to be grateful for each breath we take and for the warmth of the sun on our skin. For each hardship we face that teaches us what we desire to learn or for each memory of a hug with someone we lost. When we let go of anger and judgment, practice forgiveness of others and ourselves, and shine our God-given light into the darkness.

When we choose love in all of our responses.

Perhaps it is then we will see 'Eden' again.

What if you understood that only you can make it happen in your life? When will you start?

The good news is that the same God that was patient with me will be patient with you. The same God that is there for me, is there for you.

If you have read this far into the book and find yourself cringing at the word God, then go back to the beginning and change it to love, or whatever feels right to you. The same patient love that waited on me, waits on you.

It's an intriguing thought, isn't it? We wait on God, and God waits on us. We move in God, and God moves in us. I believe that we are sovereign beings with free will to choose and thus shape our own realities—but I believe we are made 100 percent of the organic and spiritual elements created by existence itself. We are made in the image of this. We cannot be separated from that which has connected everything to everything.

I started this book with an excerpt from the story of Adam and Eve in the Old Testament of the *Holy Bible*. Two people who believed they were separated from their Creator and as such, suffered terribly,

I will end this book with a reminder that is also in the Old Testament. When Moses asked God, "Who are you?" God answered, "I AM THAT I AM." And because we are made in the image of God, we too are who we are. Being made in the image of God—of love—gives us abilities beyond our human comprehension. We can achieve manifestation in ways that cannot be explained scientifically—just as Jesus did. It begins with understanding that we already ARE what we wish to become because we have the power of God working with us. Hence the immeasurably powerful statement "I AM THAT I AM."

The greatest teachers in our history have tried to deliver this message to us.

To me, there is no message offered in this book more important than what you will find in this chapter.

Since childhood, my path has led me toward a certain knowing as it pressed on my heart. The more I sought to identify the source of this pressing, the further away I became from the material life I had created.

I have conducted my life not by listening to the bountiful opinions around me, as well-intentioned as most of them were, but to the quiet whisper within me.

Tuning out the voices of the world is not an easy feat because it means going against societal norms. From childhood, our lives are built on what others tell us are proper thoughts, responses, and etiquettes. It is built on what we can see, hear, and touch—the physical and measurable. As a result of this early conditioning, even when it is our spirit that is seeking, we tend to gravitate to these things first.

Everything around us caters to this, and the temptation to slip into the flow of its current is as strong as the current itself.

Overcome that temptation and you will be well on your way to living by your spirit. Overcome your fear and you will overcome the world.

Don't expect it to be easy. And never give up.

Throughout the years, the roles I once held as a successful business person, significant other, caregiver to the homeless, community volunteer, founder of a running club, and a host of other titles vanished when I made the choices to change my life to honor my spiritual self. The ease in which I acquired material things changed as well, because although they once brought me peace and comfort, they no longer held their places of importance in my life.

I had to learn to source my comfort from that which could not be purchased—the things that never perish. The things sourced from God. It was hard work to break old habits. This was new territory for me and until I got used to it, I was on shaky ground with a life completely altered and no ability to see into the future.

Blind faith.

However, the more I focused on God's constant presence—the stronger in spirit I became.

My relationship with God, as it turns out, had existed all my life. My awareness of this fact was brand new. I was dealing with the stress of a life transformed, the insecurity of an unknown future, recovering from loss and festering anger at the abuses of another person, and serious doubt about what was real and what was not. What more perfect time could there be for me to focus only on the rage and to feed my hunger for revenge? What more perfect time could there be for me to turn away from thoughts of love and light?

I chose the opposite. I chose to look for beauty in the midst of unthinkable ugliness. I chose to search for truth in the midst of lies.

When it came time to learn even more, my empath dial was turned to off—consciously or subconsciously, I may never know.

Allison's deception and betrayal are only one small thread in the beautiful and vast tapestry that is my life, and it was a necessary experience. The understanding it awakened in me is massive, and although I will never condone lying, it turned out to be a gift as beautiful as a gift could be. That's what God does, He turns ugly to beauty and darkness to light.

Throughout my life, I have consistently experienced that in every moment, in every situation, the only thing we can actually control are our responses. We get to choose every thought—and our thoughts are powerful!

This experience taught me that by keeping our thoughts and choices fixed on this Divine Source, we too can snatch back the light from the grips of a darkness that would attempt to conceal it and let that light be shown to the world.

I choose to believe that the e-mail I received from "the doctor" as Allison lay in front of Mitchell and I, did not come from some unknown person waiting in the wings to help her perpetrate her hoax.

Do it again. Incorporate prayer.

I choose to believe this because I know that nothing is impossible when God has a message to deliver—and even more so when that message is "I AM right here" to the soul that is seeking.

This beautiful Divine Source is unwavering and unchanging. He communicates His loving presence through everything; and His messages are basked in the perfection of love, no matter the messenger. Since mankind began chronicling stories, they have included surprising manners in which messages were delivered. God is unlimited when it comes to the methods He might choose to teach each of us what we need to learn—because the energy of God flows through all things. Because God IS all things.

I have seen God throughout my life: in the birth of my child, in the family that surrounds me, in a tattered man who gave me his most treasured possession, through a bike that vanished into thin air, in a mist that hovered around a body, reflected by a candle that burns with love, in the palpable energy that came when I needed God the most, and in the beauty of a devoted friend who has stood by my side and wishes only the best of love for me.

I also feel the presence of God in countless everyday ways like the rising sun, a baby's laughter, a budding flower, the flutter of a butterfly's wing, a dog's wagging tail, a perfectly-timed call from a friend, the clothes donated to the homeless, the food that grows from soil, the smile from a stranger, the purr of a kitten, the aroma of coffee, the person who supports your dream, the song of a bird, the church doors that stay open, and in everything my eyes land on.

During the seasons of my life, when I didn't know God, there God was. When I identified God, there God was. When I only saw the light, there God was. When I was surrounded by darkness, there God was.

The point is, God is everywhere.

As I allowed my spiritual mind to expand, my conviction became so high and my faith so complete, it led others to believe without a morsel of doubt that my hands and heart were instruments given over to God, which allowed them to *know* that healing was possible. Once they believed this, the results were extraordinary. As Jesus taught, *because of your faith, you are healed.* These everyday folks like me shared this with their loved ones, who also believed. And the cycle continued—a cycle I hope never breaks.

For me, the greatest evidence of God is found in the miracle of the love and light that exists inside of you. Yes, you too have this light.

All of us have everything we need to be warriors for this light—and to create exquisite lives that make this world a better place.

Does that mean we can change the world?

YES! We can!

We can all start by committing to one simple thing—choose love. Dr. Martin Luther King said, "Darkness cannot drive out darkness: only light can do that. Hate cannot drive out hate: only love can do that." *Don't let anyone tell you that choosing to respond from a place of love is weakness.* It takes enormous strength. The alternate is what is easy.

This is one of the many things I learned by listening to the inner-voice with its wisdom that far surpasses my own.

Let your thoughts and responses honor this choice. If we all committed to doing this one simple thing, we would change the world.

God's energy moves through everything—connecting all of us to each other and to the world around us. We are one big human family with thoughts that enable us to create spectacular lives for ourselves and the people around us.

I believe that life ebbs and flows, and one day you will learn that the greatest pleasure and wealth you will ever find is in helping others.

The greatest gifts given to us by our Creator, are an endless supply of love, and awareness of this gift. Through awareness we are given conscious choice. And if we choose to focus on the limitless potential of the Creator, we will be open to the limitless miracles of the world we cannot see. We will increase our resilience. We will forge beautiful realities. We will gain the wisdom and faith to love our Creator and to work with the gifts and talents with which we have been blessed. When we do, we can in turn, create better lives for ourselves and a better world for the generations to come.

Again, all we have to do is choose.

And it will be so.

All the light is already inside of you.

CHAPTER 42
Today

May your choices reflect your hopes, and not your fears

Nelson Mandela

More than a year had passed since I first met Everett as an 8 year-old boy on the strongest narcotics that could be prescribed. He is ten years old now and is still headache-free. He is on the wrestling team and has discovered a love for competing. "I'd love to go to a tournament one day," I tell his mother. His body is no longer subjected to narcotic strength—or any other–medications and he is no longer missing school. Stories around the dinner table segmented time into two distinct categories, during his months of headaches and after the headaches stopped.

One day, Everett could see on the face of his mother that she was experiencing a headache of her own. He approached her with his quiet manner and asked her to close her eyes. She could feel his little hands hovering around her head, until he finally paused and said "It's right here. The pain is right here."

He was spot on.

I thought back to the message I received when I worked on his energy flow, "He is like you. He has the same gifts you have embraced. I will use him to do My work. He is Mine."

I love the faith of a child.

I love this young boy.

I love this gift of God's light inside all of us.

Do you recall the nagging thought that kept popping up during the energy healing sessions—the one that said, *there is something more, something needs tweaking?* I understood what that something was during a trip to Brazil in July 2017. It was a message that was delivered without question—much more than a pressing on the heart, it was an explosion from within.

I understood that I am not to stand over someone and be God's hands in a session, although I will still do whatever my beautiful constant companion presses on my heart to do. Rather, I am to teach anyone who is willing to learn, that they too possess this gift. It is part of the birthright of every person on this planet. It is a light that is inside (and around) all of us. We are made in the image of this Divine Source from which we can draw emotional and physical healing. It is what Jesus meant with the words, "Greater works than these you will do..."

The things I have learned along my journey and throughout the many seasons of my life are accessible to everyone. One must simply remove their limited thinking and desire to see the beauty and love in their lives and to know that these things come from God. A Source of endless strength, hope, and healing. A Source that is steadfast and unchanging. A Source that has no beginning nor an end.

Immediately upon my return from Brazil, I began writing this book in earnest and set the wheels in motion for the establishment of my coaching practice. I want every willing mind to realize their full potential and the endless Source from which it stems.

I now work with groups and individuals, on both the personal side and the professional side. I bring love as the main message to both. Yes, even on the professional side. We don't check our souls at the door when we walk into work each day, and those souls are the purest form of love. I empower people to understand who they are intrinsically so they can more readily reach their goals and their highest potential and live the life they desire.

Finally, at long last, after heeding the voice to close my business and follow my soul, I am living the life I was meant to live—unimpeded and with joy.

People have told me they think I'm courageous and admirable to walk away from a lucrative career to honor that which is my spirit and they wish they had the courage to do the same.

It was not easy and the temptation to go back was enormous, which is part of what makes this story worth telling.

However, today I can say, it doesn't have to be one or the other—soul or success. We can have both. To anyone who feels the strong pull of their spirit but is facing obstacles, I say. "Don't ever give up on chasing your heart's desire."

As for Allison, I have not spoken to her since December 2015. To my knowledge, she never did tell the truth to those who gave their time and effort to supporting me while she was with me. Nor did she ever show contrition or remorse, or retract her claim that the hospital where Dr. M. works was threatening her and using her physiology illegally. To this day, when I think of the faces I saw at the cancer ward, the true cancer patients, I feel a knife in my heart. It is yet another reason to use this story for good.

She and I have very few mutual friends now, but the ones we did have for a period after her deception was revealed, often provided unsolicited information about her to me. It took nearly all of 2016 for people to stop telling me about the stories she continued to make up. Even longer for them to stop asking me why she did these things.

I don't have the answer to that—only God knows.

I use this story of betrayal and challenge to show those with whom I work that even when we are facing incredible obstacles or opposition, we have everything already inside of us to overcome any external condition, and we are supported by the most powerful force in our universe. When we keep our eyes on what is light and love, we will find our way to peace and healing much faster. I tell them that sometimes the rockiest path is the most direct route to the Source of all light. I can attest to that.

I still believe that regardless of whatever causes Allison to behave in such a way, she was used as an instrument to teach me what would otherwise have taken much longer for me to understand. Like a spiritual boot camp. My empath dial had to be turned off so that I could learn from the whole experience.

There is no longer disdain for her in my heart because this experience is now being used to help others. Writing this book was a step in that. Was it cathartic? Of course! All of the things we do that offer expression of our emotions are. Those things keep us emotionally healthy.

That said, I am immensely grateful that season of my life is over and I have chosen not to have her energy in any part of my life. My current reality is all about being in the moment of now.

I have also achieved forgiveness for myself for believing her deception. It took some time to do so, but I got there. Forgiveness of oneself is necessary before we can forgive another. It began for me when I acknowledged that none of my actions were of malice and my original intention was simply to help a person in need. It grew within me when I thought of the many ways I am forgiven by God, and it exploded within me when I looked at what came out

310

of this experience. The altered state of my home and the feeling of imbalance led me to that empty church, where I came to identify the same energy that I had felt surrounding me for all my life since I was a young child of six running through my magical woods.

God's energy.

And as Augustine of Hippo said, "To fall in love with God, is the greatest romance; to seek Him, the greatest adventure; to find Him, the greatest human achievement."

Without the desperate quest to sit in the peace of a quiet church, it may have taken a lot longer for me to make the connection.

I am going to choose to focus on the good from that.

Whether you are early on in your life or nearing the end of it, recognize this important fact: What our spirits need to sustain in life is sourced from the eternal. It cannot be purchased, and once you have it, cannot be taken away without your permission.

It is found by listening to the quiet whispers within your soul and understanding that hope, wisdom, love and endurance, is already who you are; these are woven into your very being. Reflecting those attributes to the world is a choice we make, every moment, in how we conduct our lives and our responses. There is such power in choice and even more so in our thoughts. As you have just read, the seasons of my life taught me that.

So, find calm in the moment of now. Release the sadness (violence, abandonment, rejection, mistake) of yesterday, and don't worry about that which has not yet happened. Feel the strength and vitality of your mind, and the abundance and goodness of life.

This power is yours already.

Choose to tap into it and begin it today.

After all, we are the choosers and the co-creators of this universe.

—THE END—

• • • • • • • • • • • • • • • • •

"Until one is committed, there is hesitancy, the chance to draw back — concerning all acts of initiative (and creation), there is one elementary truth that ignorance of which kills countless ideas and splendid plans: That the moment one definitely commits oneself, then Providence moves too. All sorts of things occur to help one that would never otherwise have occurred. A whole stream of events issues from the decision, raising in one's favor all manner of unforeseen incidents and meetings and material assistance, which no man could have dreamed would have come his way.

Whatever you can do, or dream you can do, begin it. Boldness has genius, power, and magic in it.

Begin it now."

Written by William Hutchinson Murray, from his 1951 book *The Scottish Himalayan Expedition* and often attributed to Goethe

• • • • • • • • • • • • • • • •

Acknowledgements

Committing to this book required examining my beliefs and why they had come to be. While this was not an easy task, it is one I believe every person should undertake, even if they choose not to publish their story.

Thank you to the members of my critique group from the Atlanta Writer's Club—Brenda, Jeremy, John, and Patricia. I am grateful for your guidance and feedback. I look forward to continuing my participation in this invaluable resource.

A deep thank you to my editor Vail Davidson of Innerlight Creations in Atlanta, Georgia. Your understanding of all things related to nurturing our soul was apparent from the first red-lined page delivered—as was your ability to add eloquence without changing tonality or a message. You are a true artist and I encourage anyone seeking an editor to contact you.

To my mother, Blanche Gibson, who with a twinkle in her smiling eyes, claims to have found me as a baby dangling from the George Washington Bridge in New York City. Mom, I love you and your perfectly refurbished heart. Your wisdom, strength, and faith continually inspire me. I am grateful for the family with whom you have surrounded me and with whom I love so much—my siblings, Kerry, Keith, Kay, and Kathy, and the beautiful families they have created. And to my BBD, Madeline, you may have lost those chubby cheeks but you will forever have my heart. Because of you, the cycle of love continues.

Finally, to Gary McCracken. I could not have accomplished this without the relentless and unwavering support of my dearest friend in Atlanta. Recognizing my propensity to put others before me, Gary turned those tables on me and chose to put me at the forefront of his priorities. He provided a haven for the year

I needed to write (and rewrite) this book, opened his heart to support my dream, and his home as my writing retreat—a quiet and comfortable space to sequester myself and pen my thoughts. He helped me set up a prayer and meditation room, provided a beautiful corner space where I established my office, and engaged in endless hours of conversation with me in his inviting den. I believe for every letter in this book, there exists one reason to say thank you to you Gary. Or as we like to tease, "No thanks to you...?" This is a model worth duplicating, so others who may need a retreat to chase a dream are given one, and those who wish to support a dream can offer one. We are in this together, right? One human family. I am honored to be connected to you.

To the readers. Thank you for buying my book. If the stories have touched you, please share that on a review on Amazon or send me a note via my website, keryloliver.com. Let's exchange our stories without judgment and with the support that comes from knowing, we are all connected.

Many blessings.

About the Author

Keryl Oliver is an entrepreneur, a speaker, a personal and professional development consultant, and mother to the daughter who stole her heart. Keryl is passionate about guiding others toward discovering their source of personal empowerment, and believes that by changing the way we think, we will change the way we live.

Through her consultancy, KJo Consulting Group, she conducts sessions and workshops to help guide individuals and groups to the discovery of their potential and to make the changes necessary to live more fulfilling lives. **Learn more at www.KJoConsulting.com**

A portion of profits from book sales will go toward her nonprofit, Storia Group, to create programs offering free personal and professional development to community members who would otherwise not have the opportunity to participate. **Learn more about the nonprofit programs at www.StoriaGroup.org**

Keryl resides in Atlanta, Georgia. She is currently working on a children's book titled, *All the Love Inside of You* to be published in 2018.

Made in the USA
Middletown, DE
09 June 2018